Argument *Revisited;* Argument *Redefined*

Negotiating Meaning in the Composition Classroom

Edited by
Barbara Emmel
Paula Resch
Deborah Tenney

SAGE Publications
International Educational and Professional Publisher
Thousand Oaks   London   New Delhi

For information address:

 SAGE Publications, Inc.
2455 Teller Road
Thousand Oaks, California 91320
E-mail: order@sagepub.com

SAGE Publications Ltd.
6 Bonhill Street
London EC2A 4PU
United Kingdom

SAGE Publications India Pvt. Ltd.
M-32 Market
Greater Kailash I
New Delhi 110 048 India

Printed in the United States of America

Library of Congress Cataloging-in-Publication Data

Main entry under title:

Argument revisited; argument redefined: Negotiating meaning in the
  composition classroom / editors, Barbara Emmel, Paula Resch, and
  Deborah Tenney.
    p.   cm.
  Includes bibliographical references (p.) and index.
  ISBN 0-7619-0184-1 (cloth: acid-free paper).—ISBN
0-7619-0185-X (pbk.: acid-free paper)
    1. English language—Rhetoric—Study and teaching. 2. Persuasion
(Rhetoric)—Study and teaching. I. Emmel, Barbara. II. Resch,
Paula. III. Tenney, Deborah.
PE1404.A72 1996
808'.042'07—dc20   96-4472

This book is printed on acid-free paper.

96 97 98 99 10 9 8 7 6 5 4 3 2 1

Sage Production Editor: Vicki Baker
Sage Cover Designer: Candice J. Harman
Sage Typesetter: Andrea D. Swanson

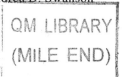

Argument
Revisited;
Argument
Redefined

Contents

We are grateful to Lucille McCarthy, Leslie Moore, and Linda Peterson for their invaluable suggestions.

For their steadfast support we thank Stephen Emmel, Richard Resch, and James Tenney.

Introduction

I suppose, Gorgias, that like me you have been present at many arguments, and have observed how difficult the parties find it to define exactly the subject which they have taken in hand and to come away from their discussion mutually enlightened; what usually happens is that, as soon as they disagree and one declares the other to be mistaken or obscure in what he says, they lose their temper and accuse one another of speaking from motives of personal spite and in an endeavor to score a victory rather than to investigate the question at issue . . .

Plato,
Gorgias

The Background of the Book

In the late 1980s, we (the editors) were asked to help redesign an entry-level writing course, changing its focus from an eclectic number of approaches to one of critical inquiry grounded in argument. We found in our discussions that there was little agreement on what the term *argument* actually meant, or how critical inquiry and the process of argument could be productively carried out in the classroom—and that there was little literature to help instructors compare, contrast, and evaluate various named approaches (the enthymeme, the Rogerian approach, Toulmin's model) to argumentative writing. Thus we originally conceived this book as a volume that would delineate argument into clearly defined approaches. Since that original conception, however, the place of argumentative writing in entry-level writing courses has been attacked by some practitioners who claim that asking students to take positions is to invite them to play a "confidence game," posing as authorities, pretending to knowledge they do not possess (Meyers 47). While some see argument as an artificial activity, others see it as too positivistic, irrelevant, and old-fashioned in a postmodern composition classroom where authorship is suspect and texts are of interest not for their content but for what they imply about the ways society distributes power and authority.

With these challenges to the term "argument" and the place of argumentative writing in composition, merely examining the different approaches to argument does not go far enough. Although textbooks with the word "argument" in their titles are proliferating, the word "argument" seldom surfaces in titles of journal articles. Still, a survey of the literature indicates that inquiry, critical questioning, and even theories about reading and writing themselves have begun to ground newly conceived writing courses and programs. In these courses, students are being asked to explore their lives and the way that their beliefs have been constructed by larger cultural forces. They are being asked not only to state their positions, but also to reflect on how they both construct those positions and are constructed, in turn, by their cultural, social, and intellectual (and sometimes emotional) milieus. These are all activities of argument. Paradoxically, those composition scholars who question the place of argument in writing courses actually write coherent arguments themselves and explicitly use the term "argument" in referring to their own essays. Despite protestations to the contrary, argument is a form of discourse practiced both in academia and in our culture at large.

In fact, the activities of academia and the political process are specifically connected in the stated goal of our profession at the 1987 English Coalition Conference: "Language arts instruction can and should make an indispensable contribution to educating students for participation in democracy" (Lloyd-Jones and Lunsford qtd. in Peterson 315). For Amy Gutmann, author of *Democratic Education,* knowing how to argue is what makes participation in a democracy possible. In her view, the mission of college is to help students in "learning how to think carefully and critically about political problems, to articulate one's views and defend them before people with whom one disagrees" (173). Disagreement is almost an understatement for what is happening in America today, where we are presently engaged in "culture wars"—the religious right vs. liberals, gun advocates vs. supporters of gun control, developers vs. environmentalists. An entry-level writing course grounded in argument can begin to address the problems of a fragmented community because it can give students from different cultures a way to begin to talk with one another and to write their way into understanding their differences. One way to begin this process is for students to understand how they came to their own ways of thinking about a given issue. As the 1987 English Coalition proposes, the first-year college writing course should "focus on the uses of language: the value laden nature of all such uses, and the ways we and our students use writing, reading, speaking, listening and critical thinking to construct ourselves as individuals and as members of academic and other communities" (Lloyd-Jones and Lunsford qtd. in Peterson 316).

Since the publication of Mary Louise Pratt's essay "The Arts of the Contact Zone," practitioners and scholars have been debating the merits of a classroom that is not a community but rather a site "where cultures meet, clash and grapple with each other, often in contexts of highly asymmetrical relations of power. . . " (444). In such a classroom, differences are not silenced, smoothed over, or suppressed; they are brought to the surface and examined. Joseph Harris has noted that Pratt offers few concrete suggestions as to "how (or why) individuals might decide to change or revise their own positions (rather than simply defend them) when brought into contact with differing views" (33). We hope this book will fill the gap. The essays in this collection have been written to help composition teachers practice "the arts of the contact zone" as our contributors explore the many facets of argumentative inquiry—developing positions, exploring difference, understanding the process of negotiating, and moving from argument as difference to argument as understanding.

This volume revisits and explains named or traditional approaches to argument—the enthymeme, evidence, classical rhetoric, Toulmin, and Rogers—and shows why these approaches are more relevant today than ever. This book also redefines argument as the chapters in the second section connect argument with movements that in some cases have been inimical to it—feminism, narratology, and reflexive reading. What unifies these two parts is that all of the contributors believe that argument does stand up both as a genre and as a process that can serve students well. In light of the recent proliferation of textbooks on argumentative writing, this book seeks to resolve the problem of having a number of apparently conflicting approaches by uniting the shared elements of these approaches into an understanding of argument that emphasizes inquiry over discord and understanding over entrenched difference.

Defining Argument: Hegemony or Negotiation?

As a rhetorical system, argument represents three essential and intertwined moments of linguistic connection among members of a community taking part in a dialogue involving differences of opinion. First, there is always a question at issue (a conflict or difference) that can give rise to any number of positions that address the issue. Taking a position is both essential and ever-present in human discourse: We make claims continuously throughout the day as we interact with each other, and seek both to make our views known and accepted. Such claims or positions may be viable only for a certain time and place, but we cannot live as human beings without making them, and without negotiating them over and over again.

Second, the positions that individuals take invariably involve a set of underlying values, many of which remain buried as unstated assumptions unless the process of inquiry uncovers them. In explaining what we believe and why, we must acknowledge which values underpin the positions we take. This process can lead to an exploration of others' values and set the stage for negotiation. As we negotiate positions, we are also negotiating values, acknowledging that some may be more privileged than others, and seeking to expand our understanding of the many different values that different peoples and different communities may hold.

Third, because argument privileges rationality as its medium of discourse, reasoning plays a role in understanding how positions and values are linked. Walter Fisher's "case for good reasons" is based on the belief that reasons serve some other purpose than logical validation alone: Reasons connect values to positions by making our values seem rational. Frans van Eemeren, a leading argument theorist, observes that ". . .we have not yet paid much attention to the question of what counts as a *rational assessment* in the context of argumentation. Yet this is a fundamental question for the whole study of argumentation" (49). Indeed, because rationality itself is value-laden, we do need to pay attention to what counts as rational, particularly now in our multicultural society. As William Covino and David Joliffe note, an assumption of rationality does not take into account "the needs of minority and oppressed groups" (56) who may operate with different cultural values and for whom a particular set of reasons may be without value. If rationality is seen as one way for a culture to assert itself over another, the concept of rationality itself may be suspect.

Each of these three aspects of argument can be problematic. Positioning can become a hegemonic struggle for power. Values that are often at the heart of difference are subject to being rejected out of hand, and reasoning may depend on a set of underlying assumptions that marginalizes the values of others.

In the preceding epigraph from Plato's *Gorgias,* we see some of the problems and misconceptions that can occur even when two parties seek to argue their way toward positions of mutual enlightenment rather than become entrenched in positions of conflict, hostility, or opposition. In the first section of Plato's *Gorgias,* Socrates and Gorgias engage in a dialogue about the nature and use of oratory—the art of persuasive public speaking. Socrates is repelled by what he sees as ethical blind spots on the parts of Gorgias, who defends persuasion as the basis of argument. While Plato did not appreciate the Sophists' understanding of truth as contingent, he does have Socrates pinpoint a perennial difficulty with argument: the desire to defeat or overwhelm the other person. In this passage, Socrates stops the conversation and steps back to ask himself and Gorgias what exactly they are doing. Should they continue their discussion? Their ideas conflict. Socrates then names some problems that arise when argument is understood as winning: tempers flare, parties become wedded to their own positions, make *ad hominem* attacks, and pursue winning at all costs.

This understanding of argument as fight is not limited to verbal exchanges. Although virtually all new textbooks on argument eschew a portrayal of argument as hostile confrontation, the language of opposition still undercuts some presentations of argument. In *Metaphors We Live By,* Lakoff and Johnson indicate how pervasive such phrases as *defend a thesis, marshall evidence, mount counterarguments,* and *confront opposing viewpoints* are in our representations of argument. Van Eemeren, too, has defined argument in terms of a defense or attack on a position in which the implied end is victory rather than understanding: "The interlocutors may adduce any desired point of view and any information which they consider relevant to the defending or attacking of an opinion" (38). Even one of the authors we cited earlier, Amy Gutmann, uses the word "defend [one's view]" in advocating that we teach our students to think critically and carefully.

In the argument-as-war metaphor, the move to accord is open to charges of power play. Moving beyond difference becomes a matter of one side winning to the exclusion of another side, thus preserving the status quo of an existing power system. In such a construct of argument, if one prevails one does so at the expense of others and loses the opportunity to create an inclusive community. The problem with the war metaphor is that it highlights opposition and winning and hides other ways argument might be understood. Argument does not have to lead to victory or stalemate.

Here we would like to propose a very different epistemological underpinning for argument. Understood as inquiry, the argumentative process can move parties from disagreement to negotiation and, if not to accord, then at least toward an understanding of what their differences are and why they exist. For this to happen, the parties have to understand what their positions are and how they were formed, explore the value systems underlying each position, make these values explicit, and have the good will to move beyond difference to understanding. This last activity is the most critical: Understanding and transcending difference define what argument is as a whole rhetorical system. Values are at the heart of argumentation and how values get played out, are heard, and are treated has everything to do with whether argumentation is viewed as hegemonic and positivistic or as a means of generating new viewpoints. Argument can allow parties to function as a community rather than a group of sparring individuals. Wayne Peck, Linda Flower, and Lorraine Higgins's definition of "community literacy" could fit a definition of argument as well, when they claim that

> community literacy means more than simply representing different views in conversation. It seeks to restructure the conversation itself into a collaboration in which individuals share expertise and experience through the act of planning and writing about problems they jointly define. The goal is not to resolve the myriad of differences that arise in a mixed, working group, but to treat diversity as a resource for solving specific problems. (205)

"Treat[ing] diversity as a resource" means recognizing that the different perspectives and values that individuals hold are essential to community life because "our ability to understand and address complex social problems depends on expertise and experience that is often distributed across various cultural, economic and racial groups" (Peck, Flower, and Higgins 204). In short, we need to listen to each other because our very existence depends on our ability to do so. As Kenneth Burke would have it, the function of rhetoric is to help us "maneuver through life" (Foss et al. 177).

We realize that viewing argument as an act of community literacy may sound naive at a time when differences in the multicultural classroom are manifested as power relations. Yet it is precisely because so much is at stake in the success of arguing toward agreement that argument as a construct is worth revisiting and redefining. Although taking a position is essential to argument, an entrenched position as an endpoint brings with it the pitfalls of isolation and deepened conflict. Pratt uses the "safehouse" metaphor to describe "social and intellectual spaces where groups can constitute themselves as homogenous, sovereign communities . . ." (455). If venturing out of the safehouse leads to conflict and acrimony, then the result, Joseph Harris argues, will be retreat to the safehouse where individuals will find like-minded others clinging to their individual perspectives, never moving beyond their initial beliefs.

Teaching Argument:
Postmodern Influences on the Pedagogy of Argument

As we locate the teaching of composition within the larger contexts of literacy and multiculturalism, an increasing emphasis has been put on asking students to question what they read, to find places of intersection with the various "texts" they read (a conversation, an essay, an event), and even, as Salvatori, Bartholomae and others have suggested, to use difference and "misreadings" to enter into a dialogue with these texts and understand themselves and their cultural backgrounds in relation to them.

Without naming this process as argument, or presenting any of the formal terms of argument, composition teachers are nonetheless asking their students to engage in argument when they ask them to reflect on their own responses to texts and the origin of their ideas in a nexus of cultural and social beliefs and values. The work of compositionists such as Kurt Spellmeyer, Mariolina Salvatori, and Kathleen McCormick indicate that students are increasingly being asked to be reflexive—to explore and question the ways in which they not only construct responses but also are themselves constructed as readers and writers by the worlds in which they live. Thus, as with argument, students are being asked to position themselves, to locate themselves within the larger issues embodied in whatever kind of text they are encountering, and to identify what issues are thus raised, on their terms as readers and on the writer's terms and on larger community and cultural terms.

Although postmodern theorists rarely use the term *argument,* we maintain that this kind of questioning is compatible with the first stage of argumentative inquiry. In the postmodern world, the constructed subject with its metaconscious and reflexive habit of mind is privileged (as in Susan Miller's *Rescuing the Subject*) over the process of argumentative inquiry as a whole rhetorical act. The questioning subject is a necessary point of departure for inquiry into the construction of knowledge and hence an important first step. Yet it is important to acknowledge that reflexivity is a starting point and not an end point, unless we perceive composition and argument to be a means of understanding the self above all else.

Postmodern compositionists have challenged the field of composition in other ways that connect to argument. If composition continues to teach writing as a matter of organizing "out there" knowledge, then according to Kurt Spellmeyer, "what disappears . . . is any sense of how human subjects struggle to preserve their life-worlds against the imposition of alien values" (1993 271). This struggle—of the individual's attempt to construct a self in the presence of other authorities—is, according to Spellmeyer, "arguably the central issue of education [and] nothing less than the central issue of postmodernity itself" (1993 271). In asking those who teach writing to understand composition on these terms, postmodernists have helped move composition away from the teaching of any systematic representation of discourse, including argument, and toward the conditions and contexts that ground such discourse. Spellmeyer and others insist that our students must engage in genuine discourse. Just how they enter into that discourse and what makes it genuine is the core of the debate in much of the literature and criticism in the field of composition today. Our particular interest lies in argument's position in that debate and its contribution to connecting pedagogy and theory. Yet argument is often rejected as being an artificial and formulaic construct, rather than an activity of inquiry essential to any genuine discourse.

What is being rejected in composition is not so much argument itself (or process theory or expressivism or cognitive theory), but rather any kind of system that would seem to preserve the status quo rather than challenge it. Whenever our pedagogies teach representation (of knowledge) over actual engagement (construction of knowledge), then we risk a metamorphosis of actual doing into instructions for doing. Once the representation (a model, a process, a form) becomes reified, then its production, rather than the knowledge construction it was originally meant to inspire, becomes the goal. Because of this conundrum, past breakthroughs, such as Flower's cognitive paradigm, become today's problems. Jill Fitzgerald's careful study of how we revise, in *Towards Knowledge in Writing,* reveals just how easily we can transform, through predictive and prescriptive pedagogies, points of entry into real inquiry into patterns of imitative production. When this happens, we are teaching students primarily a way to organize "out there" knowledge, rather than engage in their own knowledge construction. As Darsie Bowden has observed, any representation of writing can act like a container, one in which "texts (and minds) exist in a void" (374). When we teach argument as a container for truth rather than as a means to construct contingent truth for temporal communities, the whole of the rhetorical situation is undermined. Containers draw a boundary around truth as if it is something independent of our beliefs, our lives, the very challenges of our daily existence. In such an approach, the procedures of argument become an end rather than a way of understanding how communities and the individuals who comprise them communicate and construct knowledge.

Such distortions of argument have led compositionists such as Sheree Meyers to argue that those who continue to teach students to write argumentation do so because argument

> can be seen as empowering—empowering those students who by successfully imitating it convince their readers that they really 'know' what they are presumed to know. . . . Rather than risk losing their place in academe, students try to play by the rules of the confidence game. . . . Conformity may appear safer than the alternatives. (52)

This view of argument leads to charges that argument is hegemonic, preserving power systems rather than challenging them. Furthermore, students who play the "confidence game" are taking on what they see as the authority of the academy, an authority that is now suspect for its claim of autonomy. Students can write more valid arguments for today's world if they engage in "insistent questioning" and recognize their own and others' interestedness (Mortensen and Kirsch 559). Teaching argument as a mastery of conventions sidesteps important issues the postmodernists have raised—in particular, their challenge to the notion that argumentation is a dispassionate and objective form of discourse. A postmodern view of argument maintains that the questioner is never a disinterested party and that critical distance is itself a trope.

In its worst manifestation in the classroom, argument functions, its critics maintain, to teach students to enter into the power structure of existing knowledge. At its best, we argue, argument is precisely that system that permits a full challenge to such existing, positivistic, hegemonic systems. Only by engaging in the full act of argumentation can students challenge those systems and engage in the construction of new knowledge with foundations that rest on values that are not only shared but also newly constructed by the community at hand.

This book specifically addresses issues that have emerged from the postmodern challenge to argument. As illustrated, some of these challenges portray argument as a closed system for students to master rather than a more open-ended inquiry that engenders knowledge. But when argument is misrepresented or excluded from the composition classroom, we deny composition a powerful system of literacy in which students engage in reflexive questioning of self and others and then progress to decision making and negotiations of meaning that grow out of that initial reflexivity.

In Part I, "Argument Revisited," John Gage begins the discussion about argument's role in the contemporary composition classroom with his defense of the *thesis* as the means by which we take stances, understand our positions, negotiate with others, change positions, and construct new positions. In Gage's view, the thesis is not a statement of what one knows, but rather an articulated and mental construct that tentatively positions the self as one seeks to understand what one believes and why. The thesis makes it possible to connect to others in this process of inquiry into belief (because the thesis is a test) and to understand how belief and knowledge are mutually constructed by the activities of questioning, responding, and reasoning toward conclusions. Treated thus, the thesis ceases to be a construct that represents an organization of "out there" knowledge, or Meyers's "illusion of mastery," (47) and becomes a medium of dialogic exchange and knowledge construction. Finally, this construction of the thesis is most accessible through the paradigm of the enthymeme, which shows how the thesis becomes a point of entry into the whole process of argument.

To construct positions, we must know from where our positions derive. Traditionally, evidence is treated as information that one looks for to support a position one wants to defend. Barbara Emmel's chapter suggests that the organic nature of argument reverses that process: Evidence is information that writers construct and shape as they are thinking through their ideas. This information becomes evidence only when the writer/rhetor begins to shape a conclusion that uses that information as its support, as part of the reasoning process. Thus evidence is an important stage in the construction of knowledge; yet we rarely teach students to explore the relationship between their conclusions and the evidence that led to those conclusions. Emmel uses the work of art historian Jules Prown to show how arguers, especially art critics, must create the very information that will, in the end, become evidence for their conclusions. Evidence then becomes a stage of creativity in its own right in the process of argument.

Toulmin and Rogerian argumentation both find their origin in twentieth-century figures from disciplines outside of English or composition studies. Stephen Toulmin is an English philosopher, Carl Rogers an American psychotherapist. Neither one began their work in argumentation and communication with the goal of providing a model for college writing courses; yet many textbooks on argumentation contain a Toulmin or Rogerian section. In examining Stephen Toulmin's model of argumentation, Richard Fulkerson cautions against a wholesale adoption of a model that is highly appealing but which was intended primarily as an analytical tool. Nevertheless, it is more flexible than any other import from logic and epistemologically suited to a postmodern age as a revision heuristic that can help students examine and understand their various claims and the assumptions and reasons behind those claims. This chapter discusses the usefulness of Toulmin's model for helping teachers of writing understand the relationship between argument, composing, and knowledge building—and what can be reasonably expected of this model in classroom application.

Whereas Toulmin sought to understand how argument acts paradigmatically, Carl Rogers was concerned primarily with how communication was carried out among those who had genuine differences of opinion. Douglas Brent's chapter explains the foundations of Rogerian rhetoric and explores its attention to the ethics of argumentation as a means of engaging in mutual inquiry toward shared meaning and understanding rather than as a means of achieving victory. In doing so, Brent looks at how Rogerian rhetoric has been misused in the past in the writing classroom and shows that Rogerian rhetoric's major contribution is its pedagogical application, in which students learn to hear each other and to take into account different perspectives as they seek to understand their own positions and beliefs. Through dialogue, in which listening is as important as speaking, Rogerian rhetoric can help students move beyond entrenched positions to new understandings.

In their chapter on classical rhetoric, Jeanne Fahnestock and Marie Secor call for a "radical restructuring of the composition classroom," one in which students learn how to negotiate differences and positions as a whole system of inquiry. Here Fahnestock and Secor argue that argument is an art, one that students are unfamiliar with, yet one that is tied to how we construct knowledge, how we interact in that construction, and how the processes of agreement and disagreement become part of the overall process of constructing knowledge. Fahnestock and Secor conceive of a broad and formally defined way of teaching, and carrying out the processes of argumentation. Their conception of the freshman writing course interweaves techniques of argumentation (from classical rhetoric) with the normative processes of argumentation that students already possess. Under this approach, students learn how difference and agreement (activities they already engage in) form the basis for shaping new knowledge when they begin to ask what does it mean that we disagree? That we agree? This chapter raises questions about the contexts, values and assumptions that produce rhetorical discourse. Such confrontation is the only way to deal with rhetoric's capacity for appropriation and to escape the charges of "sterile formalism" and the suspicion of "mere rhetoric."

Part II, "Argument Redefined," begins with a chapter on what women have had to say about argumentative writing. In their chapter on feminist perspectives on argument, Pamela Annas and Deborah Tenney survey the effect of feminist scholarship on argument pedagogy. Although some feminist scholars eschew argument altogether as an antagonistic, alienating mode of discourse, other feminists have broadened our understanding of what argumentative inquiry involves. Annas and Tenney examine the activities by which all students learn to ground argument in intellectual inquiry and in experience and personal opinion, and to establish themselves as a community wherein they can find both the necessary support and the opportunity to negotiate their positions in argumentative writing. This approach can serve as a model for any disenfranchised group learning to challenge existing power structures, assert individual viewpoints, and develop arguments that grow out of the processes of inquiry described in this chapter.

One result of the misrepresentation of argument is that composition teachers sidestep argument as too hegemonic and revert to what seems the safer course of "storytelling" (Trimbur 112). Judith Summerfield shows us that there is nothing safe about storytelling. To narrate, from the Latin *narrare,* to make known, is to bring writers and readers into a dialogic encounter where an exchange of knowledge and of values is always implicated. Drawing from the broad interdisciplinary venture of narrative theory, Summerfield demonstrates how complex narrative is and therefore how wrongly it is often put forward as the "easy genre" for students to write early in a course. She prepares us to see that every narrative is an act of composition, an epistemological venture, and an argument for framing the world in a particular way.

The last chapters by Mariolina Salvatori and by David Bartholomae examine reading as an essential part of composition. Salvatori discusses the theoretical and practical appropriateness of using reading as a means of teaching argumentative writing. Her approach to the teaching of reading posits as necessary a teacher's commitment and ability to understand the processes that students use to create their texts. Among other things, such an approach, she argues, necessitates a reexamination of the kind of "knowledge" students can be said to produce through reading and through written responses to assigned texts. Her approach calls for students to become self-reflexive readers, to learn to see how their individual "moments of reading" determine what they write about a text. Salvatori answers those who claim her approach is too demanding by demonstrating how being a self-reflexive reader allows one to actively engage in education, rather than be "passively led" through it.

Bartholomae calls for close reading as a form of argumentation in the composition classroom. He cites its historical and often misunderstood roots in New Criticism, and maintains that close reading is both linked to and differentiated from the kind of reading Salvatori advocates in her chapter. Arguing for an approach that pays close attention to language rather than issues, Bartholomae makes a case for the good that results from students getting under and turning over words. Looking at two courses that in past decades taught this kind of argumentation, Bartholomae finds that then, as now, the point of close reading was to enable students to argue with the forms of understanding they were meant to take for granted and to learn to define themselves at the immediate point of contact with the arguments built into the "common sense" of the mass culture.

Placing argument at the center of the composition course shows respect for students' capabilities as language users, as inquirers, and as people who can challenge existing knowledge and construct their own. Having granted them such respect, our contributors expect much of their students. Teaching a course in argument makes considerable demands on the instructor as well. Both the increasingly diverse student population and postmodernism have posed significant challenges to composition and to our sense of community. But redefining argument as we have in this volume offers a way to meet these challenges. Because the diverse classroom replaces the notion of a single authority with multiple viewpoints, it becomes a place to learn how to negotiate difference. With postmodernism comes the loss of certainty but the opportunity to write arguments that reflect a richer, more complex world view.

BARBARA EMMEL
PAULA RESCH
DEBORAH TENNEY

Works Cited

Bowden, Darsie. "The Limits of Containment: Text-as-Container in Composition Studies." *College Composition and Communication* 44 (Oct. 1993): 364-79.

Covino, William and David Joliffe. *Rhetoric: Concepts, Definitions, Boundaries.* Needham Heights: Allyn and Bacon, 1995.

Fisher, Walter R. "Toward a Logic of Good Reasons." *The Quarterly Journal of Speech* 64 (Dec. 1978): 376-84.

Fitzgerald, Jill. *Towards Knowledge in Writing: Illustrations from Revision Studies.* New York: Springer-Verlag, 1992.

Foss, Sonja K., Karen A. Foss, and Robert Trapp. *Contemporary Perspectives on Rhetoric.* 2nd ed. Prospect Heights, IL: Waveland Press, 1991.

Gutmann, Amy. *Democratic Education.* Princeton: Princeton University Press, 1987.

Harris, Joseph. "Negotiating the Contact Zone." *Journal of Basic Writing* 14 (Spring 1995): 27-42.

Lakoff, George, and Mark Johnson. *Metaphors We Live By.* Chicago: University of Chicago Press, 1980.

McCormick, Kathleen. *The Culture of Reading and the Teaching of English.* Manchester: Manchester University Press, 1994.

Meyers, Sheree L. "Refusing to Play the Confidence Game: The Illusion of Mastery in the Reading/Writing of Texts." *College English* 55 (Jan. 1993): 46-63.

Miller, Susan. *Rescuing the Subject: A Critical Introduction to Rhetoric and the Writer.* Carbondale: Southern Illinois University Press, 1989.

Mortensen, Peter, and Gesa E. Kirsch. "On Authority in the Study of Writing." *College Composition and Communication* 44 (Dec. 1993): 556-72.

Peck, Wayne, Linda Flower, and Lorraine Higgins. "Community Literacy." *College Composition and Communication* 46 (May 1995): 199-222.

Peterson, Jane. "Through the Looking Glass: A Response." *College English* 57 (March 1995): 310-18.

Plato. *Gorgias.* Trans. Walter Hamilton. Middlesex: Penguin, 1985.

Pratt, Mary Louise. "Arts of the Contact Zone." *Ways of Reading.* Ed. David Bartholomae and Anthony Petroskey. New York: St. Martin's, 1995. 442-56.

Spellmeyer, Kurt. *Common Ground: Dialogue, Understanding, and the Teaching of Composition.* Englewood Cliffs, NJ: Prentice Hall, 1993.

———. " 'Too Little Care': Language, Politics, and Embodiment in the Life-World." *College English* 55 (Mar. 1993): 265-83.

Trimbur, John. "Taking the Social Turn: Teaching Writing Post-Process." Review of *Academic Discourse and Critical Consciousness* by Patricia Bizzell; *Critical Teaching and the Idea of Literacy* by C. H. Knoblauch and Lil Brannon; and *Common Ground: Dialogue, Understanding, and the Teaching of Composition* by Kurt Spellmeyer. *College Composition and Communication* 45 (Feb. 1994): 108-18.

van Eemeren, Frans H., Rob Grottendorst, and Tjark Kruiger. *Handbook of Argumentation Theory: A Critical Survey of Classical Backgrounds and Modern Studies.* Dordrecht, Holland/ Providence, RI: Foris, 1987.

ARGUMENT
REVISITED

1

The Reasoned Thesis

The E-word and Argumentative Writing as a Process of Inquiry

John T. Gage
University of Oregon

I

Perhaps because I have some notoriety with regard to the subject, the editors of this volume have asked me to write about the enthymeme. Say what? Come again?

The question, "What's an enthymeme?" clearly illustrates the formidable obstacle to the successful teaching of argumentative writing that is so often raised by the vocabulary used to discuss it, whether that vocabulary derives from logic or from rhetoric. I will address this problem in relation to that Greekish e-word *enthymeme* that to some is merely a useful term but to others is an absolute roadblock. But before I address this word specifically, we might go beyond the question of those specialized technical terms that rhetoricians are so fond of using and that others are so fond of slamming.

> For all a rhetorician's rules
> Teach nothing but to name his tools.
> His ordinary rate of speech
> In loftiness of sound was rich,
> A Babylonish dialect,
> Which learned pedants much affect.
>
> *(Samuel Butler,* Hudibras *I, 89-94)*

The language of learned pedants isn't all that obstructs the teaching of argument. What about that more common word used in the title of this book to unite its several unpedantic concerns? A more basic obstacle is faced by many teachers in the term *argument,* or its descendant *argumentative writing.*

Although to many *argument* is a useful and necessary term, to others it just isn't nice. "Don't be argumentative," we sometimes say to someone who is trying to obstruct the flow of ideas. "Objection, your honor, counsel is being argumentative," one TV lawyer might say to stop another from putting words in the mouth of a defenseless witness. Most of us respond at some level to the word *argument* as if we were remembering the pain of those gut-tearing, domestic arguments that, at best, we hope never to relive or, at worst, we feel lucky to have survived. Yet the same word is also used to describe the practice of cooperative, productive, even friendly discourse as an alternative to verbal violence. Argumentative writing is not only perceived by most writing teachers as a necessary part of the composition curriculum, it is often held up as the goal or even the ethical justification of that curriculum. Richard Larson, for instance, prefaced one popular textbook on argumentative writing by claiming that such books help us "become well-informed, fair-minded, and skillful participants in the dialogue by which defensible beliefs are reached and wise actions decided upon" (x).

Clearly, a distinction is in order. Short of altering usage, we need to be clear about the relationship between one kind of argumentation and another. Without such clarity, not only may students misperceive the task of learning to write arguments, but teachers and specialists in composition theory can make claims about one kind of argument that only really apply to another. The field of composition theory at present is rife with such claims. When an approach to writing—such as "dialogism," "collaboration," "interpretive communities," "inclusiveness," "social construction," or "subjectivity"—is alleged to be an alternative to argument in the most confrontational sense, you can be fairly sure that the alternative will boil down to some kind of advocacy (or argument in another sense) and that the new approach will be justified by means of something like the kind of argument that has allegedly been discarded. The phenomenon is at least as old as Socrates's use of rhetoric to denounce rhetoric.

The distinction I think we need is explicitly rendered in the title of an essay by Jack Meiland: "Argument as Inquiry and Argument as Persuasion." In that essay, Meiland demonstrates that many pedagogical uses of "argument" explicitly or implicitly equate the word with "persuasion." Those two words are likewise wedded in history. Rhetoric, defined historically as the art of persuasion, is the primary source of thinking about the nature of argument. Although linking argument with persuasion is historically and lexically accurate, it exposes argument to criticism from a pedagogical point of view. Students who believe that they are being taught to argue to prevail over opponents in situations of conflict may believe in consequence that this end justifies any rhetorical practice that leads to winning over or silencing another. Indeed, one may find many advocates of such a success model for rhetorical proficiency, especially in textbooks. But it is not the only model, and any— even casual—linking of argument with persuasion detracts from the potential advantages of seeing cooperation rather than victory as the goal of rhetorical activity and competence. Perhaps by unlinking argument from persuasion we can focus attention on the need to teach argumentative writing as part of an education that foregrounds respect and consideration of the ideas of others.

Meiland defines inquiry as "the process of discovering what (if anything) it is rational to believe about a topic" (187). Associating argument with this definition accomplishes two things (at least). First, it moves argument away from the goal of victory over another and toward the goal of deciding what beliefs are justified. Thus, it redefines the "process" of argument as one that may begin before one knows where to stand, as opposed to one that begins only when one is focused on justifying a stance already believed. Persuasion implies prior commitment to an idea; inquiry implies a search that may or may not lead to such commitment. Second, Meiland's definition ascribes to this process, this search, the fundamental role of rationality. Whereas students of persuasion may believe that rhetorical maneuvers are tested on the basis of whether they are effective, students of inquiry must distinguish between those aspects of rhetoric that constitute reasonable grounds for holding an opinion from those that are unreasonable.

Consequently, argumentative writing defined as inquiry will look different from argumentative writing defined as persuasion, even though both may use similar means. Meiland discusses several potential differences, such as whether one is obliged to consider alternative views and objections, whether one may choose not to draw a conclusion, or whether a conclusion is stated conditionally. We may wish ultimately to reconnect the two types of argument because to persuade oneself may involve using the same means one would choose to persuade another. But in constructing a pedagogy of argument, the distinction is especially useful because it provides a context for focusing on rationality as the foundation of argumentative writing, and it is necessary to keep rationality from being thrown out of that process. Without such a distinction, those who seek alternatives to teaching students to use language as a means of gaining power over others may be tempted to search for that alternative only in nonrational processes. But, as the history of rhetoric clearly demonstrates, emotional appeals can be appropriated for manipulation as readily as rational ones. The alternative sought is one that redefines the purpose to which the "available means of persuasion" are applied. Applying them for the sake of inquiry is a matter of how one views one's relationship to an audience (see Crosswhite 47, 251-68).

The distinction between persuasion and inquiry may be traced to alternative views of the role of the audience in rhetoric that arose during the classical era. Meiland's distinction resembles in many respects a distinction drawn by Thomas Conley between "asymmetrical" and "symmetrical" theories of rhetoric in classical Greece and subsequently throughout the European rhetorical tradition (*Rhetoric* 5-7). *Asymmetrical* (or *unilateral*) theories presuppose an active speaker and a passive audience, a speaker whose rhetorical task is therefore to do something *to* that audience. In such a rhetorical situation the mind of the audience may be changed if the rhetoric is successful, but the mind of the speaker is not. Conley ascribes this kind of asymmetry to Gorgias, whose advocacy of the practice of rhetoric depends on a radically skeptical attitude toward "truth." But the same asymmetrical rhetoric may be justified by radical belief in a single, unchangeable truth: The process of converting others to a deeply held belief without being willing to change one's own mind may also be seen as a form of asymmetrical, unilateral communication.

Symmetrical (or *bilateral*) theories, on the other hand, presuppose both an active speaker and an active audience, a speaker whose rhetorical task is therefore to do something *with* that audience. In such a rhetorical situation, the beliefs (as well as the words) of the speaker may need to be adjusted given understandings derived from the audience. Thus, a symmetrical rhetorical situation is one in which the speaker seeks assent by connecting to, rather than overcoming, the beliefs of the audience, and thus the audience may be said to participate in the formation of the substance of the argument itself. The situation is one in which speaker and audience influence each other's ideas. Conley ascribes this kind of symmetrical rhetoric to Protagorus and to

Aristotle. In contrast to Gorgias's skepticism, Protagorus conceived of debate as a condition of negotiation among *dissoi logoi,* conflicting truths that coexist and give rise to conditions of dissonance that can only be resolved by harmonizing them. Aristotle's concept of rhetoric is that of a dialectical process (not excluding emotions) that takes place in situations where stable truths are unavailable but where cooperative, rational agreement is sought (see, e.g., Grimaldi).

I invoke the history of rhetoric here simply to suggest that our own search for an approach to argumentative writing that stresses inquiry over persuasion is hardly new. The same tensions we feel between persuasion and inquiry have motivated thinking about rhetoric from the beginning. The problem is not unique to the pedagogy of composition. The problem is inherent in the nature of rhetoric itself: What is the relationship between the process of using language effectively and the process by which warranted belief is attained? Thus, anyone who is today interested in the relationship between writing and thinking is to some extent involved in a controversy that is permanently inscribed in the history of rhetoric. Although this does not mean that we are bound by the terms of that controversy in history, neither does it mean that we can presume to have found a way to escape the controversy. (See, for instance, the descriptions of how argument has recently been seen as gendered using distinctions similar to those I have been discussing, in the essay by Annas and Tenney in this volume.) In that sense classical rhetoric has relevance to composition today: not because we should teach the techniques of ancient rhetoric to our students, but because in teaching any techniques we necessarily engage ancient but still compelling issues, such as whether we imply a symmetrical or an asymmetrical concept of the rhetorical situation.

It is in this spirit, I think, that I have sought to apply Aristotle's concept of the enthymeme to the teaching of argumentative writing. That concept has seemed to me to provide a useful way to treat the writing of arguments as a bilateral, symmetrical transaction between the writer and the writer's audience in such a way that writing arguments becomes a process of "discovering what (if anything) it is rational to believe about a topic." I do not think that my adaptation of this Aristotelian concept makes me "stubbornly classical," as a recent essayist phrased it, if that means that I am opposed to his allegedly modern sense of writing as "an active means to transform the existing social inequities . . ." (France 600, 593). But my insistence on the relevance of the enthymeme to modern composition (which is reiterated, for instance, by Fulkerson's statement in this volume that even Toulmin's model is "essentially enthymematic") has produced understandable misgivings of several kinds.

Because the word *enthymeme* is unfamiliar to many teachers and students, its use can suggest a process alien to our experience. And because defining it as "a rhetorical syllogism" or in terms of a "basic deduction" (see my "Teaching the Enthymeme") invokes logical categories, the word can suggest an overly technical or formulaic application of logic to writing. Thus, one otherwise friendly reader of one of my earlier descriptions of the enthymeme called it a "silly-gism." Fair enough. These misgivings have resulted not only from the use of the term, but from the formulaic way "enthymematic invention" is sometimes taught. A final misgiving (of interest perhaps only to those who have studied classical rhetoric) is illustrated by Thomas Conley's remark to me after a presentation at a Conference on College Composition and Communication Convention. "John," he said, "you have a great theory of composition. But don't hang it on Aristotle." Because I am in no position to refute Conley on the subject of Aristotle, I must take his ribbing to heart. My own sense of what Aristotle meant by "enthymeme" has been enriched and complicated by recent studies (see esp. Conley, "Enthymeme," Green, Poster, and Walker).

Consequently, I am interested here in completing this discussion of argumentative writing without using the troubling e-word. (Perhaps by this means I am moving my own discourse in the direction of "bilateral symmetry," but what misgivings does that ugly phrase arouse?) Lest my readers sigh too deeply with relief at this point, let me say that at the end of this discussion I wish to return to the enthymeme briefly because my ideas about teaching argumentative writing raise the issue of the relevance of historical concepts of rhetoric to contemporary pedagogy.

II

Teaching argumentative writing as a process of inquiry does not depend on knowing or applying logical categories but does require some sort of method of assessing reasons. By saying this, I have implied that there is a method of assessing reasons that is different from the methods of logic, and that of course depends on what we mean by both *method* and *logic*. Formal symbolic logic, at any rate, is not the means by which we ordinarily assess reasons, especially when we are engaged in trying to find grounds for agreement in real argumentative situations. The work of Chaim Perelman and Lucie Olbrechts-Tyteca, among others, draws our attention to the difference between the structures of real arguments and the patterns of symbolic logic. In *The New Rhetoric,* for instance, "quasi-logical" appeals characterize some of the things we do when we argue, but many other things we do bear no resemblance to the forms of syllogisms or inductions. Rhetoric, in that work, differs from logic primarily insofar as real arguments cannot be reduced to the structures of syllogisms, do not conform to validity rules, do not depend on "self-evidence," and are always expressed in language susceptible to ambiguity. But the absence of logical purity need not be taken to mean that our arguments are irrational. This absence merely means that the way we conceive of and practice rationality is not confined to the perspective of formal logic. (For a full treatment of assessing reasons, in the context of *The New Rhetoric,* see Crosswhite, esp. 79-80 and 141-48.) Although we rarely judge our own and others' inferences in terms of formal validity, we often judge them according to whether they seem "strong" or "weak." This does not mean that we have no criteria for making such a judgment.

Teaching argumentative writing as a rational process apart from formal logic requires substituting for formal logical categories an informal, fluid, audience-situated focus on reasons in natural language. Such a focus stresses the giving of reasons as a process that we engage in naturally and spontaneously even when we have no conscious sense of doing so. If we take this to mean that "anything goes" when it comes to giving reasons, then of course we would have nothing to teach. But because when we unself-consciously engage in argument we know that "anything" does *not* "go," we can approach the question of what to teach from the perspective of what we do when we choose one reason over another, when we intuitively ground our arguments in what we consider to be "stronger" reasons than some others we might have chosen. The process is not "governed" by rules though it may be "guided" by principles. The principles generally include a felt sense of relevance, a felt sense of connectedness, and a felt sense of relative precision. These "felt senses" exist in the atmosphere of our awareness of other minds. That is, we judge our reasons in part according to whether they make sense to us and in part according to whether we believe they will make sense to others.

The student writer can be invited to appreciate and measure reasons according to these "felt senses" by undertaking to address a real audience on questions that for that audience have genuine salience. We might call them "questions at issue": the kinds of questions that people engaged in discourse pursue because they believe together that answers to them are needed. In such a context, arguments depend fundamentally on a shared belief that some particular idea is worth getting right. For pedagogy, this implies that students not be told what issues they must write about but be invited instead to discover those issues in their own conversations. The context for such teaching, then, is "symmetrical" and "bilateral" from its outset, in the sense that the creation of "questions at issue" is itself a merging of what matters for a writer and what matters for an audience. I mean only that students should enter into argumentative writing by discovering mutual grounds for dissent as a prerequisite to discovering mutual grounds for assent—that is, that they have a shared sense of a problem needing a thoughtful answer. What we do not know together forms the basis for any search for what we can know together. Teaching argument entails not only the opportunity for conversation but also the opportunity for mutual inquiry because conversation has called it forth.

Just as the perception of "questions at issue" grows out of the presence of a writer in a situation circumscribed by the ideas of others, the construction of arguments in response to such questions grows out of that presence. To enable students to think about the construction of arguments in this way, we might adapt the traditional concept of "thesis statement" to this end. Much of the resistance these days to teaching this concept comes from its conventional association with formalism, and an "organic" or "functional" view of the thesis is less common. The "thesis statement" is ordinarily taught as a structural aid but it can function more basically as an argumentative principle if it is seen not as a single reductive statement of a prerequisite "main idea" but as a multipart statement that contains not only a central claim but central reasons for that claim as well, and that evolves as a response to a "question at issue" as mutually defined by a writer and that writer's audience. Thus, it is possible to see the "reasoned thesis" as a way to connect one's own thinking to the thinking of others both in the way it proposes a solution to a mutually felt problem and in the way it accommodates the reasons of others into the formation of its own reasons for the claim. This aim in itself will give rise to both a more fluid and a more complex idea of what a "thesis" is and how it functions.

The reasoned thesis is one that functions operationally, and hence tentatively, to define the "whole case." That is, at whatever point one is thinking through a problem in the presence of others with whom one shares that problem, one can assess the status of one's thinking by writing it down in some form and asking for a response. If the task is to write it down as a potential solution to the problem, together with the reasons that make it a potential solution, such a statement becomes available for scrutiny: What is its potential to become a more fully developed line of argument? The reasoned thesis is similar to a pencil sketch, then, that one might use as the basis for deciding whether to commit oneself to a whole design in paint. A thesis statement that is not necessarily final, in other words, and that contains both an idea and reasons for the idea, can function as a focal point for inquiry. The thesis can be used to represent the thinking one has done up to a point and it can be used to direct the way toward further thinking one might pursue. This pedagogical use of a reasoned thesis can be likened to "taking the temperature" of one's thinking at any point in its development as an aid to its further development. By virtue of being written down, it becomes something the writer may assess carefully in terms of adequacy while enabling the audience to do the same. Writing may function, then, not only as the culmination of a process of thought, but as the representation of that process at any stage.

One purpose for writing a reasoned thesis as part of the process of argumentative writing is to enable the writer and the audience to focus the inquiry collaboratively on the question of what constitutes a reasonable case. No formal criteria need to be prescribed for such a statement for it to fulfill this purpose, other than the informal criterion of including reasoning. If one's reasoning is not "good enough," presumably the writer and the audience (here I mean by *audience* those with whom the writer is engaged in conversation and to whom the writer may show such a statement) can make that judgment according to whether they find it adequate. No formal logical apparatus need guide this judgment if the informal criteria of the felt senses of relevance, connectedness, and relative precision are applied. This means only that students (especially if they are already engaged by a "question at issue") are brought to ask whether the reasoning found in the statement is relevant to them, whether the potential conclusion seems to follow, and whether the writer's meaning is clear enough.

The conditions for this inquiry are built into the nature of a reasoned thesis as a written claim and supporting reasons. Clarity is addressed by asking whether all who should understand the statement and the reasons do understand them. The result of testing a thesis by this criterion may be the need to revise the statement for precision. Relevance is addressed by asking whether the statement adequately responds to a question at issue. The result of testing a thesis by this criterion may be the need to revise not only the language of the thesis but the claim itself. Connectedness is addressed by asking whether the reasons provide an adequate basis for accepting the claim in the thesis as the case. The result of testing a reasoned thesis by this criterion may be to revise the reasons or the claim that they support. Connectedness, in this sense, is a twofold quality. *Connectedness* refers to the connectedness of the reasons to the conclusion and to the connectedness of the reason*ing* to the beliefs of its intended audience. (The process of revising a reasoned thesis under pressure from teacher and peers is illustrated by Emmel).

This last sense of connectedness derives from the implied conditions that govern any statement "that connects an idea with reasons for believing it and that relies on its audience's inferential powers" (Walker 63). Any statement that is asserted as the consequence of belief in another statement will rely on beliefs already held by its audience for the inference to seem to follow. These beliefs—let's call them *assumptions*—are the unstated but necessarily implied preconditions that make a reasoned connection feel warranted. No discourse in which ideas are related as reasons to conclusions will be without implied beliefs of this kind. Looking for them and then asking whether they are assumable by the audience is a way for students to examine their reasoning from the point of view of its connectedness to the reasoning of others. The give-and-take of such an inquiry among students is meant to lead them not only to a better phrasing of the ideas they wish to argue but to better ideas as well.

This inquiry, as part of a process of discussion and writing, does not depend on a reasoned thesis taking any particular form. Notice that I do not say that such a thesis should have one reason or that it should have three reasons. The goal is to find better reasons, and that goal is accomplished not by the addition of formal conditions but by asking questions designed to provoke further inquiry. Some teachers prefer a more constrained version of the reasoned thesis to guide students toward such questions. But if the constraints become arbitrary and students believe they are fulfilling a formal rather than an intellectual task, that inquiry is hindered. So, until teachers derive from the idea of a reasoned thesis guiding constraints that work for them, I am here recommending only an approach to the reasoned thesis that keeps those constraints to a minimum. The constraint I am advocating is of the intellectual kind only: The thesis should include reasons for believing it. Once such a thesis is in writing, it can be revised according to a process of inquiry: Does that thesis answer a question at issue? Is it clear? Do the reasons support the conclusion? Are the assumptions implied by the reasoning acceptable to the audience? As students engage each other with such questions about each others' written statements, they are simultaneously engaging in inquiry about the potential quality of the writing and of the ideas.

III

What I have been describing is a process that attempts to merge self-conscious classroom writing with what happens intuitively and spontaneously in argumentative situations outside classroom contexts. The reasoned thesis is the medium of this merger. The reasoned thesis functions to bring self-conscious attention to features of that situation and exerts pressure in the direction of inquiry by associating the writing of one's ideas as much as possible with the need to undertake a mutual discovery, *with* one's audience, of the rational grounds for coming to a conclusion. What the composition of a reasoned thesis can do for students as they move toward structuring a further-developed and further-differentiated argument depends fundamentally on what we consider to be the basic parts of such an argument.

This consideration can flow in various directions. Argument is only one of the many complex phenomena of living that reveal their "basic parts" to be different depending on the point of view or mode of analysis one adopts. That is why logic cannot be totally excluded from consideration even while we may wish to minimize attention to it; it will appear more or less "basic" according to what kind of a line of force we draw through the phenomenon of argument. So too will "grammar;" so too will *"topoi;"* so too will "personality," you name it. Aristotle drew a line through argument from the point of view of "artistic proofs" and perceived the basic parts to be "ethos, pathos, and logos." Roman rhetoric, famously, drew a line of "duties" through argument and perceived "invention, arrangement, style, memory, and delivery." George Campbell in the eighteenth century drew a line of "mind" through rhetoric and perceived it as consisting most basically of "understanding, imagination, passions, and will" (1). Stephen Toulmin in the twentieth century drew a line through argument from the point of view of its "physiological structure" and came up with "data, claim, warrant, backing, qualification" (94ff). None of these views is the same; each may comprehend the others. Perelman's insight, as I understand it, is to have seen argument as not comprehended by any such basic set of parts but to have seen all such sets as necessarily derived from a process of association and disassociation, linking and unlinking, rendering argument as a "web" of parts in relationships of infinite variety. An argument consists of a selection from a perceived array of potential associations and disassociations among ideas. (In terms of composition, these may take the form of qualifications, analogies, antitheses, further reasons, examples, anecdotes, summaries, refutations, implications, and so forth.) Perelman's view at least speaks to the complex of interrelations inherent and potential in any aspect of an argument. Like Kenneth Burke's philosophy of language, his is a perspective of perspectives. But for that very reason, like Burke's theory, it is often perceived as less practical for pedagogy than other schemata. Perhaps so. I would not advocate any attempt to make a prescriptive model of the anatomical detail presented in *The New Rhetoric*. But what might be lost in terms of formal modeling may well be compensated for in terms of richness in an attempt to bring such a point of view to bear on the reasoned thesis (see Crosswhite 107-12, 129-32).

If a student is engaged in the composition of a reasoned thesis that responds to the perceived needs of a reasoning audience, that thesis will gain relevance, connectedness, and relative precision for its readers as it is rewritten in light of their responses. At some point, that thesis can be viewed in terms of its potential to be developed into an extended discourse according to the field of potentialities for more writing (associations and disassociations) it implies. Thus, such a thesis is subject to questions about those potentialities: What connections does it make? What disconnections? What connections or disconnections does it suggest need to be made? These questions are not the same as questions of formal "arrangement" as such, though answers to them lead to formal considerations. These questions merge such considerations with the inquiry itself rather than treat inquiry and arrangement as separate "stages" of the writing process.

So, while revising a reasoned thesis in response to classmates' comments, a related task is to see in that reasoned thesis its potentialities. Two questions seem to me to guide that inquiry: What *must* an essay that argues this thesis do? What *might* an essay that argues this thesis do? These questions enable the associations and disassociations that a fully developed argument will make to be seen as potential within the reasoning of the thesis either as necessary qualities conditioned by the thesis or as sufficient qualities made possible by the thesis. Thinking about this distinction necessarily directs a student's attention to form because the perception of the necessary and sufficient parts of any argument will be what gives it an intuitive sense of wholeness. But such thinking is not about "form for form's sake" because the questions relate directly to the content of the reasoned thesis as an argument one seeks to make.

All of this is admittedly hard to talk about and one has to see it in practice to get the best sense of how a reasoned thesis can provide students with intuitive knowledge of what shape their argument needs to have to do justice to their ideas. I was amused but chastened when Richard Fulkerson reviewed the first edition of a textbook in which I tried to illustrate how a reasoned thesis statement gives rise to a developed structure of ideas, an outline for an essay. What he said was that despite the merits of the approach, when it comes to showing students how to move from a thesis to a structured argument, it gets "damned near mystical" (366). I pled guilty and in the next edition I tried to make amends (see *The Shape of Reason,* Chapter 5). But the problem represented by Fulkerson's jab is intriguing: How do we enable students to acquire a *sense* of form as generated from a "forming principle" or "shaping cause" (see Crane 140), as opposed to acquiring a limited stockpile of prefab forms? If we prescribe forms for them, we deprive them of the intuition that provides this sense and they will fall back on those prescribed forms when they are not appropriate—as in the case of the five-paragraph essay, the "keyhole" introduction, or even the fair-minded "format" prescribed for a "Rogerian argument" (see, e.g., Coe 342). But if we do not, there is no guarantee that they will perceive the forming principles in their ideas. Rather than view this as a double bind, my preference is to try to use the reasoned thesis to create conditions that will encourage the intuition of form to happen, on the assumption that unless students can first conceptualize the case they wish to make there will be nothing for them to be intuitive about when it comes to forming a whole argument. I am basing this assumption in part on what I have seen students do and in part on my own reflections on learning to compose: Until I have a sense of my argument as a whole and how it fits into a larger context of inquiry, I have no sense of what parts it must or might have and what order is right for them; but when I do have that sense, I need no external formal model to follow. We teach form best, as much else, by indirection. Readers of this volume will encounter a contrasting view of teaching form in the essay by Fahnestock and Secor, an attempt to rehabilitate formal categories from classical rhetoric. This approach is one that I find compelling but would finally resist in favor of the more "generative" approach I am advocating here. At the very least, whatever approach to form is used, we ought to be concerned about whether we teach it as separate from the inquiry represented in the reasoning or whether we teach it as an outgrowth of that inquiry.

To summarize: A reasoned thesis enables argument to be taught as inquiry rather than as persuasion, because it responds to a "question at issue" and because its claim and reasons are subject to revision (rethinking and rephrasing) based on the responses of an audience that shares that question. The process of this revision does not require that a reasoned thesis be subjected to strict logical tests because we judge reasoning by other means, which I have outlined as relevance, connectedness, and relative precision. A reasoned thesis will imply assumptions and those assumptions connect the reasoning to the thinking of others. A reasoned thesis that undergoes such a process of revision will provide the writer with an intuitive sense of what needs to be said and what might be said in any essay written to that thesis as a basis for structuring a whole argument.

IV

The preceding qualities that I have summarized are not the same qualities that Aristotle defined for the enthymeme, even though I and others have used that word to describe what is here called a "reasoned thesis." I am offering an alternative to *enthymeme* for anyone who can't get past the word or who finds it misapplied. I hear the echo of Conley's voice: "Don't hang it on Aristotle." Yet there is a sense in which I want to continue to think of the reasoned thesis and the enthymeme as related, because as I read further inquiries into Aristotle's and others' "enthymeme" I never fail to think more about what might be meant by "reasoned thesis." To the degree that Aristotle's sense of rhetoric yields further examination of what it means to communicate, and especially what that implies about knowing, then we might take whatever we can get from investigations of what he meant by "enthymeme." To the degree that Aristotle does not apply to us, we should un-hang ourselves from his view of argument.

The risk we take in rejecting Aristotelian or any historical categories outright is illustrated for me in the following statement from Kurt Spellmeyer's *Common Ground: Dialogue, Understanding, and the Teaching of Composition*:

> The most important part of any conversation, the most revealing part—the most freeing—is the search for the substratum, the hidden ground, that will enable all participants to recognize what they hold in common. Aristotle's "lines of argument" or topics, often mistaken for transhistorical organizing principles, are nothing more than a partial inventory of this substratum, the common sense of his day. But Aristotle could not have foreseen the conditions of discourse now. The common sense whose minutiae he recorded in the *Rhetoric* was the *Weltanschauung* of a single class, a minority of wealthy males with nearly identical schooling, private habits, and civic obligations. By contrast, a genuine *sensus communis* is for us far more difficult to pursue, or even to conceive, when the authority of "public" institutions has so often been directed against the public itself, and when so little common ground seems to have survived two centuries of almost perpetual change. (267-68)

Indeed, to expect Aristotle to speak directly to our needs is absurd. And our "more difficult" task of pursuing a *sensus communis* adapted to our sense of equality, justice, and human rights is one that demands we look elsewhere. But do we look elsewhere at the same time that we try to understand Aristotle or do we assume that Aristotle is wholly irrelevant to our search? If we do not *also* look back for answers, we fail to perceive something about the shape of our own discourse and its connectedness to a past. Although some of Aristotle's "lines of argument" may not be transhistorical, Spellmeyer's statement offers no reason to believe that none of them are. In fact, Spellmeyer proves the transhistorical nature of those *topoi* that he himself has used in this passage just as Aristotle defined them. And Spellmeyer has actually created, here, a wonderfully wrought enthymeme. So let us beware, in our enthusiasm for how different we are, that our own indictments of Aristotle's irrelevance do not rub off on us and stand as indictments of our own irrelevance. Yes, we are different, but note that Spellmeyer's term for what we ought to seek, a *sensus communis,* is itself a term from rhetoric's ancient past. So, being different, we are also the same. That dialectic between how we are different from the past yet continuous with it is what makes our own search for "common ground" necessary and poignant.

Call it a "reasoned thesis" or an "enthymeme," then, or something else again. But whatever you call it, the task is the same: to find a way of teaching the process of argumentation in writing that enables students to see their intellectual differences from others not as a rhetorical occasion for persuasion by any means, but as fruitful ground for mutual inquiry.

Works Cited

Butler, Samuel. *Hudibras.* Ed. John Wilder. Oxford: Clarendon Press, 1967.

Campbell, George. *The Philosophy of Rhetoric.* (1776). Ed. Lloyd F. Bitzer. Carbondale: Southern Illinois University Press, 1963.

Coe, Richard M. *Form and Substance: An Advanced Rhetoric.* New York: John Wiley & Sons, 1981.

Conley, Thomas. "The Enthymeme in Perspective." *Quarterly Journal of Speech* 70 (May 1984): 168-87.

————. *Rhetoric in the European Tradition.* Chicago: University of Chicago Press, 1994.

Crane, R. S. *The Languages of Criticism and the Structure of Poetry.* Toronto: University of Toronto Press, 1953.

Crosswhite, James. *The Rhetoric of Reason: Writing and the Attractions of Argument.* Madison: University of Wisconsin Press, 1996.

Emmel, Barbara A. "Toward a Pedagogy of the Enthymeme: The Roles of Dialogue, Intention, and Function in Shaping Argument." *Rhetoric Review* 14 (Fall 1994): 132-49.

France, Alan W. "Assigning Places: The Function of Introductory Composition as a Cultural Discourse." *College English* 55 (Oct. 1993): 593-609.

Fulkerson, Richard. Untitled review of *The Shape of Reason. College Composition and Communication* 39 (Oct. 1988): 365-66.

Gage, John T. "Teaching the Enthymeme: Invention and Arrangement." *Rhetoric Review* 1 (Sept. 1983): 38-50.

————. "A General Theory of the Enthymeme for Advanced Composition." *Teaching Advanced Composition: Why and How.* Ed. Katherine H. Adams and John L. Adams. Portsmouth, NH: Heinemann, 1991.

————. *The Shape of Reason.* 2nd ed. New York: Macmillan, 1991.

Green, Lawrence D. "Situating Aristotle's Enthymeme in the 1990s." Paper delivered at the Conference on College Composition and Communication, Boston, March 22, 1991.

Grimaldi, William M. A., S. J. *Studies in the Philosophy of Aristotle's Rhetoric.* Weisbaden: Franz Steiner Verlag, 1972.

Larson, Richard. "Foreword." *A Rhetoric of Argument.* By Jeanne Fahnestock and Marie Secor. New York: Random House, 1982.

Meiland, Jack. "Argument as Inquiry and Argument as Persuasion." *Argumentation* 3 (1989): 185-96.

Perelman, Chaim, and Lucie Olbrechts-Tyteca. *The New Rhetoric: A Treatise on Argumentation.* Trans. J. Wilkinson and P. Weaver. Notre Dame: Notre Dame University Press, 1971.

Poster, Carol. "A Historicist Recontextualization of the Enthymeme." *Rhetoric Society Quarterly* 22 (Spring 1992): 1-24.

Spellmeyer, Kurt. *Common Ground: Dialogue, Understanding, and the Teaching of Composition.* Englewood Cliffs, NJ: Prentice Hall, 1993.

Toulmin, Stephen. *The Uses of Argument.* Cambridge: Cambridge University Press, 1958.

Walker, Jeffrey. "The Body of Persuasion: A Theory of the Enthymeme." *College English* 56 (Jan. 1994): 46-65.

2

Evidence as a Creative Act

An Epistemology of Argumentative Inquiry

Barbara Emmel
University of Wisconsin-Eau Claire

When I ask students in my advanced composition course in argumentative writing what the word *evidence* means, I can predict their answer: Evidence is something you find in the library. If I push further, I hear that evidence takes a specific form, that of "facts, statistics, data." For my students, evidence is an absolute: information obtained solely for the purpose of serving as proof in some form. Evidence can be found in encyclopedias, graphs, tables, census studies, surveys, almanacs, reference books, and so on.

The result of this misconception is that when we ask students, "What is your evidence?" to get them to think more about the origins of their various claims and conclusions, the question comes across as one of diligence: "Did you do enough research?" we seem to be asking. Yet in using the word *evidence,* we are asking an epistemological question instead: How did you arrive at your conclusion? What other conclusions were necessary along the way? What kinds of information and ideas did you first need to recognize? How are your various thoughts hierarchically connected? In short, we want our students to see that evidence is a function of their own thinking, their creative act of realizations that earn the name "evidence" in a piece of writing only when their ideas are transformed into that role by the assertion of conclusions that in turn depend on these ideas for their very formulation.

The ideas that function as evidence as we think our way to conclusions may well contain information found in books. Or such information may be "created information," such as derives from observation, conversation, or experience. The point is not where we get the information, but rather what we do with it and how we act on it to make it part of our own and others' knowledge.

Some compositionists, most notably Peter Elbow and Ann Berthoff, have developed theories about how we interact with information, either in its creation or in its discovery, to transform it into a stage of discovery in our epistemological and dialectical journey toward knowledge and understanding. But neither of these composition scholars gives the name "evidence" to the processes that they have uncovered as essential stages in idea development. Elbow, for example, gives the name "first-order thinking" to a creative, intuitive (and initial) stage in writing that is then shaped by a more critical, self-reflexive stage called "second-order thinking" (58). Berthoff's dialectic of the double-entry notebook seems to function as the creation of a body of information that can then serve as a basis for exploration into further thought and inquiry. Nor does either of these two approaches use the word *evidence* to refer to the relationships thus developed—even though in both instances the use of language to create a body of ideas that play an epistemological role in the development of other ideas is, in fact, the essence of evidence as a function of knowing and knowledge construction.

Further, such creative naming does little to help rescue the word "evidence" from the realm of the pedantic, where it is typically associated with dry research. That association is part of the problem: If the creation of evidence is determined to be primarily a prescriptive move rather than one organic to our very processes of thought, then we are placing a limit on a conceptual activity essential to understanding how we use language to create shared meaning and knowledge. As part of the epistemological process of coming to know, transforming information into evidence is part of the process of constructing not only an understanding of a subject, but the very subject itself; it is an activity that contains within it the potential for further realizations and without which those realizations cannot take place. Thus it is both more defined and more integral to the shape of inquiry than terms such as *cooking* or *freewriting* or *prolific writing* imply. As a term, *evidence* is tied up with the process of inquiry as that inquiry is shaped by our need to know, and in turn shapes the structure of our knowledge. In recent years, some composition scholars have sought to understand the generative processes by which writing functions both as a system of inquiry into what and how we know and as a system for concretizing that knowledge (see, e.g., John Gage, Louise Phelps, and Jeffrey Walker). Yet as Richard Fulkerson has noted both in his chapter in this book and elsewhere, the balance between form and process (for evidence as a term invariably invokes notions of form) is delicate and difficult to sustain in the classroom and, without close attention to the pedagogies that sustain that balance, is constantly threatened by a reversion to formalism.

What we need is a theory of evidence that makes it possible for us to invoke the full implications of the word "evidence" as a generative and conceptual heuristic, one intimately connected with possibilities for idea exploration, creation, and development. We need to teach "evidence" as an activity of discovery connected with the self and others, one that connects thinking to writing and process to product. In so doing, we will be teaching that expressivism is a form of inquiry, that writing has its origins in both the self (as discovery) and in rhetorical form (as knowing), and that products of writing are shaped by, as Stephen Fishman and Lucille McCarthy have shown, an "interaction of personal and disciplinary languages" (659). If students in my writing classes are any gauge, they are eager to feel knowledgeable and to feel connected to their knowledge. Yet they are frustrated in that connection because they are so little skilled in the process of assimilating or generating information and transforming it into their own knowledge through their own processes of inquiry—and so limited in their knowledge of a universal language with which to discuss this process.

Prown's Methodology

Any number of paradigms exist that can make important contributions to our understanding of the relationship between what we do in writing and how we think. Frank D'Angelo's work in *A Conceptual Theory of Rhetoric*, published over 20 years ago, has become more recognized in recent years. John Gage's work with the enthymeme theorizes that structure in argumentative writing is organic to reasoned discourse. Richard Fulkerson's work with Toulmin also explores the relationship between writing and thinking, and between inquiry and structure, as does the work of the other authors in this book. I would like to add to these paradigms one that comes from outside the field of composition but that also has implications for how we can better understand and teach writing as argumentative inquiry. Developed by Jules Prown, art historian, this paradigm has two notable features that can add to our understanding of composition in general and argument in particular. First is the paradigm's emphasis on an individual intellectual engagement required by the formation of our ideas and its detailed exploration of the nature of that engagement. Second is its attention to the relationship between intellectual inquiry as a whole and the activity of inquiry into and creation of what becomes evidence in the process of that larger inquiry. Prown hypothesizes that evidence is always organic to the construction of knowledge. Constructing evidence is not just a matter of finding information in a book; it can involve an act of creating and shaping information. Even if we are working with information found in a book, the act of composing requires that we transform it from found information into a part of our thinking before it can take on any epistemological implications. In its focus on the smallest increments of ideation and realization, Prown's paradigm examines what an idea is and how ideas are formulated through the use of language, perception, and cognition. Yet because his concern is with writing, he does not stop at microcosmic levels of meaning but goes on to propose a whole structural paradigm based on inquiry from its most basic to its most sophisticated levels.

When Prown first developed his paradigm, he was primarily concerned with representing how art historians interpret and theorize about art and how they subsequently construct disciplinary knowledge. But early in his work he came to recognize three ways in which the process of inquiry into art is inherently connected to the processes of written composition. First, the methodology is based in the perceptual/cognitive[1] and semantic processes of observing and naming, and thus language (and eventually writing) is its essential medium of expression. Second, Prown perceived a relationship between the different activities of inquiry (or stages, as he called them) defined in his methodology and the shape of reasoning (a shape that, as Gage has shown, is visible in a finished piece of writing), a relationship that he taught to his graduate students both to benefit them as critics and writers and to enable them to teach their own students how to write about art and society. Third, he saw a broad relationship between the perceptual/cognitive process of inquiry into objects and the way we view writing as epistemology. He then went on to teach this methodology as a general methodology of inquiry and writing to high school teachers through the Yale-New Haven Teachers Institute.[2]

In the methodology Prown developed, art historians use both inherent features of the object and historical knowledge about it and its cultural context as evidence for constructing knowledge. First, however, they need to *create* the information that will become evidence in the construction of that knowledge.

The methodology is divided into three coformative and consecutive activities or hierarchies of inquiry centered around an object or pictorial representation (e.g., a photograph or a painting): a descriptive inquiry, a deductive inquiry, and a speculative inquiry (see the Appendix). By connecting these different types of inquiry, Prown has created a set of epistemological moves in which each kind of thinking, each an end in itself, becomes both a heuristic for the creation of and evidence in support of the conclusions realized in the other levels. Thus, for the formation of its own insights and conclusions the final activity of speculation depends on, both epistemologically and structurally, the findings of each of the first two areas of inquiry. Prown uses the term *stage* to refer to each focus of inquiry because of the hierarchies of realization implicit in his schema; nonetheless, all three activities are ultimately mutually informative.[3]

Stage I: Description

The descriptive activity is the starting point both methodologically and epistemologically. One cannot start with either of the other two activities of inquiry because the information they work with or build on must be created in this first stage. Conclusions achieved in the later activities of *deduction* and *speculation* (levels two and three) depend on the kind and range of observations that grow out of *description*, observations which then become evidence toward the deductive and speculative ends. Thus, an exhaustive and encompassing descriptive inquiry is essential to the generation of information that will eventually be transformed into evidence. Any deductive or speculative conclusion ultimately depends on the kind and range of observations developed through description, and one's conclusions will be differently formed (or even indefensible) if this first act of inquiry is cut short.

In this stage, the investigator engages in *synchronic inquiry,* descriptive observation in which, as Prown notes,

> description is restricted to what can be observed in the object itself, that is, to internal evidence [which is] read at a particular moment in time. In practice, it is desirable to begin with the largest, most comprehensive observations and progress systematically to more particular details. . . . [At this point] the analyst must continually guard against the intrusion of either subjective assumptions or conclusions derived from other experience. (7)

The synchronic exercise of description (synchronic because investigators draw on their own observations and interactions with the object only in the here and now and do not have access to others' observations [or even their own] over a historical, diachronic period of time) is made up of three substages (see Stage I in the Appendix): (1) an analysis of the object's substance (called *substantial analysis*), (2) an analysis of its content (*content analysis*), and (3) an analysis of its features of form (*formal analysis*). In each substage the goal is to observe and to name those observations. In short, the investigator focuses on the object, limiting awareness of the self as much as possible (because responses to these observations form the next stage of the inquiry).

The nature and kind of the object dictate which categories of analysis are most valuable, although the investigator should not ignore any category because to do so is to conclude, a priori, that there is no information to work with there, thus undermining the epistemological and structural value of the inquiry.

Although Prown's methodology can be illustrated through the use of virtually any artifact or painting, I have chosen as an object of inquiry George Stubbs's *Reapers,* a British painting of the nineteenth century. Because this painting is owned by the Yale Center for British Art, I have used it to teach Prown's methodology in composition classes at Yale. Students respond well to the narrative it contains because its iconography is a highly accessible one: The painting portrays a group of peasants at work harvesting wheat and being observed by a mounted overseer, who is both well-dressed and well-mounted (see Figure 2.1).

Showing a descriptive inquiry into, or analysis of, *Reapers* is best in nonnarrative style, for a note-taking kind of open-ended writing is the style in which such inquiry would be carried out by students themselves. The following organization fulfills the stages of inquiry outlined in the Appendix, although the ensuing detail and initial deductive conclusions appear more ordered and arranged by virtue of the categorical guidelines than they would be in the actual process of descriptive inquiry, which is recursive in nature. Typically, students observe first in one category, then another, then another, and then perhaps revisit the first, revisit another, and so on. The categories themselves help both to define the range of observations and to order those observations into meaningful units.

Stage I, Substage C. Formal Analysis[4]

1. Two-Dimensional Organization:
   a. Lines
      (1.) Horizontals: All horizontal lines are discontinuous. Although all are broken by some other line, they do establish a series of unrelenting horizontal planes. One can observe either three or five horizontal "lay-

Figure 2.1. George Stubbs's *Reapers.*
SOURCE: Yale Center for British Art, Paul Mellon Collection. Reprinted with permission.

ers." The earth, trees, and sky (which is vertically bisected) make up three layers. Or, there are five horizontal layers: the ground, the row of people, the low line of green behind them, the thin background line of distant blue, and the sky and taller trees (vertically bisected).

(2.) Verticals: The verticals interact with the horizontals to create many insights into the painting (and also to create the cognitive and semantic evidence that would support those insights). But the verticals must first be perceived and named apart from their interactions with other lines in the painting. This is true of all the lines (verticals, horizontals, diagonals, etc.). The verticals are: the towering trees, the figure on horseback, the distant spire of the church in the background, the haystack, the standing man and woman, the horse and its tail, legs, and so forth.

(3.) Diagonals and Triangles: All horizontal and vertical lines are crossed by a number of diagonal lines and triangular shapes, including the following: the major diagonal line formed by a movement from the trees in the upper right moving to the lower left (a line that also divides the painting into darker and lighter color schemes); the triangular shape of the haystack; the diagonal lines formed by the workers' backs; the diagonal line of the dog; and an imagined diagonal of the worker's gaze to overseer's gaze.

(4.) Curves and Circles: Framed by an oval inner frame, the entire picture forms a curved line. The picture contains many curved and circular lines: the circles and curves of the clouds, the circles and curves of the trees, the circles of the faces, the circles of the eyes, the curves of hats, the curves of the workers' backs, the curves of the sickles, the curve of the horse's neck, the circle of the cask lying on the ground, and so forth.

The generation of detail (through the medium of language) creates awareness of the existence of the detail and its potential for meaning. This process engages the investigator in a cognitive and semantic activity, that of seeing, perceiving, and naming what is seen and perceived. The act of observing (and the detail articulated therein) lays the groundwork for development of further ideas and insights.

In its first stage, the process of descriptive observation is deceptively simple—yet investigators are creating awarenesses that become incrementally and hierarchically more important as the process of inquiry unfolds. In the more interconnected stage of perceiving designs created by the two-dimensional lines the process—and its ends—become more interesting, as the following details reveal.

    b. Designs: repeated lines that form patterns
        (1.) The curve of the hats: a long curve across the entire picture, in which the hat of the overseer creates a high point at the right end.
        (2.) The bottom of the curve is represented by two workers who themselves form downward curves. The black hats rhythmically punctuate the curve and their blackness draws attention to the various positions of the workers and the overseer.
        (3.) The white sleeves of the workers and the downward curves they make, lines pointing to the ground. There are also other downward curves, all pointing to the ground: the curve of the cask, the dog's body, the clouds, the trees, the sickles. The ends of these, like a rainbow, tie each entity to the ground.
        (4.) The curve of the horse's head, a curve that also pushes downward, pushing on the head of the worker curved to the ground.
  2. Three-dimensional Organization: "forms in space, whether actual in a three-dimensional object or represented in a pictorial object" (Prown 8).
    a. Shapes
        (1.) Most predominant are the *figures,* the workers who themselves are placed into various positions and relationships.
    b. Relationships between shapes
        (1.) All of the figures are on the same plane, all working in a fairly straight line. Why? This arrangement is an unlikely one—would the workers have been so close together in real practice?

(a.) The workers are all facing the same direction—they are all looking toward the overseer.

(b.) The overseer himself is facing from the opposite direction. Is this a deliberate opposition?

At this point, it is worth noting that Prown is aware that the lines between descriptive and deductive inquiry may begin to blur as the mind jumps ahead to create conclusions. "Deductions," he notes, "almost invariably creep into the initial description" (9). Prown warns against this because deductions cut short the process of observing that will give a wealth of material to work with, but he also notes that the investigator can take advantage of the act of jumping to conclusions by asking why. Why am I so quick to want to see this? What is at issue here?

(2.) There are two triangles that dominate the picture, the triangle of the overseer, his horse, and the worker curved under the head of the horse (with the overseer's hat at the apex of the triangle), and the triangle formed by the woman and the man on either side of the stack of sheaves. The two triangles weight each side of the picture.

(a.) The triangle on the left breaks the plane of the wheat by virtue of the hats of the man and woman, but their hats do not reach as high as the apex of the overseer's hat.

(3.) The male figures are all touching in some fashion. The woman is divided from the men by the intrusion of the haystack, but her hat reaches higher than those of the male workers.

All of the foregoing descriptions become details from which the next activities of idea formation are created. Thus the detail of the descriptive stage becomes, epistemologically, evidence for the formation of insights, realizations, ideas, and conclusions drawn in the deductive stage, which in turn functions as another hierarchical level of evidence from which the conclusions of the speculative stage can be drawn.

Before we examine the relationship between descriptive inquiry and deductive inquiry, I want to anticipate the power of Prown's methodology to illustrate how we construct knowledge in writing by transforming descriptive detail into evidence. This can be done by setting up a contrast between the carefulness of observations and conclusions gained through the use of Prown's methodology and conclusions presented in such a way that we have no grounds for accepting them because they lack the detail that would serve as evidence in support of them. For example, in a recent review of an art show at Yale (which included *Reapers,* and was titled "Toil and Plenty: Images of the Agricultural Landscape in England, 1780-1890"), Michael Rush wrote that:

British landscapes, people[d] with well-dressed, serene and pious-looking peasants, are fakes. That is, they do not at all reflect the reality of peasant life as lived
on the farmlands south of London. Peasants were a starved, overworked and
rebellious lot whose plight anticipated the rise of socialism. The painters who
created such serene landscapes were consciously distorting the truth of what they
observed for the sake of perpetuating a myth about peasant life. Often borrowing
from classic mythology in a literal way, they were heralding rural life over the
cruel life of the cities. In truth, many of these artists were adhering to a prescribed
scenario, set forth by the Royal Academy of Art in London, about how farm life
should be portrayed. The artists also were providing their patrons, the landed
gentry, with the unthreatening [sic] and optimistic scenes the rich folk wanted to
adorn the wall[s] of their manors. (E1, E7)

This passage is filled with a series of thesis-type claims that beg for substan-
tiation and the review is weakened by the lack of any direct detail that would
function as evidence to support its many claims—as is much student writing
that attempts to be critical without understanding the origins of critical insight.

Stage II: Deduction[5]

Even a brief discussion of deductive inquiry as an epistemological next step
reveals that students are led, through their intellectual engagement with the
picture, to construct a different interpretation of *Reapers* than Rush's, one
more informed by the observations made during the descriptive stage and thus
more obviously grounded in supporting evidence.

One possible interpretation is that the painting is a subtly conscious effort,
perhaps even a subversive one with ominous overtones about the ongoing
relationship between the gentry and their workers. An idea that emerges
through deductive inquiry is that of the subjugation of the worker. Details
from the painting become evidence in support of this idea: The worker closest
to the overseer is pressed visually into the ground by the powerful line of the
diagonal that connects the overseer's head to the horse's head and continues
through the worker to the ground. Both this worker and the worker next to
him are bent low, their backs pushed into the ground by the horizontal line of
the far-reaching field of wheat. Their gazes and their sickles draw them to the
earth through an invisible diagonal line connecting the two.

The powerful theme of subjugation belies the more prettified theme of workers
at leisure suggested by Rush. The workers' clothes may not look dirty, ragged,
or even mussed, but their positions and postures, especially in relationship to the
vertical power of the overseer (a power heightened by his position on the horse
and by the heavy mass of trees behind him) tie them to the earth.

Yet we may also deductively conclude that there is an implicit challenge within this atmosphere of oppression: The workers are all aligned against the overseer. This conclusion also has its origins in a wealth of detail. Two of the workers confront the overseer directly with their gazes (a horizontal line that suggests equality); standing farthest from the overseer, they are free to stand upright and even break the unyielding horizontal line of the wheat field with their hats. Their hats symbolize an implicit equality in another way, too: The overseer wears the same black hat as the workers. Although his hat is in the higher position now, possibly he too will have to join them some day, for he too is linked by the broad u-shaped curve of hats that pulls him to the ground as well.

Furthermore, although the workers and the overseer appear to be lined up on a single plane, and thus all connected, their different relationships lead to further deductive insights. The worker on the left and the overseer hold each other in their gazes as if in challenge. If we shift our focus to the two men immediately in front of the overseer, their subservient positions become a major theme. By contrast, the man and woman working with the sheaves of wheat seem more free, more upright, more equal.

Students have also observed that the characters in the painting all seem frozen in a single moment of time on a single plane. Their positions are fixed, not fluid. They seem static, not active. Perhaps it is a position that reflects a moment in British history that is about to pass—as it did.

Finally, as one student writer noted, the oval shape of the painting and its inner frame,

> tipped on its side as it is, is redolent of the human eye in shape. In this respect, the form calls attention to the act of seeing itself, echoing, or perhaps even parodying, the viewer's own vision. The raised wood carvings, placed strategically in each corner of the frame, direct our vision inward to the center of the painting, to the subject matter itself. It is a device which asks that we recognize the way in which our own vision is directed, and hence constructed. (Rosalsky 5)

The observation of detail is a heuristic for the generation of deductive insights and conclusions. Yet as art critic John Berger has observed,

> To look is an act of choice. We never look at just one thing; we are always looking at the relation between things and ourselves. Our vision is continually active, continually moving, continually holding things in a circle around itself, constituting what is present to us as we are. (8-9)

Berger's words anticipate Prown's speculative stage, the final stage that asks the investigator to explore the meaning of what has been observed and deduced—and understand why these observations and responses are important. Speculation creates a context for the foregoing epistemological activities, thus linking epistemology to dialectic.

Stage III: Speculation[6]

By the time the investigator questions the meaning of the foregoing activities of observation and deduction—and thus moves into Prown's "speculative stage"— most of the generative work has been done. Speculation takes up the task of shaping the foregoing observations and deductions into a conscious whole. Speculation asks, "So what?" What is the meaning of what I have now observed (which will now become evidence toward my conclusions), what are my responses to those observations, and why are those responses important? Who else is concerned and why? What is at issue here?

Speculative inquiry enables a writer to begin to explore and develop "theories that might explain the various effects observed and felt" (Prown 10). In doing so, the writer draws heavily on the details of the first two stages to support these final conclusions. In this way, Prown's methodology is similar to the enthymeme insofar as the final claim or conclusion does not create new information but rather gives logical shape to a body of underlying information. The information generated through descriptive and deductive inquiry becomes evidence in support of the conclusions of the speculative stage—but evidence is itself, as we have seen, a created phenomenon.

Thus, in the structure of a piece of writing the epistemological shape of knowledge is inverted, as Frank D'Angelo sought to show in *A Conceptual Theory of Rhetoric* years ago and as John Gage and Richard Fulkerson illustrate in this book in their respective chapters on the enthymeme and Toulmin's paradigm of argument. Speculation is the argument that controls the movement of a piece of writing from beginning to end, and the descriptive and deductive details that support that argument are subordinated to it throughout as evidence— even though it is the creation and realization of these details that first set the whole argumentative process of inquiry into motion. The process of creating, developing, and constructing arguments is an epistemological journey made up of several hierarchical levels of realization and reasoning—as Prown's methodology shows (and a dialectical journey when the argument is contextualized).

Speculation thus shapes a piece of writing, although the details generated in the descriptive and deductive stages are visible throughout. Speculation may also grow from information gained through another kind of "observation," that of reading, a stage of inquiry and insight that would parallel the hierarchical growth of the foregoing descriptive and deductive stages—and thus would connect reading to the contexts of inquiry. Thus Prown's paradigm includes a program of research as well, one that might help substantiate or widen the ideas created during the stages of perceptual inquiry (or even, as we adapt this model to composition, generate those ideas).

In the instance of *Reapers,* it might be useful to know more about the painterly conventions, cultural expectations, and social conditions of the time. Investigators who turn to social history would learn, for example, of the tremendous economic and social unrest going on in England in the 1700s and 1800s, unrest that would eventually lead to the kind of opposition between classes depicted in *Reapers*: the Swing riots with their destruction of threshing machines and property, arson of the harvest haystacks and wheat shocks, the creation of the Corn Laws, the Poor Laws, the Game Laws, and the Enclosure Acts. Each of these laws gave greater power to the gentry and worsened working conditions for the laborer, setting the stage for increased confrontation between classes. If there is a need for library research, there is now a reason for it, a question to be answered and an epistemological framework within which to place one's findings.

Whatever the origins of our thinking, speculation is an essential last act of inquiry, for it functions (both as a stage and as a statement) to define and shape the process of discovery into an argumentative whole that exhibits a certain exigency and thus a need for resolution (see, e.g., the chapter in this book by Fahnestock and Secor). Through its sense of purpose, speculation transforms all foregoing generative detail and insight into evidence in support of a position. The role of speculation as a defining and shaping end is apparent in writing; we can see how speculation transforms and subordinates description and deduction to its own end.

For example, art historian Christiana Payne, like Rush, speculates that many of the British landscape paintings of the 1700s and 1800s "are vehicles for myth rather than accurate reflections of reality" (23). The difference between Payne's and Rush's conclusions is not so much one of content as of development: The origins of Payne's speculations are more visible throughout her book-length study of the imagery of the paintings of this time and it is this visibility of substantiating detail that makes it possible for readers to test their assent to her conclusions.

Based on the same evidence (that is, working through the same descriptive and deductive hierarchies), art historian John Barrell comes to a different speculative conclusion: although he agrees at first with Payne that "for the most part the art of rural life offers us the image of a stable, unified, almost egalitarian society," his concern "is to suggest that it is possible to look beneath the surface of the painting, and to discover there evidence of the very conflict it seems to deny" (5).

Curiously, Barrell positions Stubbs outside this tradition of "unity as artifice, as something made out of the actuality of division" (which is also a speculation), and claims that Stubbs's paintings are "the most refined and artificial images of the rural labourer that the century produced" (23), a deductive conclusion that is essential to his overall speculative thesis that the paintings often represent views that the artists themselves did not consciously embrace (conclusions that he substantiates with detail from Stubbs's paintings).

Both Payne and Barrell are proposing book-length arguments about the cultural and social significance of the art of the 1700s and 1800s. Both are "speculating" about the meaning of their own mental engagement with the artifacts of those cultures, as a way not only to gain *evidence* towards their conclusions, but also to understand, first, what their conclusions are and, second, why what we call *evidence* does, in fact, carry out the function *of* evidence. And, because they come to very different conclusions, both are in the position of having to substantiate their arguments through a mastery of detail, deduction, and induction that we typically call *evidence* (or *reasons* or *support*) when we talk about writing either as a process or as a product.

Whatever an individual's reading of the details that will eventually become evidence toward a hierarchy of conclusions, the point is that such a hierarchy does exist and that a final speculative conclusion (in any discipline) must have an origin. The process of understanding and learning to work from origins to conclusions represents the organicism of thought that has been explored by D'Angelo (and by Alexander Bain before him), and teaches us that the structure of our writing—and especially of what we call argumentative writing—has its architecture in that organicism. Such an approach is pedagogically more interesting than the fill-in-the-blanks type of approach implied by Edward P. J. Corbett's statement that "the basic strategy of arguing is to assert or deny something and then give some reason or evidence to support the assertion or denial" (11). Speculation also subordinates evidence to a position of support for an assertion, but Prown's approach links structure to epistemological exploration. Thus, according to Prown's paradigm, an effective piece of writing will always reveal the origins of its structure in thought as inquiry—and thus reveal structure in writing to be both organic and formal in nature.

The Prown Model in the Composition Classroom

The Prown model has implications for teaching students how to write because it contains within it both a generative and a critical system of inquiry in which students learn to use language both as a means of bringing into existence a series of observations and insights and as a means of questioning the meaning of that body of information. In this way, the paradigm is remarkably similar to Elbow's two levels of thinking—first-order and second-order—in which *second-order thinking* is "thinking about our thinking" generated in freewrites and *first-order thinking* is "first-draft exploratory writing" (58).

There are important differences, however, between Elbow and Prown (and between Elbow and other compositionists). First, Prown does not hesitate to use the word "evidence" to discuss the transformation of one set of ideas (descriptive observation) into support for another set of ideas or realizations (and thus a kind of metadiscourse) that grows from it. Second, Elbow does not pursue the full range of critical implications for his paradigm: His two-part system has its fullest expression in teaching students to write personal narratives and then explore the meanings of those narratives (see, e.g., Workshops 2, 3, and 4 in Elbow and Belanoff's *A Community of Writers*). Thus, as a critical system, Elbow's paradigm is less defined than Prown's in its explanation of how critical insight and realization are generated, how conclusions relate to their origins, and how structure grows from process.

Nonetheless, the challenge for a composition classroom is to wed structure in writing to the generative principles espoused by Prown and Elbow alike—and to show, throughout a series of writing assignments that become increasingly complex, the hierarchical nature of critical and generative inquiry and the way in which evidence is a heuristic itself, a system of invention essential to other levels of critical insight. Writing thus proceeds as a medium of inquiry throughout, a medium in which "first-order" generation of detail is essential to achieving insights that grow from that detail and where, finally, these generative details lead to realizations that will be substantiated in the end by the very detail that led to their formulation.

One way to connect Prown's methodology to the writing classroom is to use actual artifacts to focus student inquiry on visual/tactile objects, the symbolism of which contains potential for cultural insights and argumentation about those insights. Cultural icons such as a Coca-Cola can, a tube of lipstick, a photograph frame, and Valentine's Day cards (examples my students have used) contain a wealth of possibility for discussion and any number of points of entry into cultural analysis. Images from the media provide another kind of text, one that also focuses inquiry on visual text as a starting point. Inquiry can then progress more and more broadly into the contexts and cultures in which these texts exist. Whether we are asking questions about a series of rape scenes from current movies, scenes that Robin Warshaw examines in "Ugly Truths of Date Rape Elude the Screen," or wondering why television sitcoms wrote mothers out of their scripts, as Joy Horowitz does in "Poof! The Mommies Vanish from Sitcomland," Prownian levels provide a useful way for students to begin to understand how their writing grows both from their responses and from an analysis of those responses. As with writing about paintings, the many details observed during the descriptive stage are transformed into evidence as the writer seeks to formulate and substantiate further deductions and speculations.

Yet writing classes typically are not centered on inquiry into objects, but on written texts. Classes in sociology, psychology, and education may ask students to observe behavior, people, and the dynamics of social and psychological interaction; thus, the core of Prown's methodology may seem to be more appropriate for such disciplines because visual or artifactual texts are similar to behavior and events as texts. Likewise, the centrality of Prown's artifact shares similarities with the basis of inquiry in the physical sciences: Observing, measuring, and engaging with the physical realities of tests, experiments, and other such data provide a useful parallel with Prown's descriptive stage. Scientists know that to cut short their engagement with the subject on its own terms (the descriptive inquiry) before beginning deduction and speculation can be hazardous to the construction of knowledge in their fields (and thus hazardous to their reputations). Even though the conventions of disciplinary knowledge are of the utmost importance for students to grasp, the academy expects all students to be able to write in response to what they read—to read at length and to propose arguments that not only grow from their knowledge and understanding but also avoid regurgitating that reading. If Prown is to be useful to the writing classroom, with its emphasis on written texts (even if the text is one of the student's own creation, as in Elbow's methodology), we need to understand how reading itself involves descriptive inquiry, how our responses to what we read—Prown's deductive and speculative hierarchies—grow from what we read even as they provoke rereadings, and how these hierarchies are evident in the structure of our writing.

Because writing and thus reading are multifaceted acts, engagement with reading can be differently described depending on the nature of that engagement. Just as an investigator can interact in any number of ways with an artifact during the descriptive stage of its examination, so too do we read differently depending on our purpose for reading. Most basic is reading for information, for access to the raw data of detail from which our own arguments will eventually grow through deduction and speculation, and for mastery of the detail that will be transformed into evidence to support those as yet unshaped arguments (just as those who investigated *Reapers* needed to master a wealth of detail internal to that painting before discussion could begin). Just as *Reapers* helped illustrate Prown's theories about visual/tactile texts, a written text can illustrate how information gained during reading can serve as a basis for realizing and shaping arguments and for inquiring into one's own arguments derived from that reading.

In the following passage taken from an article titled "Heathens and Angels: Childhood in the Rocky Mountain Mining Towns," the author, Elliott West, explores portrayals of childhood on the frontier, particularly in mining towns in the Colorado Rockies during the late 1800s. This passage is particularly useful not only to illustrate how detail is transformed into evidence in support of a series of conclusions, but also to illustrate how much awareness we need to have of our own acts of interpretation if we are to gain readers' understanding of and assent to our arguments. In a series of vivid paragraphs, West speculates about the ways in which frontier life shaped children's lives and affected their growth and development. In the following passage, he claims that:

> Boys [unlike girls] found jobs that took them away from the influence of the home. . . . By twelve or thirteen, many were performing the more menial tasks of the town—'forking' along the sluices, feeding pack mules, peddling bills, selling newspapers, washing dishes, and seeking out odd jobs. Others took on remarkably difficult and occasionally perilous duties. 'Pretty dangerous business, ain't it?' Walter Smith, age thirteen, wrote his mother from Tellurium, Colorado, where he was dodging rocks blown out by explosives, pounding out drills in a blacksmith shop, and throwing his ninety-five pounds behind a heavy miner's sledge in the tunnels. The brightest and most ambitious were given surprising responsibilities. As a clerk for a grocer in California Gulch, Colorado, the twelve-year-old Bennet Seymour often was left in charge of the store, and by the next year he was freighting goods for his boss from South Park. At thirteen, Charles Draper was so successful at selling books in Red Lodge, Montana, that a publishing house offered him an annual salary of $1,000 to serve as its field representative; at the same age, Willie Hedges, son of a Helena attorney and judge, received forty dollars a month as head of the capital's public library; and when only fourteen, another Montanan was running a ferry. (370)

West goes on to tell the story of a boy named Francis Werden, whose diary records his increasing "independence and ambition," both in his willingness to take on more and more work and his interest in becoming increasingly responsible at a young age. His diary records his efforts to stake a claim on one Christmas Day:

> "Today I stampeded [sic] off after a claim . . . (200 ft. each). I did not succeed in getting one. Heard tonight that they were made smaller so that gives me another

chance." In his impulsive optimism, this teenager could be mistaken for men twice (or four times) his age. . . . Children, especially the boys, often seemed to take on the acquisitive, aggressive, economically individualistic values characteristic of the mining frontier . . . . (371)

Details observed from primary sources (texts such as diaries, letters, reports, journals) and transformed into evidence in support of West's conclusions make up much of the substance and content of this article, and the move from descriptive detail to deductive (or inductive) interpretation of that detail is obvious in West's propositional style.

Yet midway through this article, West makes a curious move: He challenges his own conclusions (and thus his own act of reading as both a descriptive and deductive, interpretative act) by observing that any conclusion can be shaped from a willful misreading of only part of the detail obtained from primary sources. West uses the comments of a visitor to the Rockies to question his own act of selectivity during the descriptive stage of reading, an act of selectivity that Prown warns against and that turns reading into an act of finding and filling in information that supports preconceived conclusions rather than grounding inquiry (and reading) as an act of intellectual engagement. First, West cites a visitor to the Rockies whose superficial observations led her to exclaim at length on the absence, even extinction, of childhood. She exclaims, "I have never seen any children, only debased imitations of men and women, cankered by greed and selfishness, and asserting and gaining complete independence of their parents at ten years old" (374).

West then questions this observation and consequently his own—presumably, such a setup is behind his purpose in drawing such a dire portrait of children's lives in the first half of his article. "Was she correct?" he asks. "In fact, such conclusions should be drawn cautiously . . . if a reasonably accurate picture is to be drawn" (374). The whole of a body of evidence needs to be examined, according to West, before investigators can be satisfied that they have fully understood and accurately interpreted the subject.

In taking this step, West criticizes the first half of his own article and the "pattern" of interpretation constructed from "the evidence considered thus far": that the frontier deprives children of their childhood (373). West is echoing Prown's concern that whatever we inquire into first be separated from our own uses for that information *as evidence,* because only then can we begin to understand what we are seeing as itself a response that needs to be inquired into through deductive and speculative inquiry. Both West and Prown ask students to examine carefully the bases for their own conclusions and to make those bases clear in their writing: What information or what details from the texts they have read lead them to interpret as they do? How do their realizations and conclusions grow out of that detail? How are their claims substantiated by that detail? Finally, what do they make of their own conclusions, their own responses to what has *become* evidence in their writing? Offering detail is not just a matter of livening up our writing; it is the very basis for substantiating and revealing the origins of our thinking. I find myself constantly asking my students for more detail in their writing because their claims (often in the form of broad generalizations) seem so ungrounded to me. I want to know from whence their arguments are derived: What information did they process (either through observation, reading, talking, or experiencing) to come to their conclusions? How does this detail substantiate those conclusions?

This kind of reading is equivalent to Prown's descriptive stage: Texts can function as the equivalent of the visual/tactile object, and writers' engagement with any text have implications for their own writing. But, just as Prown's hierarchies of deduction and speculation ask investigators to question their own observations and to engage in the metadiscourse of examining and responding to their own thinking, so too do they need to understand how the act of reading is itself a "text" that bears examination. What we do when we respond to reading, the equivalent of Prown's descriptive stage, becomes a "text" that we can in turn read.

One way to understand the relationship between reading and constructing knowledge from and because of our reading is to locate the act of reading itself as the focus of our inquiry. Kurt Spellmeyer shows us how Richard Rodriquez's acts of reading to absorb but not to question (as Rodriquez himself describes in *Hunger of Memory*) are not acts of argument because they are *not acts of inquiry*. By contrast, Spellmeyer's own inquiry into reading as inquiry emphasizes how knowledge is (according to Foucault's terms, as Spellmeyer notes) "an activity rather than a body of information" (71). Similarly, Richard Miller reports on a student's attempt to read Gloria Anzaldua's "Entering into the Serpent." What ensues is the student's attempt to understand his own act of reading: "Not only must I lessen my own barriers of understanding, but I must be able to comprehend and understand the argument of the other" (406). If we are to understand the connections between the act of reading as a text and argument as an act of constructing knowledge in response to the "texts" created by our reading, then such inquiry into how we read is important. Yet I am concerned about a twist in the focus of our arguments as a result: Reading theorists make it possible to argue more fully and eloquently about how we read, but not necessarily about how we argue about subjects other than reading, *because of* what and how we have read. The parallel in Prown is that "reading" the text of *Reapers* makes it possible to argue about the larger social and cultural issues of the times and not about how we read *Reapers* per se (which nonetheless could be a fascinating subject itself). Similarly, Kathleen McCormick hypothesizes that texts are always embedded in their cultures and thus can always serve as a starting point (like visual/tactile objects) from which inquiry proceeds in ever-increasing circles outward, until what we are inquiring into are the conditions, cultures, and periods (both synchronous and dichronous) in which a text exists.

Any number of ways of reading a text (including, but not limited to, examining the way in which we read that text) exist and have the potential for embarking us on journeys in which we examine both the text itself and the knowing that we might want to argue for as a result of reading. We may read for an awareness of the writer's whole argument. For example, when West concludes at the end of his article that two forces had come into conflict ("that childhood was a distinct, unique, and valued time of life" that was challenged by the requirements of survival in mining camps) and thus tradition and innovation existed in the frontier in a "delicious irony" as communities sought both to protect their children and flaunt their survival skills (a mentality of toughness, so to speak), we may wish to understand the logic of his argument, the process of reasoning by which he came to this conclusion. If we agree with him, we may wish to understand why we agree. Or, we may challenge his conclusions through our own criticisms of his argument (do his own deductive and speculative conclusions, for example, seem manipulative of the information at hand?). In either event, we need to understand what is at issue in our acceptance or disagreement and why either position is important both to observe and understand. Or, if we ask questions about the difference in perspectives between West's interpretations and those of other scholars, or between dichronous and synchronous interpretations of the age, then we would want to question our own attention to perspective and ask why perspective is an important feature to examine. What is at issue in our examination of any text? That question provides the parallel with Prownian questions about the deductions that we may come to about our readings, and about the speculations about our own deductions.

That there is a relationship between reading and arguing seems inevitable, as Bartholomae observes in this book when he argues that "close reading is an exercise in argument." Yet the point, ultimately, of looking at Prown's work is not to add to the growing body of reading theory or to insist that the focus of inquiry in a composition class is always a written text, but rather to understand how we construct arguments out of an engagement with inquiry *with any number of different kinds of texts through any number of different kinds of "reading"* and how that construction grows out of (and is shaped by) a number of informative, hierarchical acts of cognition, language, naming, defining, and interpreting.

The difference between reading theory (as a specific branch of composition theory) and Prown's methodology is that, like Frank D'Angelo before him, Prown is interested in the entirety of conceptual inquiry, whether we "read" written texts, visual images, tactile objects, or the dynamics of interactive social and cultural events. What is at issue, as always, is this: What happens when we engage in intellectual inquiry into anything? How can we inquire into our own inquiry? What does an intellectual engagement with inquiry imply about our understanding of writing not only as an extension *of* that engagement but also as structured *by* that engagement? What are the structural parallels? And how can our understanding of writing as a conceptual act shape our pedagogies as teachers of writing?

Conclusion

My purpose in reviewing Prown's paradigm at length is not to give us a new methodology to import into our composition courses but to examine its implications for composition. One of those implications, I believe, is that as yet we have no methodology worked out for teaching our students about the *creation* of evidence (and the transformation of information into evidence) and the epistemological role that evidence plays in all writing. That is, we lack a theory of evidence that addresses how we create and use information to understand the processes of our own minds.

We are not alone in this: Apart from departments of philosophy, which teach evidence as part of symbolic logic, few, if any, departments teach the concept of evidence as part of their discipline's epistemology and as a heuristic. One recent book, *Questions of Evidence,* notes that "surprisingly little attention has been directed toward the central concern of what constitutes evidence in research and scholarship" in the disciplines. Larry Laudan of the University of Hawaii notes that other than in departments of philosophy, evidence is typically taught only in law schools where, paradoxically, its study is offered in courses on what constitutes inadmissible evidence.

These charges are serious ones, just as is the charge I am making against composition: that it lacks a theory of evidence, a theory that should be essential to our discipline. We lack a theory of evidence in part because we lack methodologies for teaching and for creating evidence, and the two go hand in hand. But let me temper that charge a bit: I do think that there are approaches to composition, such as those in this book, that teach students how to write and create evidence—but they are not so named. Evidence, evoking the worst of the old current-traditional paradigm, is an out-of-favor word, one that smacks of prescriptive formalism: the old reason 1, reason 2, and reason 3. What we teach may in fact have potential to contribute to our students' understanding of evidence as epistemology, but if we don't give it that name *and* connect that name to a process, they cannot make the connection.

In the end, I would argue that it is not just a matter of terminology, but of the very way in which we understand writing as an epistemological act, an understanding or approach that sees the entirety of the writing process as a mental journey in which the writers learn to recognize the individual landscapes of their own minds; a landscape they both create and explore, the creation of which is intimately tied to further exploration, further ideas, further insights. The "further" is what seems of essence here: If they cannot understand the importance of the initial epistemological stages of this journey of knowing and writing, how can they progress to the final stages of knowing what they think and why—and how can they know the entire process as one of their own creation?

Notes

1. I am using a broad definition of "cognition" here as Bizup and Kintgen do in their definition of cognitive science as the study of "all varieties of human intelligence and *cognition*, from 'basic' functions such as perception and motor control to those 'higher' faculties such as language use and reasoning which we tend to view as integral to our humanity" (841, emphasis added).

2. In 1985, I worked with Jules Prown as a writing advisor (through Yale's Bass Writing Program) for the Yale-New Haven Teachers Institute seminar and for a graduate seminar that he taught in the Department of Art History, titled "American Art and Artifacts: The Interpretation of Objects" (History of Art 725a/American Studies 804a). The curriculum units that resulted from the Yale-New Haven Teachers Institute seminar are published in a book titled *Time Machines: Artifacts and Culture* (New Haven, CT: Yale-New Haven Teachers Institute, 1985).

3. At this point, I would like to use the word "stage" to refer to Prownian levels of inquiry. Although I would not want the use of the word "stage" to imply that I am attempting to resurrect a stage theory of composing here, Prown himself uses the word *stage* in order to distinguish between the different activities that occur in each area of inquiry, and particularly to show how interdependent and hierarchical these activities are.

4. I have omitted discussion of substages A and B here because they do not contribute as significantly as substage C to the development of conclusions about *Reapers*.

5. Prown's use of the term "deduction" to label a stage in the thinking process may or may not involve deduction in its entirety. While it is true that many of the ideas created in this stage (especially the substage of "intellectual engagement") do require a deductive move from descriptive detail, sometimes that move might well be inductive instead (as in the "sensory engagement" substage). See, for example, the discussion of the West passage included in this chapter.

6. Compositionists might well ask what the term "speculation" means and how speculation as an activity differs from deduction. Speculation is a more self-reflexive act than is deduction, according to Prown. Deduction, as an act of inquiry, takes into account one's responses to what one has observed—that is, what we deduce (or even induce) from what we have seen. Speculation involves questioning the importance and meaning of our initial deductive/inductive responses. Thus speculation may mean a kind of further deductive insight, one that is more wide-reaching and which transforms initial deductions into another level of evidence.

APPENDIX:
OUTLINE OF METHODOLOGICAL PROCEDURE
FOR ART AND ARTIFACTS

Stage I. Description

The descriptive stage is a synchronic one in which "description is restricted to what can be observed in the object itself, that is, to internal evidence [which is] read at a particular moment in time" (7). Prown recommends beginning with general and larger observations first, then moving toward an increasingly detailed investigation. Prown urges the investigator to observe as dispassionately and disinterestedly as possible, thus making the artifact the object of inquiry first and delaying inquiry into our own responses until the later stages of deduction and speculation.

The descriptive stage consists of three substages.

A. Substantial Analysis: Large-scale description of the physical attributes of the artifact, whether two- or three-dimensional.

1. *Physical Dimensions:* measurements (weight, height, etc.)
2. *Materials:* type, use, pattern of distribution
3. *Articulation:* "the ways in which the materials are put together in the fabrication of the object" (8).

B. Content Analysis: Inquiry into the content and subject of the artifact, whether three-dimensional or pictorial. "The procedure is iconography in its simplest sense, a reading of overt representations" (8).

1. *Overt Subject Matter:* what the picture or object shows
2. *Symbolic Embellishments:* "decorative designs or motifs, inscriptions, coats of arms or diagrams, engraved or embossed on metal, carved or painted on wood or stone, woven in textiles, molded or etched in glass" (8).

C. Formal Analysis: Formal analysis begins an inquiry into the specific detail of the artifact. Although this level of inquiry provides the fine level of observation that can give rise to deductive and speculative insights, Prown warns that too much detail can obscure those insights as much as too little.

   1. *Two-dimensional Organization:*
      a. Lines: horizontals, verticals, diagonals, curves, etc.
      b. Designs: repeated lines that form patterns
      c. Areas: size relationships
   2. *Three-dimensional Organization:* These may be actual, as in an artifact, or pictorial
      a. Shapes (pyramids, squares, spheres, etc.)
      b. Relationships between shapes
   3. *Other Formal Elements:*
      a. Color
      b. Light
      c. Textures

Stage II. Deduction

"The second stage of analysis moves from the object itself to the relationship between the object and the perceiver. It involves the empathetic linking of the material (actual) or represented world of the object with the perceiver's world of existence and experience" (8).

A. Sensory Engagement: What you the investigator see, hear, smell, taste, and feel when you look at, touch, or otherwise interact with the object.

B. Intellectual Engagement: Here the investigator needs to determine whether his or her ideas arise from the observation and inquiry—and thus from the observed details of the artifact. Any knowledge that adds to but does not derive from the artifact should wait until the speculative stage. For example, Prown observes that

> In the case of a pictorial object, there are a number of questions that may be addressed to and answered by the object itself, especially if it is representational. What is the time of day? What is the season of the year? What is the effect on what is depicted of natural forces such as heat and cold or the pull of gravity? In the relation between the depicted world and our world, where are we positioned, what might we be doing, and

what role, if any, might we play? How would we enter pictorial space? What transpired prior to the depicted moment? What may happen next? (9)

C. Emotional Response: How you respond to the object, what feelings it arouses.

Stage III. Speculation

A. Theories and Hypothesis

In the speculative stage, investigators can now begin to react to their observations and deductive reactions. This step functions as a kind of meta-analysis in which investigators begin to add existing knowledge to the knowledge gained from observation of the elements intrinsic to the object of inquiry.

B. Program of Research

Having explored both the artifact and one's own existing knowledge for the insights it provides, investigators might now decide to go elsewhere to increase their knowledge about the culture of the artifact and the conditions of its production. Prown calls this step "the search for and investigation of external evidence" (10). Clearly, however, the integrity of inquiry depends first on the construction of knowledge and insights to which a broader program of research could contribute.

Finally, Prown notes that these three levels of inquiry—description, deduction, and speculation—should not be seen as a separate and distinct kind of research in and of themselves, but rather there "should be continual shunting back and forth between the outside evidence and the artifact as research suggests to the investigator the need for more descriptive information or indicates other hypotheses that need to be tested affectively" (10).

Works Cited

Barrell, John. *The Dark Side of the Landscape: The Rural Poor in English Painting 1730-1840.* Cambridge: Cambridge University Press, 1980.
Berger, John. *Ways of Seeing.* London: Penguin, 1972.
Berthoff, Ann. *The Making of Meaning: Metaphors, Models, and Maxims for Writing Teachers.* Upper Montclair, NJ: Boynton/Cook, 1981.
Bizup, Joseph M., and Eugene R. Kintgen. "The Cognitive Paradigm in Literary Studies." *College English* 55 (Dec. 1993): 841-57.

Chandler, James, Arnold I. Davidson, and Harry D. Haroofunian, Eds. *Questions of Evidence: Proof, Practice, and Persuasion across the Disciplines.* Chicago: The University of Chicago Press, 1994.

Corbett, Edward P. J. *The Elements of Reasoning.* New York: Macmillan, 1991.

D'Angelo, Frank J. *A Conceptual Theory of Rhetoric.* Cambridge, MA: Winthrop, 1975.

Elbow, Peter. *Embracing Contraries: Explorations in Learning and Teaching.* New York: Oxford University Press, 1986.

Elbow, Peter, and Pat Belanoff. *A Community of Writers: A Workshop Course in Writing.* 2nd ed. New York: McGraw-Hill, 1995.

Fishman, Stephen M., and Lucille Parkinson McCarthy. "Is Expressivism Dead? Reconsidering Its Romantic Roots and Its Relation to Social Constructionism." *College English* 54 (Oct. 1992): 647-61.

Fulkerson, Richard. "Technical Logic, Comp-Logic, and the Teaching of Writing." *College Composition and Communication* 39 (Dec. 1988): 436-52.

Gage, John T. *The Shape of Reason: Argumentative Writing in College.* 2nd ed. New York: Macmillan, 1991.

———. "A General Theory of the Enthymeme for Advanced Composition." *Teaching Advanced Composition.* Ed. Katherine H. Adams and John L. Adams. Portsmouth, NH: Boynton/Cook-Heinemann, 1991.

Horowitz, Joy. "Poof! The Mommies Vanish from Sitcomland." *The New York Times* 26 May 1991: 23, 25.

Laudan, Larry. "The Concept of Evidence." NEH Summer Seminar for College Teachers, University of Hawaii, 1994.

McCormick, Kathleen. "Task Representation in Writing About Literature." *Poetics* 16 (1987): 131-92.

———. *The Culture of Reading and the Teaching of English.* Manchester: Manchester University Press, 1994.

Miller, Richard E. "Fault Lines in the Contact Zone." *College English* 56 (Apr. 1994): 389-408.

Payne, Christiana. *Toil and Plenty: Images of the Agricultural Landscape in England, 1780-1890.* New Haven, CT: Yale University Press, 1993.

Phelps, Louise Wetherbee. *Composition as a Human Science: Contributions to the Self-Understanding of a Discipline.* New York: Oxford University Press, 1988.

Prown, Jules D. "Mind in Matter: An Introduction to Material Culture Theory and Method." *Winterthur Portfolio* 17 (Spring 1982): 1-19.

Rodriquez, Richard. *Hunger of Memory: The Education of Richard Rodriquez: An Autobiography.* Boston: D. R. Godine, 1982.

Rosalsky, Susan. "George Stubbs' *Reapers*." Duplicated paper provided for a revision workshop, Department of Art History, Yale University, New Haven, CT.

Rush, Michael. "The Earth Won't Move When You See Yale's 'Toil'." *New Haven Register* 30 Jan. 1994: E1, E7.

Spellmeyer, Kurt. *Common Ground: Dialogue, Understanding, and the Teaching of Composition.* Englewood Cliffs, NJ: Prentice Hall, 1993.

Stubbs, George. *Reapers.* Yale Center for British Art, New Haven, CT.

Walker, Jeffrey. "Of Brains and Rhetorics." *College English* 52 (Mar. 1990): 301-22.

Warshaw, Robin. "Ugly Truths of Date Rape Elude the Screen." *The New York Times* 5 May 1991: H17, H22.

West, Elliott. "Heathens and Angels: Childhood in the Rocky Mountain Mining Towns." *Growing Up in America: Historical Experiences.* Ed. Harvey J. Graff. Detroit, MI: Wayne State University Press, 1987. 367-84.

3

The Toulmin Model of Argument and the Teaching of Composition

Richard Fulkerson
East Texas State University

In the late 1970s and early 1980s, when composition teachers and scholars first learned about the six-part argumentation model of British philosopher Stephen Toulmin, they were attracted by the model's potential to describe the processes by which arguments were generated in real discourse. Composition-ists soon embraced Toulmin's model as a promising new approach to argu-mentation and adapted it to their classrooms and textbooks. Introduced to composition studies in 1978 by Charles Kneupper in *College Composition and Communication,* the model began to show up in books like Maxine Hairston's *Successful Writing.* The model still has cachet: it remains the foundation of two of the most popular books on argumentative writing, Annette Rottenberg's *Elements of Argument* and John Ramage and John Bean's *Writing Arguments.*

But composition was not the first field to adapt Toulmin's model to its own needs, nor did the model come without a history of controversy. When he introduced the model in 1958 in *The Uses of Argument,* Toulmin was engaged in a critique of formal logic at large; the model was simply a means of illustrating the inadequacies he saw in philosophy's view of both argument and epistemology. *The Uses of Argument* received universally negative reviews[1] and aroused hostility in his colleagues, who called it an "antilogic" book (Olson 288). Toulmin recounts that his own doctoral adviser virtually refused to speak to him for the next twenty years ("Logic" 375), and he expected the book to die a quiet death. He was thus perplexed by its continuing to sell at a steady pace, until he learned during a visit to the United States that American departments of speech communication had discovered and adopted his model in courses in argument ("Logic" 375).

Wayne Brockriede and Douglas Ehninger first introduced the Toulmin model to American speech scholars in 1960 ("Toulmin on Argument"). They then popularized the model by using it as the foundation for a highly successful argumentation textbook, *Decision by Debate* (Ehninger and Brockriede 1963). By 1987, the model had appeared in at least twenty speech textbooks (for titles see van Eemeren, Grootendorst, and Kruiger 186; Kneupper 237; Ortiz-Seda 17), and Kneupper maintained that it had replaced deduction as the dominant approach to the principles of argument in the field of speech (237). For his enduring contribution to speech communication, Toulmin received, in 1990, the first Wayne Brockriede Milestones in Argumentation Award from the Speech Communication and American Forensic Associations. He remarked at the time,

> More than thirty years ago, when I sat down to write my book, *The Uses of Argument,* the last thing I had in mind was to revive the theory of rhetoric. My own concern with "substantive inferences" sprang directly from my dissatisfaction with the current state of the theory of knowledge, and my target was other philosophers. . . . Only when I came to understand the reason why the American speech communication and forensic communities took the book so seriously could I even (so to say) grasp the significance of my own work! ("Editors' Column" 36)

The Toulmin model has been used and debated for nearly forty years now. Its prominence and the length of time it has held sway in both speech communication and in composition might suggest that the model has become part of the canon by which we understand and teach argumentative writing. But this is not the case: The model is becoming more, not less, controversial, albeit on different terms than those of philosophy's debate with it. After composition's almost twenty years' experience using Toulmin to teach argumentation, we still have questions about it and issues to debate: How does the model work? What exactly is a warrant? What does the model's use contribute to the composition classroom? Can it be used to generate arguments? To describe them? To assess them? To organize student papers? What are its advantages as a composition model and its defects? Do the former outweigh the latter? Our experience fails to settle such questions. Instead, experience and research have made the model seem more problematically complex than it first appeared.

Toulmin's Criticism of Traditional Logic

Toulmin wrote *The Uses of Argument* as an argument itself, an argument challenging the core of traditional philosophical logic. Ever since Aristotle, logicians had been concerned with distinguishing *valid* arguments from *invalid* ones. By *valid,* philosophers mean properly formed deductive arguments, arguments in which the premises logically entail the conclusion: that is, arguments in which it is impossible for the premises to be true and the conclusion false. Let me illustrate: "If I do not have the keys to my car, I will not be able to get home from the airport. I do not have the keys. So I will not be able to get home." If the first two sentences (the premises) are true, then purely because of the syntactic form of the argument (a hypothetical syllogism following a valid form known as *modus ponens*),[2] the final sentence (the conclusion) inevitably follows. That is what is meant by *validity/entailment.* Of course, there are much more complex forms of valid argument than this simple example.

But because many, probably most, good arguments in actual discourse do not purport to be deductively valid, Toulmin criticized philosophy's fixation on logical entailment. In these everyday arguments the conclusion is asserted to follow from the premises *with probability,* but not to be entailed by them. Toulmin calls such arguments *substantial,* but following Aristotle, we can call them *contingent* in that their credibility depends on contextual factors (discussed on following pages), not just on their internal structure. Though technically *invalid,* such arguments nevertheless function appropriately and nonfallaciously to achieve "proof" in their real-world contexts. Consider, for example, a medical diagnosis based on a patient's symptoms of fever, runny nose, and coughing. Or consider a composition teacher's argument that a paper should receive the grade of C. These situations involve conclusions that are not logically contained in the premises but represent a leap from known premises to a more or less problematic, that is, *contingent,* conclusion. Such arguments are also traditionally called *inductive,* and philosophers largely ignore them.

In *The Uses of Argument* Toulmin attacked this entire philosophic structure. He called the traditional distinction between deductive and inductive arguments "a crude muddle" (147) and went further to assert that no "substantial argument" is in practice deductive (218). By this he meant that no argument about real-world concerns can be equated to the purely analytical arguments philosophers deal with. When people argue in the real world, they rarely formulate their arguments with universally correct premises, absolutely dependable factual information, and fully precise terminology, all of which are required for traditional logic to produce its certifiable ("entailed") conclusions.

We can help keep the differences between traditional philosophical views of argument and Toulmin's "substantial" view clear by remembering two paradigm cases. Euclidean geometry with its axioms, postulates, and proofs is the best illustration of traditional formal logic. In contrast to such formal systems, as Toulmin pointed out, are contingent legal arguments with their case law precedents, interpretations of ambiguous texts, and attempts to cope with conflicting evidence. The goal in contingent argumentation is not absolute proof but, within the given epistemic conditions, proof beyond a reasonable doubt, or in civil suits, proof that is stronger than whatever case can be made for the opposing view. With a proper geometry proof there can be no disagreement. But the very best legal argument depends on contextual issues and thus is open to challenge.

One can understand why philosopher-logicians would not take kindly to Toulmin's criticism, especially given his frequently severe tone of voice. Toulmin further compounded the insult by claiming that the quality of an argument does not depend on whether it fits certain preset, abstractable forms (such as the correct forms of the classical syllogism, or the *modus ponens* form of the hypothetical syllogism). Instead, he said, an argument's quality must be assessed as appropriate or inappropriate, stronger or weaker, within its relevant field. He thus denied a view that has been the keystone of philosophic study of argument for 2,500 years.

Toulmin's Argument Model

As a counter to formal logic, Toulmin developed his own six-part model of argumentation. Unlike models of formal deductive logic, which seemed irrelevant to practical argumentation, Toulmin's model specifically suited contingent arguments the substance of which was grounded in knowledge of a given field (what Toulmin called "field dependence"). Given the concerns of the speech and composition communities with contextually-grounded, real-world argumentation, there seems little doubt that the Toulmin model more accurately reflects their interests than does formal deductive logic.

The Toulmin model says that every argument (whether traditionally inductive or traditionally deductive) involves a movement from some premises called data (or grounds) to the argumentative claim. The movement is justified by another, more general, premise that Toulmin designates as the warrant. Toulmin uses the analogy of an "arrest warrant," a document that authorizes certain actions (Toulmin, Rieke, and Janik 48). He has also used the metaphor of a "bridge" to describe what a warrant does (*Uses* 98). For example, in the preceding argument about the car keys, the warrant reveals the assumption that connects data to claim:

Claim: I will not be able to drive home from the airport. [because]

Data: I do not have my keys.

Warrant: Keys are necessary to drive a car.

All arguments, no matter what the field, have these three elements, although frequently not all three are explicit. In actuality the preceding argument might sound more like this: "Damn, I've lost my car keys. Now what? I guess I'm going to have to call Lee to bring me another set." Here both the warrant and the claim are taken as so obvious as not to need stating, and a further step in argument is introduced, leading to the second claim about phoning.

But going further, Toulmin asserts that substantial arguments often have some or all of three other features: backing, qualifier, and rebuttal conditions.[3] Let's complicate the previous argument a bit.

Given the electrical circuitry with which modern automobiles are constructed, it's necessary to have a key to operate them, unless you know some procedure like hot-wiring or how to get a substitute key. I have lost my key, so I won't be able to drive home, unless I can find a replacement key, hot-wire the car, get someone else to hot-wire the car, or borrow a car from someone else.

Here the full Toulmin model is in operation. We still have the data (lost key), the claim ("I won't be able to drive home"), and the warrant ("It's necessary to have a key"). But we also have a short phrase ("given the electrical design of modern cars") that specifies the backing (defined as support for the warrant), and several rebuttal conditions marked by "unless."

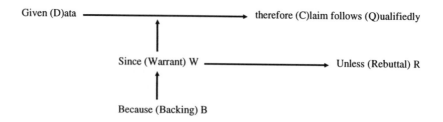

Figure 3.1. The Toulmin Model of Argument

SOURCE: Toulmin/Rieke/Janik, *An Introduction to Reasoning,* 2/e, (c) 1984, pp. 87, 98. Adapted by permission of Prentice Hall, Upper Saddle River, New Jersey.

Because exceptions to the argument are possible, the claim itself might appropriately include a qualifier, an adverb indicating the strength with which the arguer believes the premises support it. In this case we might introduce "in all likelihood" or "probably."

The abstract schema is often presented visually as in Figure 3.1.

Toulmin's point is that when people argue about issues of substance, few if any arguments have unimpeachable warrants and firm data so that conclusions can follow from them absolutely. Logical entailment is a scholarly figment. For Toulmin, real argument is inferring reasonable conclusions from "known" data by means of warrants that justify such moves with greater or lesser confidence, confidence ranging from "maybe" to "almost certainly." As Aristotle put it, "No one debates things incapable of being different" (Kennedy 41, 1357a). Real-world arguments, and more importantly the arguments composition students write, are thus contingent. They depend on what is granted as known by arguer and audience, on accepted patterns of reasoning within the discourse field, on the values assumed by the arguer and audience, and on the outcomes of prior related argumentation.

Because contingency rather than entailment accounts for the various features in Toulmin's view of argument, his model seems more likely than traditional argument forms to represent the processes by which rhetors conceive of and carry out arguments either in speech or writing. But the model holds other attractions for those trying to teach the process of writing argument. The model's stress on the tentativeness of argumentative conclusions, which need to be properly qualified and their rebuttal exceptions spelled out, fits well with modern (or postmodern) social views of knowledge as dialectically created and thus probabilistic. Denying the usefulness of traditional syllogistic or mathematical logic relieves arguers (and instructors) of the arduous and seemingly nonproductive task of mastering the philosophic rigmarole of syllogistic forms, Venn diagrams, rules for validity, and the accompanying technical jargon. And, finally, the idea that argument soundness is field-dependent harmonizes with the move to writing-across-the-curriculum and our general interest in discursive communities and constructivism.

But the question remains whether, despite its surface attractiveness, using Toulmin's model of argumentation in composition courses can help improve student argumentation about substantive issues. The research of the past fifteen years increasingly points to a distinction between the model's use to generate arguments and its use in analyzing them. Toulmin's model has been found useful as an analytical tool but problematic as a means of generating arguments, and the gulf between describing finished texts and teaching students to produce them is wide.

The Toulmin Model and Argument Analysis

Many scholars have examined the model's usefulness in analyzing existing texts, and the complexity of Toulmin's model, and some of its ambiguities, can be illustrated by examining how a real text looks when analyzed according to the model. Through such an analysis we can get a sense of how many microarguments are embedded into a full-length piece of writing and thus how many different claims, warrants, and backings any given macroargument might contain, either linked into chains or embedded hierarchically. Seeing how the model might work in relation to an extended text may in fact be the best way to understand both its workings and its limitations.

For an extended illustration, I have chosen "Violence and Domination as Metaphors in Academic Discourse" by Professor Maryann Ayim. The topic of the article, our images of argument in the academy, is appropriate to this collection, and the text, while relatively complicated, is simple enough to work with. The analysis, however, reveals the tremendous complexity of even rather straightforward argument.

The major claim of Ayim's argument—at least as I read it—is that in academic discourse in general, "Reason itself will be better served if we abandon the metaphor of the battlefield for the more humane and more human metaphor of the cooperative community" (192). I take it that the grounds for such a claim must be that cooperative metaphors are rationally superior to combative metaphors, and the unstated warrant is that in academic discourse we should adopt the metaphors that best serve reason.

So the last stage of the argument in Toulmin terms looks like this:

Warrant: Educators should use language in ways that best serve reason.

Data: Cooperative metaphors are rationally superior to combative ones.

Claim: Educators should replace combative metaphors with cooperative metaphors.

Whatever the warrant is taken to mean, it can scarcely be disagreed with and thus needs no separate backing. The problematic part of the argument is the statement functioning as data: that cooperative metaphors are (rationally) superior. Clearly, for Toulmin, *data* is not equivalent to the concept *fact* or even *evidence*. Because the *data* are open to challenge, Toulmin says they must be treated as the *claim* of a prior argument in a chain.

For this prior claim, Ayim actually presents three separate sets of data, each requiring its own warrant. That is, she has three separate lines of argument leading to the idea that cooperative metaphors are superior to combative ones. Toulmin's model does not readily lend itself to such a configuration, so we will have to treat each line as a separate argument, even though it reaches the same conclusion *mutatis mutandis.*

Ayim first asserts that in the field of science combative metaphors are harmful. That assertion functions as prior data to support the statement that, in general, cooperative metaphors are superior to combative ones. Here the warrant is a standard rule that one may generalize from evidence about a sample to a claim about the larger group, as long as certain criteria of representativeness, accuracy, sample size, and relevance are met.

So this secondary argument operates as follows:

Warrant: If several famous scientists use harmful metaphors, then one can generalize to the field.

Data: Two examples of the harmful use of aggressive and/or sexist metaphors by famous scientists are cited.

Claim: In science, combative metaphors are common and rationally harmful.

That is a rather long and cumbersome analysis of just one of Ayim's three major lines of argument, and in fact it isn't really satisfactory yet because the argument is a good deal more complex than this. The two examples are from Francis Bacon and Richard Feynman, and both are surely sexist. Bacon's refers to "hounding nature into her hiding places" (Ayim 186) and thus may also be violent. In order to show that these images are in some way undesirable, Ayim relies on yet another warrant that sexist imagery is obviously bad. Recognizing that some readers may not accept such a warrant, she provides a third warrant to go with the data about sexist/combative imagery in science. She argues that such imagery leads to a false view of science as the unemotional and objective study of "the truth"—rather than to a presumably more acceptable view of truth as socially created or discovered.

A second line of development concerns the use of combative images in philosophy (in which one *attacks* and *defends* positions, and *beats opponents* by *cutting* the support out from under them). Ayim argues that such a use of language also has harmful effects, allowing students of philosophy to focus only on small chunks of argument rather than seeing wholes, and to concentrate on spotting weaknesses rather than understanding points of view. And a third parallel line of argument concerns the use of combative metaphors within the field of education (e.g., "attack skills" in reading).

On the basis of these three lines of proof, Ayim can then assert her major data, that in academics the widespread imagery of combat is harmful.

In Toulmin's terms the argument looks like this:

Warrant: What is true of science, philosophy, and education as fields is probably true for education in general.

Data: Harmful combat images are common in science, in philosophy, and in education as fields.

Claim: Harmful combative imagery is common in education.

Finally, a generalized policy warrant tells us that "whatever is harmful should be replaced if possible," and Ayim can then propose metaphors of cooperation and nurturance as superior. In concrete terms, she suggests that we might someday cease calling an original contribution to knowledge "seminal" but call it "mammarian" or "ovarian" instead, and that we might replace our images of academic discourse as battles with images more like that of the quilting bee (192).

Now if I attempt to visualize these arguments according to Toulmin's model, I get something that looks like the schema Figure 3.2—which is still vastly oversimplified, but perhaps presents the major lines of argument.

Analyzing texts according to Toulmin's model sometimes results in useful insights, whether the analysis is part of the activity in a composition classroom

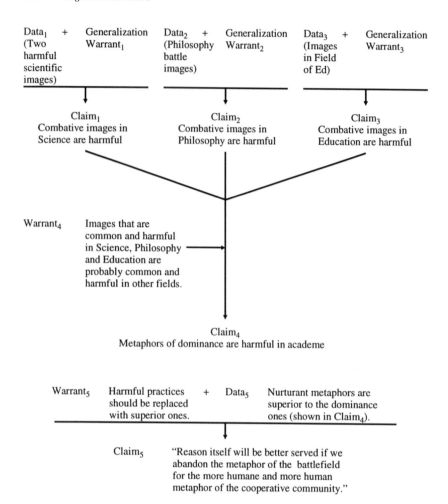

Figure 3.2. An Application of the Toulmin Model to a Full Discourse

using Toulmin's approach or part of the instructor's preparation for using the model. Like any good *explication de texte,* a careful application of the model leads an analyst to see the text more perceptively, to notice the necessary but often unstated warranting principles, and to specify the argumentative relationships among the various parts of the discourse. By forcing the analyst to go beyond claims and evidence, the Toulmin model sometimes reveals important but not obvious features of an argument (in the same way that teasing out the often unstated premise of a complex enthymeme does). I understand Ayim's argument better for having gone through this analysis.

However, on the downside, we should emphasize the problematic nature of applying Toulmin to full-length arguments. First such an application requires extensive analysis, patience, and a lot of practice with the model, which is cumbersome at best even when applied to a text carefully chosen to illustrate its uses. (I do not mean to imply that some other logical system is less cumbersome. I would have a much harder time analyzing Ayim's essay using traditional deductive/inductive logic, for example.)

Second, applying the model at the discourse level is not a routine or algorithmic procedure in which various analysts would produce the same layout. Such an application is instead a complex interpretive act that in the very process of application could either buttress or weaken the argument.[4]

Third, the Toulmin model fails to assist in making value judgments (assessing arguments). Once the model has been applied to a text, what one has is an elaborate and systematized paraphrase of the argument. From within the Toulmin model, the critic has no means of evaluating the argument, for the Toulmin scheme is descriptive, not evaluative. Any argument whatsoever can be laid out by it. So obviously I can cast any of Ayim's subarguments in such a way that by supplying the proper warrant (whether stated or not) her argument is coherent.

The model is not evaluative because Toulmin says the criteria for argument evaluation are primarily field-dependent. This feature has been part of the model's appeal to writing teachers, for it allows us to teach the model confident that its elements will show up in all fields. Yet we can admit that actually judging argument quality requires the knowledge of specialists in the field, who alone are able to assess the warrant and backing.

Certainly this idea has its appeal. I do not know the argumentative techniques for determining blood type or DNA makeup or when there will be an eclipse. But I have reason to accept that within the appropriate fields of inquiry ways exist to make such decisions and provide virtually ironclad evidence for them. Such contextuality makes the Toulmin approach to argument essentially rhetorical rather than logical.

On the other hand, when composition teachers teach argument, presumably we are not teaching the specifics of argument within a field but general principles that would apply both to public argumentation and across fields. If argument can be assessed only as a function of the field within which it exists, where Toulmin also says it is learned by acquisition as apprentices work with master craftspersons ("Logic" 378), then what sort of assessment is appropriate to arguments over abortion, health care, affirmative action, or sexual harassment?

Calling arguments field-dependent merely displaces the question of evaluation, raising first the often unanswerable question of what field an argument is in. Ayim herself is an educational philosopher, and a large part of her article deals with the metaphor of war in the field of philosophy; further, her essay appears in a collection designed for use in introductory logic courses. But it does not seem to me that this argument is "in" the field of philosophy and that philosophers must be the ones to assess it. Nor does it seem that we can usefully call all of "academia" itself a field, although that might make more sense here.

Fourth, on the other hand, some traditional principles of argument evaluation do seem to belong to the public domain and to cross fields, even though they are not addressed in the Toulmin model. One is that "evidence should be sufficient for conclusions drawn from it to avoid the fallacy of hasty generalization." If one applied this standard to Ayim's line of argument about metaphors of combat in science, her argument might be found seriously lacking. She discusses only two instances of such usage, one from Bacon 400 years ago, and one from Feynman in 1966 discussing the work that won him the Nobel prize. Both images are sexist, Feynman's more directly so than Bacon's, but only Bacon's involves aggression or dominance. Two instances from a 400-year period hardly show that scientists normally speak in such metaphors, and Bacon and Feynman are hardly typical users of scientific discourse.[5] Similarly, because Ayim is asking for a policy change in the way language is used, the general (and field-independent) criterion that "we do not change an established procedure without reason to believe the alternative will be workable and successful" is relevant. Yet Ayim does little to show that cooperative metaphors of the quilting bee, or feminist metaphors of "mammarian ideas," would actually promote a better approach to science or to philosophy or to education.

Toulmin's Model and the Generation of Arguments

In its first presentations in composition textbooks, the Toulmin model was merely described and shown to fit a simple argument, such as the one involving the lost car keys previously used. And in a number of texts, even some current ones, the model was incongruously presented side by side with traditional deduction and induction, with no apparent recognition of the essential conflict between the approaches (see Hairston, Barnet, and Bedau, Spurgin, and Vesterman).

But given our emphasis on teaching writing as a process, a number of authors soon began to work out the possible heuristic features of the Toulmin model. The question was, could students use a knowledge of the model to generate their arguments, and if so, would this approach prove more effective than other procedures?

When Charles Kneupper first introduced the Toulmin model to composition, he suggested one way that students might use the model as an invention heuristic. He proposed that students could outline their arguments before writing them by making the claim the main heading, the warrant the first level subheading, and the data and any backing they intended to cite a second level of subheading (240). That approach, however, essentially begs the question of how students are to come up with claims, warrants, and data in the first place (although no more, of course, than telling students to use a traditional outline does). No textbook that I am aware of ever suggested this procedure.

More recent textbooks have struggled to take Toulmin's work seriously, transform the parts of the model into heuristic questions, and use the model as a basis for seeing argumentative writing as essentially enthymematic (that is, built around the central pattern of a "reasoned thesis" as discussed by John Gage in this volume). The parts of the model can be transformed into the following questions, which assume that a student has already chosen a topic, identified a question at issue, and perhaps examined the available evidence by using some procedure such as the one Barbara Emmel lays out in her essay in this volume:

1. What is my *claim* about the issue?
2. What *data* (evidence, facts, examples, quotations, statistics) support my claim?
3. What general principle (*warrant*) justifies deriving this claim from the evidence? (And will the audience accept it?)
4. What exceptions to that general principle (*rebuttals*) are there?
5. Given those exceptions and my audience, how much should I hedge the claim (with *qualifiers*)?
6. If that general principle were actually challenged, what further proof (*backing*) could be cited to justify it?

But such questions both simplify and mask the possible power of the model to work as a heuristic. They simplify the model by turning it into a macrolevel formula, the operation of which presupposes that students can intuit the underlying issue[s] that would make the questions meaningful. And, they mask whatever contributions the model might make to composition if approached differently.

If the model is to have any real usefulness as a heuristic, and it will be clear that I am skeptical about this possibility, that usefulness may well depend on first understanding, in a more intuitive way, how most arguments operate as constellations of subarguments. A helpful analogy involves thinking of the Toulmin model as describing the smallest unit into which an argument can be broken, a kernel argument as it were. Just as kernel sentences can be combined in an infinite number of ways to produce real utterances, simple Toulmin kernels can join to produce essay-length arguments.

Because the model may help us understand how argument works in miniature, we may be able to show students that real arguments are more complex than the model appears because they contain multiple microarguments, either embedded within larger arguments, chained together in sequences of support, or both.

Thus students might take an initial step toward learning to generate complex arguments with the model by first using it to analyze the complexity of an existing text, as was done previously with the Ayim piece. Later, when using the model generatively, students might understand that each argument produced would probably function as a kernel or microargument within a larger discourse. Although pedagogical and cognitive moves from close analysis of sample discourses to production of student texts have always been problematic, paradoxically, Toulmin's model might well work best as a generative tool when used analytically. That is, analysis of how actual arguments operate, using the model, might lead students to make important connections between ideas when constructing their own elaborated arguments.

Complexity within the Toulmin Model

However, when we move from using Toulmin's model as an analytic tool and into using it as a generative heuristic, new problems emerge, not only because all models tend to become form bound and reductive, but also because this model in particular is more complex than it first appears: Its apparently simple form belies a number of complex underlying processes, ones not easy to apprehend or to generate consciously.

From early in its scholarly history, students of the Toulmin model have pointed out what might be called its asymmetry. That is, we can visualize the model as in Figure 3.3, with the arrows representing lines of support.

Together, the warrant plus the data "authorize" the move to the claim. If the warrant is challenged or problematic, one can then look to the backing that

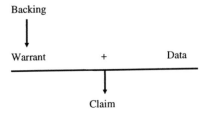

Figure 3.3. The Asymmetry of the Toulmin Model

supports it.[6] But if the data are challenged, the model itself contains no corresponding *support* for the data. Toulmin says that in such a case one must back up and treat the data as the outcome of a prior argument, complete with its own prior data, prior warrant, and prior backing. Thus an extended argument, such as Ayim's essay, will often involve a lengthy chain of Toulmin layouts in which the concluding claim of one stage becomes *data* used in the next. That is logical in certain senses, but for use as a heuristic, it is still cumbersome.[7]

In my experience, students have no trouble understanding the idea of claim and data in the abstract. That, after all, corresponds to our essential concept of what an argument is: an assertion put forth and then supported with evidence of some sort. But understanding in principle that one makes claims and supports them with data obviously doesn't guarantee that students can apply the principle and produce well-thought-out claims with adequate data.

Moreover, even in principle, students have a great deal of trouble identifying appropriate warrants to link data to claims. When Toulmin presents the model, he assumes that arguers and analysts can naturally identify an appropriate warrant to bridge the gap between a claim and the evidence/data presented for it. But apparently the cognitive act of inferring an appropriate warrant for a given argument isn't intuitive. Here, ironically, it helps to be familiar with traditional logic: Usually the warrant fits as the major premise of a syllogism or as the first (if/then) premise in *modus ponens* (see Note 2).

A warrant must somehow *reference* both the data presented and the claim drawn; that is how it bridges the two or authorizes the movement. The simplest, and algorithmic, procedure for determining the warrant is to use a hypothetical "if/then" sentence and position the data as the if-clause and the claim as the then-clause. In the lost keys example, the warrant can easily be framed as "If one lacks a key to an automobile, the automobile cannot be driven." This *always* works, but it is usually less than enlightening because all it does is to restate the move from evidence to conclusion: It doesn't tell us why that move is reasonable.

Another way to explain what a warrant requires is to note that it provides a general rule for interpreting data (Toulmin refers to it as a "rule of thumb"), in the way that a law provides rules for interpreting the facts in a legal controversy. Like a law, a warrant must be a general principle for interpreting the data it applies to, not itself a claim of fact. Nor may the warrant be an argument in which one clause supports another. Here are some examples of possible warrants:

- "In general, in an inhabited area, an earthquake measuring 6.0 on the Richter scale can be expected to cause extensive damage."
- "Usually, American college students find mathematics more difficult than English."
- "In the U.S., people are free to practice any religion they wish as long as they do not harm others."
- "Other things being equal, student essays that lack supporting evidence are inferior to those with evidence."

The cognitive difficulty of extricating an appropriate warrant either from a potential argument during the process of composing or from an existing text is illustrated by the difficulty several English scholars who have used or supported the model have themselves had in analyzing warrants. Because my experience with both students and scholars indicates that this is perhaps the point at which uses of the model are most likely to go astray, I want to document it at some length here.

Instance: In an appendix presenting the Toulmin model, Barnet and Bedau use it to interpret an essay from their collection, Susan Jacoby's "A First Amendment Junkie." Jacoby argues against the position that pornography should be censored because it inherently attacks women. Because the piece is a several-hundred-word column, it makes several interconnected claims; thus several applications of the model are necessary. Barnet and Bedau identify six related claims. Then, curiously, they identify three "warrants" even though the Toulmin model would require one warrant for each claim. One of the proposed "warrants" is as follows: "Feminists ought to see that *they risk losing more than they can hope to gain* if they succeed in censoring pornography, because antifeminists will have equal right to censor things they find offensive but that many feminists seek to publish" (qtd. in Barnet and Bedau 287-88, emphasis in original). This complex sentence cannot be a warrant because it is a full argument. The claim is that "feminists risk losing more than they gain," which is grounded in the assertion that antifeminists would be able to censor materials that feminists want published. (Because the sentence itself contains both claim and support, it also relies on an unstated warrant.) In other words, the "warranting principle" explicated by these two composition scholars doesn't come close to fitting the Toulmin model.

Instance: In "Visualization of Arguments; or, How to Get Through the Labyrinth to Right a Text," Anne Gervasi and Betty Kay Seibt propose using magazine advertisements as paradigm cases of argument for students and using the Toulmin model to analyze the ads. Of course that simplifies the issue considerably because it doesn't involve working with full-length texts. As the authors explain their pedagogy, when students analyzed ads, they learned that every ad claims that

> This is the best product for _____ (fill in the blank with "washing clothes," "brushing teeth," "diapering a baby," etc.). The warrant, the underlying assumption, for each advertisement was the same—consumers want to have the cleanest clothes, the brightest teeth, the driest baby. (99)

As a test case, let's lay out that analysis more precisely, using detergent X.

Warrant: Consumers want to have the cleanest clothes.

Data: [whatever test or testimonial the ad gives about detergent X]

Claim: Detergent X is the best product for washing clothes.

Notice that consumer desire for cleanliness in no way helps establish the quality of the detergent in question. "Consumers want to have the cleanest clothes" cannot warrant any conclusion about product quality. Thus even a simple advertisement turns out to be argumentatively more complex than it seems.

Instance: As a third example, consider the following Toulmin argument about "The Cask of Amontillado," from a dissertation that uses Toulmin to construct interpretive arguments about short stories:

Warrant: Montresor prides in and boasts of his action.

Data: Montresor confesses his crime.

Claim: Presumably, pride is the motivating force behind Montresor's confession. (Ortiz-Seda 118)

Now whether this is a sensible interpretation of Montresor's motivation or not, the statement that he prides in and boasts of his action added to the data that he does confess (or at least narrate) his crime, does not support the causal conclusion that the pride causes the confession. Here the "warrant" is a fact from the narrative, not a principle about how to interpret confessions in fiction. Thus the argument begs the very question it is trying to address—what motivates Montresor's narration of his murder of Fortunato fifty years earlier.

Instance: Finally, in a thoughtful article advocating the use of the Toulmin model in teaching composition, Joan Karbach has attempted to relate it to a variety of traditional sorts of argument, such as traditional induction. As an example of a student argument she gives the following:

Data: Waitresses who make a dependable wage will be less likely to leave present employment.

Claim: A 15-percent service charge should be added to restaurant patrons' checks in lieu of tipping. (85)

Looking at those two statements, it is impossible to construct a warrant that would get from one to the other. Too many steps are involved. Presumably the warrant would have to assert that, "Having waitresses leave employment is undesirable," and that, "Owners should take whatever steps are needed to prevent waitresses leaving," plus, "A 15-percent wage increase without tips would significantly reduce turnover by providing a *dependable* wage."

Actually, the warrant Karbach proposes is "A high turnover of employees reflects unfavorably on profits" (85), which cannot justify any conclusion about *what* an employer should do to prevent the high turnover, although it could support the proposition that "having waitresses leave employment is undesirable to employers."

I have rehearsed these instances at length in order to justify my conclusion that we can hardly expect students to understand intuitively the concept of a Toulmin warrant if most composition scholars who write about it fail to understand it. If we hope to make the model useful in the classroom, we will be compelled to master it ourselves, then present it to students at some length, and discuss the contrast and connection between the apparent simplicity of the model and the complexity of extended argument.

If determining an appropriate warrant is a problem, locating suitable backing is even more complicated. Even if a warrant for a microargument can be satisfactorily identified, a student attempting to use the model may be baffled about how to validate for readers the reasons for accepting the warrant. Suppose, for example, a student wants to argue that tobacco products should be made illegal. Probably the data for that claim would be, "Tobacco causes serious health problems for users," which would itself be a claim based on prior argumentation. The warrant would have to be something like, "Whenever a product causes extensive health risks, that product should be legally banned." I suspect that to many students that warrant would seem unexceptionable. But if challenged, few of them would be able to provide backing for this warrant, which concerns an issue in political theory. (I grant that some students might see that backing could be drawn from an analogy with drug laws or with other dangerous-product laws.)

A final difficulty in adapting the Toulmin model as a heuristic concerns how one generates a full essay from the simple "claim-because-data-plus-warrant" enthymeme. This move will work if the data are extensive and need rehearsing. In the preceding example, most of the essay about outlawing tobacco could be a catalog of the studies about the health risks of tobacco. This catalog would actually be a subargument leading to the conclusion that, "Tobacco use is harmful to health." That claim would then become the data for the policy claim that tobacco should be outlawed. However, this move of simply elaborating the data into a full essay doesn't work if the data are essentially well-known and the controversy involves evaluation or policy (consider the abortion controversy as a paradigm case, or laws relating to "hate" speech). Thus attempts like Karbach's to sum up a full argument (about tipping) in one Toulmin layout are almost bound to fail and to confuse students.

But none of the preceding is a criticism of the model itself, because it was never intended for use as a heuristic device or as an analytic tool for extended arguments. Toulmin presented the model as an analytic portrait of a micro-argument. The model *describes* what happens when an arguer presents a single move from data to claim. Toulmin never suggested that the model would be useful in creating arguments. In fact, he says that one acquires the skill to create arguments by apprenticing within a field ("Logic" 378). Given Toulmin's purpose in creating the model and his development of it as an analytical tool in *An Introduction to Reasoning,* clearly if the model *can* be used to help students generate arguments, it must be *adapted,* not merely borrowed, and the adaptation must come from composition scholars.

Attempts to Adapt the Toulmin Model

So far, the most effective attempt to overcome these problems by fully *adapting* the Toulmin model is that by Ramage and Bean in *Writing Arguments.*

Examining just how they adapted and extended it is instructive. The authors first suggest to students that they create complex sentences with "because" clauses to summarize their large-scale lines of reasoning, essentially what John Gage argues for in his essay in this volume. For instance, Ramage and Bean discuss the prewriting for a student policy proposal that uses as its major reasoning this thesis: "All college students should be required to take an ethics course because most students are not effective ethical thinkers and because an ethics course would help solve this problem" (331).

Once such an argument has been created (somehow), Ramage and Bean encourage the student to identify the assumed warrants (note the plural), to ask whether they will be acceptable to readers or need further backing, and to find ways to elaborate the grounds. If students find themselves able to do this, then the questions derived from the preceding Toulmin model might function as a "critical revision heuristic"—even before students draft their papers.

Ramage and Bean use an example of a student who wanted to make the following argument: "The state should require the wearing of seatbelts in moving vehicles because seatbelts save lives" (114). After examining the warrant for that line of reasoning ("Laws that save lives should be enacted by the state"), and asking whether readers would accept it, and what conditions of rebuttal might apply, the student writer noticed that the warrant would justify a wide range of state intervention in personal behavior, ranging from requiring citizens to take vitamins, to requiring safety strips in bathtubs (Ramage and Bean 114). Realizing that a principle warranting such state regulation of personal behavior would scarcely be defensible, the student was moved to ponder what seem to be the salient differences between seatbelt laws and other life-saving laws that would seem infringements of personal liberties. The student then wrote a more persuasive paper based on a more limited warrant, something like, "The state should pass laws that save lives by governing *public* behavior when that can be done without significant cost to citizens or major limitations on their freedom of action." Such a use of the Toulmin scheme as a revision heuristic (or a postplanning/predrafting heuristic) brings Toulmin fully into harmony with the enthymematic approach to composition.

Ramage and Bean deal with the asymmetry problem as Jimmie Trent suggests by introducing an extra feature into the model, a "stated reason" (rather than data) that itself has further support and thus makes the model symmetrical. So in their adaptation, the model would be visualized as seen in Figure 3.4.

Whether such adaptation of the Toulmin model, including the elaborate procedural suggestions for using it as a prerevision critical heuristic, overcomes its inherent bias toward description rather than generation is still an open issue.

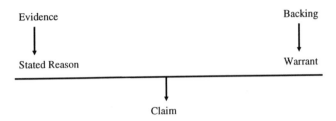

Figure 3.4. A Representation of Ramage and Bean's Adaptation of Toulmin's Model

But such enhancements are clearly necessary to make the model generatively useful. The question is whether they are sufficient and worth the trouble.

Effectiveness of the Toulmin Model for Composition

I hope the previous sections, though almost purely theoretical, have raised doubts about the inherent usefulness of any mere borrowing of Toulmin's model: It is deceptively simple. It does reasonably well what it was designed to do. But it was not designed to help students write arguments, nor to evaluate them.[8] If it is going to prove helpful in the composition classroom, then we teachers of writing must understand it and adapt it at a much more sophisticated level than has usually been the case. Which, of course, emphasizes the issue of whether the efforts needed to adapt and master the model are worth the benefits they might have.

Not surprisingly, right now, we have very little more than anecdotal evidence about whether the model can be effectively translated into the composition classroom either as a preliminary heuristic (a possibility that seems doubtful to me) or as a critical revision heuristic within a process pedagogy, which seems to me somewhat more feasible.

Ramage and Bean, and Rottenberg, find the model productive in their classrooms, and the sales of their textbooks may be signs that other teachers also find it so. Rottenberg does not use the model fully, nor does she integrate it with the other features of her text. Ramage and Bean *do* integrate it fully and thus produce the most elaborate and complex argument text available, a text that contains far too much material for one course and yet is so well integrated that it is very difficult to break into pieces. I have taught from both texts several times, and my experience with them has been mixed. A. Harris Fairbanks has also criticized the use of Toulmin in composition, and Susan Millsap has criticized it from a feminist perspective in speech.

Gervasi and Seibt claim, "Toulmin's practical approach to argument based in a dynamic rather than a static world worked well with our students" (98). But as I previously discussed, this conclusion rests on a significant misuse of the model, so it can hardly count as evidence for the model's effectiveness.

The only empirical research about using the model to teach composition led to discouraging results. Bill McCleary, believing that the Toulmin model represented a major advance over traditional approaches to argument, performed a study using junior-college students. The project included fifteen sections with several teachers. One group of students was taught composition with no special treatment of argument, a second group was taught traditional deductive logic (actually two subgroups were taught deduction in two different ways), and a third group studied Toulmin logic (again in two different ways in subgroups). When all groups were tested for gains in writing skill, no significant differences in writing quality were found among the three groups.

But, though well designed, this is only one study. Given the complexities of adapting the Toulmin model for use in producing extended arguments, no single study is likely to be definitive. In fact, as an outcome measure of argumentative writing quality, McCleary used a paper involving ethical reasoning and requiring a pre-set structure, written within a timed session. Perhaps a different sort of topic, a less restrictive form, or time to write and revise outside of class would have produced different results. In an empirical sense, then, the case for or against using adaptations of the Toulmin model in composition remains to be made. However, it is important to stress that the same can be said for any of the other approaches to teaching argument examined in this volume. No procedure for teaching written argument can currently claim any empirical proof of its effectiveness.

Toulmin and Course Design

As the essays in this volume suggest, there are many ways to build courses in argumentation. Probably the most traditional one is to base the course on readings grouped thematically around issues such as abortion, animal rights, and athletics. Obviously one could introduce the Toulmin model in such a course and invite students to use the model's features in their own writing, as discussed previously, or to use Toulmin as a critical reading lens, as I have attempted to do with the Ayim essay. I have attempted to teach students to read a text through Toulmin—in an introductory logic course—and it is a time-consuming and laborious procedure, one my students and I are frequently unable to make work. Ordinarily in such a course, Toulmin's scheme would be essentially ancillary.

However, two ways to design an argument course seem to make a theoretically more productive use of Toulmin's scheme by cross-breeding it with two taxonomies of argument. The two leading argumentation textbooks, Rottenberg and Ramage and Bean, illustrate the two approaches.

In nonformal logic, the acronym GASCAP is sometimes used to help students recall what are essentially six *modes* of argument, that is, six different ways that one can go about supporting a claim. The letters stand for *generalization, analogy, sign, cause, authority,* and *principle.* Each mode of argumentative support is fairly easy to explain in terms of the Toulmin model. In arguing for a generalization, for instance, the data are a sample from a larger group. The warrant is the presumption that, "Whatever is true of a well-chosen sample will be true of the larger population" (which I designated as a "generalization warrant" in my analysis of the Ayim essay). That warrant allows one to draw conclusions about all sorts of topics in connection with large groups. If the warrant is challenged, both theoretical and empirical ways to back it exist. Because one is leaping from a small sample to a large population, a strong qualifier and explicit rebuttal conditions are needed. (For more extensive analysis of how the Toulmin model fits with each of the modes, see Toulmin, Rieke, and Janik, Chapter 22.)

Annette Rottenberg presents a variation of GASCAP and ties it to the Toulmin scheme by discussing different types of warrants (151-59). She does not use the acronym, and alters *principle* to *values,* while adding comparison as distinct from analogy. However, she does not make the connection a structuring feature of her textbook or, presumably, of courses using it. There are good reasons for that. GASCAP may be a useful analytical tool for students studying argument; it may even be a useful generative/revision tool. But because it deals with *methods* of argumentative development rather than *purpose,* any writing course built on it is open to all the criticisms of modes courses in general (such as courses built on EDNA). There is no inherent progressive order to the six modes of arguing, they do not build on each other, and if teachers assign students to write "an argument by authority," they distort the process of writing arguments in at least two ways—by having the students begin with a mode rather than with some topic and by artificially restricting them to using only one sort of proof.

Potentially more interesting would be crossing the Toulmin scheme with a taxonomy of argument based on some version of stasis theory (as discussed in this volume and elsewhere by Fahnestock and Secor). Rottenberg uses a simple version of stasis theory in claiming to distinguish among arguments of fact, value, and policy. But, again, she does not use this as a central structuring principle. Ramage and Bean, on the other hand, devote approximately the middle one-third of a long book to a sequence of stasiastic argument types, one chapter per type, with their adaptation of the Toulmin model featured in each chapter. In such an approach the model is presented macroscopically and a generalized warrant associated with the type of claim might be presented (e.g., for a claim of policy, "if the positive consequences of a proposed policy are more significant than the negative ones, the proposal should be adopted"). Jeanne Fahnestock (who, with her frequent coauthor Marie Secor, is one of our leading experts on modern stasis theory), has described an advanced composition course in which students pursue the same public topic all semester, working on it from four different stases and using a simplified version of the Toulmin model in connection with each one. Such syllabi have all the virtues and problems of stasis approaches but with still another layer of apparatus. Yet they represent the most sophisticated attempts so far to adapt, not merely to borrow, the Toulmin model of argument for our needs.

To borrow Steve North's terms, at this point we have a good deal of lore about the Toulmin model, a considerable amount of theorizing and philosophizing. What we do not have much of and what we need is further careful research (including experiments, ethnographies, and case studies) that examines the effectiveness of the Toulmin model when adapted accurately yet creatively, either alone or in tandem with other approaches.

Notes

1. Logicians had many objections to the Toulmin "approach" to argument and to the model. One of them is that the model simply doesn't handle a number of basic argument forms. Consider a wife who reasons as follows: "If he loves me and understands my wishes, he would do what I want. He hasn't done what I asked. But I know he loves me. So he must not have understood. Thus I need to tell him again and make myself clearer this time." The line of reasoning can be easily analyzed using formal symbolic logic, but the Toulmin model cannot account for it. (The example is adapted from Tannen 31.)

This is not the place for an extensive analysis of Toulmin's philosophical critique or the reasons the philosophical community rejected it. The best analysis from this perspective is van Eemeren, Grootendorst, and Kruiger's chapter in *Handbook of Argumentation*. See also the extensive critique by Freeman in his section "Toulmin's Problematic Notion of Warrant" (50-90).

2. In general, *modus ponens* is any argument of the following form:

If P, then Q.

P

Therefore Q,

where P and Q represent full declarative sentences. This is a deductive argument because the truth of the two premises necessitates ("entails") the truth of the conclusion.

That logical entailment of the conclusion is the distinguishing trait of deduction indicates what is wrong with the common definition that "deduction is reasoning from the general to the specific" or "applying a general rule to a specific case." (See my "Technical Logic, Comp-Logic, and the Teaching of Writing.")

3. The claim of a Toulmin argument corresponds to the decision reached in a court of law. The Toulmin data correspond to the evidence in the trial and the warrant corresponds to the statute itself or to accepted precedent. Toulmin backing corresponds to the cases that have previously interpreted a law or even perhaps to legislative debate over the statute. The Toulmin rebuttal condition fits with legal exceptions such as "temporary insanity" or "self defense" in what would otherwise be a clear case of murder or assault. And because legal arguments are rarely absolute, rationally one should see the conclusion as hedged with some adverbial qualifier, including perhaps the phrase "beyond a reasonable doubt."

4. Given the problematic nature of applying Toulmin with precision to full texts, it is surprising to learn of the wide variety of research applications the model has led to. (None of them have been replicated as far as I know, so there has not been an accepted procedure of research using the Toulmin model.)

Jimmie Trent, in his doctoral dissertation, examined a large body of courtroom argument using the Toulmin model. Trent found no arguments in which the claims were qualified even though the premises would have warranted only qualified, not absolute, conclusions (259). (That is hardly a surprising finding because in the adversarial and triadic situation of American law neither side is expected to suggest any weaknesses in its own argument.)

Roderick Hart studied fifty-four persuasive speeches, some given to overtly hostile or skeptical audiences, and others to friendly ones. He somehow applied Toulmin macroscopically to the entire speeches, and concluded "the amount of commonality a speaker perceives [with the audience] will affect the claims he makes, the data he offers, and the warrants he provides" (83). More specifically, Hart found "pronounced differences in the numbers of warrants explicitly supplied by speakers facing committed audiences and those facing collective distrust or disagreement" (84). Speakers facing hostile audiences used an average of two explicit warrants for each data-claim move, and "each warrant was stated, on the average, almost four times" (89). Generally, speakers facing already committed audiences neglected to supply warrants at all.

Michael Hazen used the Toulmin scheme to analyze the rebuttal speeches of fourteen Japanese high school debaters in comparison to those of five American debaters. He found that "compared to the arguments used by American debaters, the Japanese version is more complete and uses more evidence." Hazen cautions against drawing any significant conclusions about Japanese uses of logic or rhetoric, however, because these speakers were trained in traditional Western debate and were speaking English.

Finally, in the only textual application of Toulmin done by an English (as opposed to speech) scholar, Darnyd Ortiz-Seda wrote a doctoral dissertation reporting on the effects of using the Toulmin argument scheme to help interpret short stories. "The use of the model allows readers and students alike to search for logical and rational explanations to their reactions and conclusions from the stories they read. It also helps them to formulate informed and rational questions that in turn help to clarify their doubts. As a result, readers of the short story can better understand, appreciate, and enjoy a story" (viii). Because literary interpretation consists of making claims about literary texts, and supporting the interpretative claims with evidence from the text, one would expect that interpretations could be examined or perhaps generated using the Toulmin model. Variations in literary theory might then account for different claims about the same textual data, because interpretive warrants would be derived from the theory. However, as I discussed previously, Ortiz-Seda's applications of the model are problematic indeed, so the question of whether it is useful to see literary interpretation through the lens of the Toulmin scheme remains open.

5. In fairness to Ayim, she situates the Bacon and Feynman quotations as part of an ongoing discussion by citing in her own footnotes other feminist scholars who have offered other evidence of the use of masculine metaphors of power to describe the scientific endeavor.

6. A further problem inherent in the model has never been pointed out, to my knowledge. The move from backing for a warrant to the warrant is itself an argument. That is, the backing plays the role of data for the warrant considered as a claim. If that is the case, then there is necessarily another warrant that authorizes the move from the backing to the first warrant. But that second warrant would require backing itself, which would be the data in yet another argument. The analyst is caught in an infinite regress. The general vagueness and complexity of Toulmin's treatment of backing may explain why most attempts to use the model, such as Rottenberg's, either omit or gloss over backing. Toulmin himself has acknowledged that his analysis of backing was the greatest weakness in *The Uses of Argument* (Olson 291).

7. Jimmie Trent proposed modifying the model by adding a different sort of "backing"—backing for the data, and this suggestion has been adopted by Ramage and Bean, whose *Writing Arguments* is the most thoroughgoing attempt to use Toulmin in a composition textbook. Annette Rottenberg, in *The Structure of Argument,* the second most extensive adaptation of Toulmin, omits backing, and presents the model as having three parts: claim, data, and warrant. (It reveals something about the composition community's affinity for the model that, as of this writing, these two textbooks are the best-selling argument rhetorics.)

8. Joseph Moxley is the only writer who apparently believes that the Toulmin model implies an evaluative dimension. He analyzes an artificial argument he used to test student knowledge of argument and says the "passage is not a complete argument because it lacks an explicit warrant. The claim expressed in the first sentence is followed only by data and by one qualifier" (14). But there is no reason why the warrant of an argument should be explicit, any more than the major premise of a syllogistic argument should be included overtly. Given the conclusion and the data, a knowledgeable analyst can always recover the unstated warranting premise.

Works Cited

Ayim, Maryann. "Violence and Domination as Metaphors in Academic Discourse." *Selected Issues in Logic and Communication.* Ed. Trudy Govier. Belmont, CA: Wadsworth, 1988. 184-95.

Barnet, Sylvan, and Hugo Bedau. *Critical Thinking: Reading and Writing.* 2nd ed. Boston: St. Martin's, 1996.

Brockriede, Wayne, and Douglas Ehninger. "Toulmin on Argument: An Interpretation and Application." *Quarterly Journal of Speech* 46 (Feb. 1960): 44-53.

"Editors' Column." *Informal Logic* 13 (Winter 1991): 36.

Ehninger, Douglas, and Wayne Brockriede. *Decision by Debate.* New York: Dodd, Mead, 1963.

Fahnestock, Jeanne. "Teaching Argumentation in the Junior-Level Course." *Teaching Advanced Composition: How and Why.* Ed. Katherine Adams and John Adams. Portsmouth: Boynton/Cook, 1991. 179-93.

Fahnestock, Jeanne, and Marie Secor. "Teaching Argument: A Theory of Types." *College Composition and Communication* 34 (Feb. 1983): 20-30.

———. "Toward a Modern Version of Stasis." *Oldspeak/Newspeak: Rhetorical Transformations.* Ed. Charles W. Kneupper. Arlington, TX: Rhetoric Society of America, 1985. 217-26.

Fairbanks, A. Harris. "The Pedagogical Failure of Toulmin's Logic." *The Writing Instructor* 12 (Spring/Summer 1993): 103-14.

Freeman, James B. *Dialectics and the Macrostructure of Arguments: A Theory of Argument Structure.* New York: Foris, 1991.

Fulkerson, Richard. "Technical Logic, Comp-Logic, and the Teaching of Writing." *College Composition and Communication* 39 (Dec. 1988): 436-52.

———. "Some Uses and Limitations of the Toulmin Method of Argument." *The Toulmin Method: Exploration and Controversy.* Arlington, TX: Liberal Arts, 1991. 80-95.

Gervasi, Anne, and Betty Kay Seibt. "Visualization of Argument; or How to Get Through the Labyrinth to Right a Text." *The Toulmin Method: Exploration and Controversy.* Arlington, TX: Liberal Arts, 1991. 97-104.

Hairston, Maxine C. *Successful Writing: A Rhetoric for Advanced Composition.* New York: Norton, 1981.

Hart, Roderick P. "On Applying Toulmin: The Analysis of Practical Discourse." *Explorations in Rhetorical Criticism.* Ed. G. P. Mohrmann, Charles J. Stewart, and Donovan J. Ochs. University Park: Pennsylvania State University Press, 1973. 75-95.

Hazen, Michael David. "An Analysis of the Use and Structure of Logic in Japanese Argument." Paper presented at Speech Communication Association, Chicago, November 1984. ED 253905.

Jacoby, Susan. "A First Amendment Junkie." *Critical Thinking, Reading, and Writing: A Brief Guide to Argument.* 2nd ed. Ed. Sylvan Barnet and Hugo Bedau. Boston: St. Martin's, 1996. 22-24.

Karbach, Joan. "Using Toulmin's Model of Argumentation." *Journal of Teaching Writing* 6 (Spring 1987): 81-91.

Kennedy, George, Ed. *Aristotle, On Rhetoric: A Theory of Civic Discourse.* New York: Oxford, 1991.

Kneupper, Charles W. "Teaching Argument: An Introduction to the Toulmin Model." *College Composition and Communication* 29 (Oct. 1978): 237-41.

McCleary, William James. "Teaching Deductive Logic: A Test of the Toulmin and Aristotelian Models for Critical Thinking and College Composition." Diss. University of Texas, 1979. DA 790168.

Millsap, Susan P. "A Feminist Perspective on Argumentation: An Examination of the Toulmin Model." Speech Communication Association, Miami Beach, Nov. 18-21, 1993. ED 367038.

Moxley, Joseph M. "Reinventing the Wheel or Teaching the Basics: College Writers' Knowledge of Argumentation." *Composition Studies* 21 (Fall 1993): 3-15.

North, Stephen. *The Making of Knowledge in Composition: Portrait of an Emerging Field.* Upper Montclair, NJ: Boynton/Cook, 1987.

Olson, Gary. "Literary Theory, Philosophy of Science, and Persuasive Discourse: Thoughts from a Neo-premodernist." *Journal of Advanced Composition* 13 (Fall 1993): 283-309.

Ortiz-Seda, Darnyd W. "A Critical Approach to the Short Story in English: Toulmin's Rational Model of Argumentation." Diss. Florida State University, 1990. DA 9118495.

Ramage, John D., and John C. Bean. *Writing Arguments.* 2nd ed. New York: Macmillan, 1992.

Rottenberg, Annette T. *Elements of Argument: A Textured Reader.* 4th ed. Boston: St. Martin's, 1994.

Spurgin, Sally Dewitt. *The Power to Persuade.* Englewood Cliffs, NJ: Prentice Hall, 1985.

Tannen, Deborah. *You Just Don't Understand: Women and Men in Conversation.* New York: Morrow, 1990.

Toulmin, Stephen. *The Uses of Argument.* New York: Cambridge University Press, 1958 [paperback 1964].

———. "Logic and the Criticism of Arguments." *The Rhetoric of Western Thought.* 4th ed. Ed. James L. Golden, Goodwin F. Berquist, and William Coleman. Dubuque, IA: Kendall/Hunt, 1989. 374-88.

Toulmin, Stephen, Richard Rieke, and Allan Janik. *An Introduction to Reasoning.* 2nd ed. New York: Macmillan, 1984.

Trent, Jimmie D. "Toulmin's Model of an Argument: An Examination and Extension." *Quarterly Journal of Speech* 54 (Oct. 1968): 252-59.

van Eemeren, Frans H., Rob Grootendorst, and Tjark Kruiger. "Toulmin's Analysis Model." *Handbook of Argumentation Theory: A Critical Survey of Classical Backgrounds and Modern Studies.* Dordrecht, Holland/Providence, RI: Foris, 1987. 162-207.

Vesterman, William. *Reading and Writing Short Arguments.* Mountain View, CA: Mayfield, 1994.

4

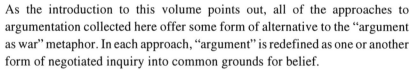

Rogerian Rhetoric

Ethical Growth Through
Alternative Forms of Argumentation

Doug Brent
University of Calgary

As the introduction to this volume points out, all of the approaches to argumentation collected here offer some form of alternative to the "argument as war" metaphor. In each approach, "argument" is redefined as one or another form of negotiated inquiry into common grounds for belief.

Rogerian rhetoric also moves away from a combative stance but is distinct from other models of argumentation in three ways. First, it goes even farther than most other models in avoiding an adversarial approach. Second, it offers specific strategies based on nondirective therapy for building the cooperative bridges necessary for noncombative inquiry. Third, and in my opinion most important, it has the potential to offer students an opportunity for long-term cognitive and ethical growth.

Ever since Young, Becker, and Pike introduced the discipline of composition to Rogerian rhetoric in 1970, our profession has remained deeply divided over whether such a rhetoric is conceptually sound, useful in practice, or even possible. Some have argued that it is nothing but warmed-over Aristotelian rhetoric (Lunsford); others, that it is untrue to Carl Rogers's principles (Mader) or that it is a cumbersome welding-together of persuasion and nondirective therapy, two fundamentally incompatible processes (Ede). All of these criticisms point to real problems with the model, problems that often reflect the way it has been conceptualized by its proponents. Nonetheless, the literature of composition studies reflects a continuing fascination with Rogerian principles. Textbooks continue to suggest these principles as alternative methods of persuasion (Coe 1990; Flower), and a recent collection edited by Nathaniel Teich (1992) presents a wide variety of both philosophical and pedagogical investigations into Rogerian perspectives.

In this chapter I will try to account for this continuing fascination with Rogerian rhetoric and explain what it can offer that no other approach to argumentation can quite match. To do so I will briefly survey the history of Rogerian rhetoric and outline its basic principles. Then I will discuss some of the ways in which Rogerian principles can be used in practice to teach both a *technique* of inquiry and an *ethic* of inquiry.

Background: Rogerian Therapy and Rogerian Rhetoric

Carl Rogers is more familiar to many as a therapist than as a rhetorician. However, the goal of therapy, like the goal of rhetoric, can be broadly described as "attitude change." Whereas rhetoricians may want their audience to adopt certain specific beliefs, therapists may not—in fact, should not—have a clear model of specific behaviors that they want their clients to adopt in place of the dysfunctional ones that brought the clients into therapy in the first place. Rather, therapists aim for a broader change in the way their clients interact with the world. Nonetheless, the essence of both arts is to induce change through verbal means— Plato's "art of influencing the soul through words" (*Phaedrus* 48).

Rogerian therapy informs rhetoric by offering a new way of thinking about the means of inducing change. Rogers ("Communication") describes how, as a young practitioner, he quickly discovered that he could not change the attitudes or behavior of his clients by rational argument. The ideal rhetorical situation as described by Plato involves an audience that, like his hero Socrates, is "not less happy to be refuted than to refute" (*Gorgias* 17). Alas, this attitude is rare among real, vulnerable human beings who are not characters in a Platonic dialogue. Clients in therapy, at the peak of their vulnerability, are particularly unhappy to be refuted. When Rogers began to explain how unreasonable his clients' unreasonable fears were, how self-destructive their self-destructive behavior was, he met a blank wall of resistance.

The problem, he decided, was that rational argument of this type always implies a form of evaluation. Argument may convince a person to buy this kind of car or to vote for that politician, but the closer the subject of the argument comes to the beliefs that constitute the core of a person's sense of self, of identity, the more any attempt to change beliefs is perceived as a threat and met with walls of defense.

The way around these walls, Rogers discovered, was to change the role of the therapist. The therapist, in Rogers's view, is not a healer, but rather a *facilitator* of healing. Therapists do not explain their point of view to their clients, but instead listen actively to their clients as clients get in touch with their own thoughts and emotions and do their own healing.

For the art of rhetoric, the most immediately useful aspect of Rogerian therapy is the specific technique that Rogers developed to facilitate this self-healing process. This technique is called "restatement" or "saying back." Rogers is quite explicit that this is not simply a passive process (*Therapy* 27). Therapists continually repeat back their understanding of the clients' words in summary form to check their understanding of the clients' mental state. Thus the therapist might say, "It sounds as though what you are really saying is that you hate your father." The client might respond, "No, that's not quite it," and the therapist would continue with more probes such as, "Well, perhaps you were just angry with him at that moment." Always therapists must walk the fine line between giving their clients words to express hitherto inexpressible feelings and putting words in their mouths. As a therapeutic tool, Rogerian reflection is both difficult—it can quickly degenerate into an irritating echo-chamber of voices—and breathtakingly successful when done well.[1]

In this "pure" form, Rogerian therapy is not "argument." Rogerian therapy is antiargument, a form of discourse in which the speaker must specifically *avoid* stating a point of view either directly or indirectly. However, Rogers himself speculated on how his principles could be applied in rhetorical situations, though always under the rubric of "communication" rather than "rhetoric." In his 1951 paper, "Communication: Its Blocking and its Facilitation," Rogers proposes that the empathy and feedback model could be used to facilitate communication in emotion-laden situations outside the therapeutic relationship, such as political or labor negotiations. His formula is simple: "Each person can speak up for himself only *after* he has first restated the ideas and feelings of the previous speaker, and to that speaker's satisfaction" (332). In later articles he details Rogerian-style negotiation sessions that have produced astonishing results, including the Camp David negotiations conducted by Jimmy Carter, a conference involving health care providers and impoverished and embittered health care consumers, and even opposing sides in Northern Ireland (Rogers and Ryback).

This power to create an atmosphere of cooperation is what led Young, Becker, and Pike to propose an alternative form of rhetoric based on Rogerian principles.[2] Rogerian rhetoric as recreated by Young, Becker, and Pike is aimed at those situations in which more confrontational techniques are most apt to fail: that is, in highly emotional situations in which opposing sides fail to establish even provisional grounds for discussion. Young, Becker, and Pike recommend that rather than trying immediately to present arguments for their point of view and refute their opponents, writers should first undertake a task similar to that of the Rogerian psychotherapist. They should try to reduce the reader's sense of threat by showing that they have genuinely listened to the reader's position. This reduction of threat will in turn induce an "assumption of similarity": The reader will see the writer as a human being more or less like herself and therefore be more likely to listen to what the writer has to say.

Although they argue that it should not be reduced to a mechanical formula, Young, Becker, and Pike outline four basic stages through which a Rogerian argument should pass:

1. An introduction to the problem and a demonstration that the opponent's position is understood.
2. A statement of the contexts in which the opponent's position may be valid.
3. A statement of the writer's position, including the contexts in which it is valid.
4. A statement of how the opponent's position would benefit if he were to adopt elements of the writer's position. If the writer can show that the positions complement each other, that each supplies what the other lacks, so much the better. (283)

Not every version of Rogerian rhetoric emphasizes exactly these stages, but the common denominator among all versions is that writers must state the opposing viewpoint *first*, before stating their own, and do so honestly, with understanding, and without either overt or covert evaluation.

Rogerian Rhetoric in the Writing Classroom

Beginning with Maxine Hairston's seminal article, a number of writers have recommended Rogerian rhetoric as an alternative form of argument to be used, as Young, Becker, and Pike originally recommended, when emotions and a sense of threat preclude direct debate in the classical mode (Bator 1989, 1992; Coe 1992).

Lunsford and Ede, Gage (this volume), and others have argued that those who view classical rhetoric as inherently combative have been misled both by later misreadings of Aristotle and his contemporaries and by an incomplete understanding of the role of the enthymeme. They argue that the enthymeme, the heart of Aristotle's structure of argumentation, differs from the logical syllogism precisely in that it involves the rhetor in building an argument from the opinions of the audience. Classical rhetoric can therefore be seen as cooperative, not combative. This in fact is the basis for Lunsford's argument that a Rogerian "alternative" to traditional rhetoric is unnecessary.

Regardless of the merits of these arguments, the traditional conception of rhetoric still poses limitations. Traditional rhetoric as envisioned by Aristotle and by most modern textbooks on argument is typically triadic; that is, it is aimed at a third party who will judge the case on the basis of the arguments presented by competing advocates, politicians, researchers, advertisers, or other partisan arguers. In this case it matters little if one arguer threatens the beliefs and self-esteem of the other, for it is not the opponent the arguer is trying to convince, but the audience as third party. The process of inquiry claimed for the enthymeme creates cooperation between rhetor and audience, not between rhetor and opponent.

But what about the instances—far more common in everyday life—in which two parties are directly trying to convince each other? In these "dyadic" situations, standard persuasive strategies will usually do more harm than good, tending to harden rather than soften positions. In such cases of dyadic argument, a technique is required that will create the grounds for reasonable discussion that classical rhetoric presupposes. Rogerian rhetoric offers such a technique (Coe 1992).

The challenge for the composition teacher, of course, is how to teach students to put Rogerian principles into practice. Rogerian rhetoric is often tried and dismissed as impractical, too difficult for students to use, too difficult to teach, or too easy for students to misinterpret as a particularly sly form of manipulation.

I believe that some of these problems stem from a failure to recognize just what Rogerian rhetoric really is. The basic model of Rogerian argument, particularly when abstracted from the rich context of heuristic techniques in which Young, Becker, and Pike originally embedded it, looks like a form of *arrangement:* a recipe for what to say first. But arrangement is only part of the business of any rhetorical system. Logically prior to arrangement—and as I will argue, embedded in the process of arrangement, not separate from it—is the process of *invention*. In Rogerian terms, this means exploring an opposing point of view in sufficiently rich complexity to make it possible to reflect it back convincingly to an audience.

The problem of invention is accentuated by the written medium. A writer is in a much worse position than the therapist, for writing does not allow the back-and-forth movement of face-to-face conversation that makes possible the continual readjustment of the discourse. But if we are content to relax our standards somewhat, it is still possible for students to learn how to apply a form of Rogerian principles in writing. To do so, they must learn how to imagine with empathy and how to read with empathy.

By *imagining with empathy,* I mean more than teaching students to imagine another's views. This would be little different from classical audience analysis. I mean teaching students to think carefully about *how* another person could hold views that are different from one's own. This is what Young, Becker, and Pike mean by finding the contexts in which the opposing viewpoint is valid. Rather than simply imagining an isolated set of arguments for an opposing viewpoint, the writer must imagine the entire worldview that allows those arguments to exist, and that makes them valid for the other.

By *reading with empathy,* I mean teaching students to use the printed words of another as a guide to this imagining process. In a sense, this is no more than what is usually known as *research.* When preparing any written argument it is useful to do one's homework. But whereas students often associate research with the mere looking-up of facts, *research* in a Rogerian context emphasizes the looking-up of facts in the context of the arguments that support them and looking at those arguments in the context of other worldviews, other ways of seeing.

This kind of imaginative reconstruction does not come easily. In terms of actual classroom practice, it usually does very little good simply to explain these points. Rather, the teacher must set up situations in which the students can practice Rogerian reflection and the Rogerian attitude long enough for it to sink in. For instance, the teacher can set up a dialectical situation in which students can practice on real, present people in a context more like the original therapeutic situations for which Rogerian principles were originally designed. The oral, face-to-face conversation serves as a bridge to the more difficult imaginative task of the distanced written conversation.

Though these tasks are in one sense designed to serve as preparation for another, they are in no sense mere warm-up drills or "prewriting" activities separate from the business of argument itself. They are integral parts of what Rogerian rhetoric understands by "argument": a process of mutual exploration that may culminate in a written text but that may also take oral and other pathways. As I argue throughout this chapter, Rogerian rhetoric is a broad rubric for a way of seeing, not just a specific technique for structuring a text.

Rogerian Rhetoric in Action: Some Close-Ups

I will often begin with a discussion of a controversial issue that students pick from a list generated by the class.[3] For this exercise I usually depend on the knowledge that students already possess on the subject, though in more advanced classes I ask students to research the topic beforehand. I get students to identify themselves with one side or the other. Then I will call on a volunteer from each side to engage in a public Rogerian discussion (since my disastrous first experience with this technique I am careful not to use the word "debate").

The discussion is organized according to Rogers's own rules as suggested in "Communication: Its Blocking and its Facilitation." Neither person can mention their own view until they have restated the other person's *to that person's satisfaction*. Thus the first "round" would consist of student A stating an argument, student B *restating* that argument in summary form, and student A either agreeing that the summary is accurate or attempting to correct it. This goes on until student A is happy with the summary; then student B gets a turn to state his or her own point of view (*not* to refute A).

The exercise often breaks down into a traditional debate in which one person either tries to refute the other's views or restates them in a way that will make them easier to attack. Emotional hot buttons get pushed and more straw men begin flying about than in the monkey attack from *The Wizard of Oz*.

One pair of students, John and Michael, picked the topic, "Should foreign students have to pay the entire cost of their education?" Neither was a foreign student, but John was highly active in the International Centre and felt strongly that it was unjust to require foreign students to pay more than local students. He stated his reasons, including basic principles of equity and the important contribution that foreign students make to the university. Michael opened his "restatement" along the lines of, "So, you think it's okay to make our taxpayers pay for the education of a student from Singapore who won't even stay in this country?"

Obviously, this is hardly Rogerian reflection. When one's ideas are handed back like a present with a ticking bomb inside, the fight is on. But this is exactly the point. I want students to see the difference between this sort of rebuttal and true Rogerian discussion. Sometimes I involve the entire class in discussing whether a particular response is genuinely "Rogerian" or is really just a sneak attack on the other's values. After some discussion and more prompting from John, Michael eventually worked himself around to identifying the values behind John's statement:

> So, if I understand you correctly, you don't think that the cost of education should be tied directly to the amount of money one's family has paid into a given educational system, or the obvious financial returns that a country can get from educating people. Rather, you think that a more general principle of equity applies and that we need to look at a more global good.

He still didn't agree, but at least he understood John's point of view. Only John's assent that Michael had in fact got it right gave Michael permission to go on to state the reasons for that disagreement.

The process is exhausting and usually the class is over before the first exchange of views is complete. But by the end of the process, students (and the teacher) have a greater appreciation of the difference between their own default mode of argument and the process of struggling toward a genuine understanding of another's point of view.

The point of this oral exchange is not so much to invent material for a particular piece of writing as to get the general feel of Rogerian discussion in its most native mode, face-to-face communication. Once I think students have got the hang of this, I move them on to the more difficult task faced by writers: recovering underlying values from other people's written texts. Again I pair them off and they begin by writing straight-ahead, univocal arguments for their own point of view on a controversial issue. Students exchange papers and try to write summaries that satisfy the original author, who in turn may write countersummaries that extend and correct the reflected image of their ideas.

Kathy, for instance, felt quite passionate about the Young Offenders Act, a controversial Canadian law that severely limits the sentencing of criminals under sixteen years of age even if they have committed violent crimes. Her statement began like this:

> I feel that we must dispose of the Young Offenders Act. It is a useless piece of legislation practically promoting crime. Hasn't our society enough evidence that the YOA doesn't work? The use of weapons in schoolyards, an unprecedented amount of car thefts, break-ins, even children selling other children for prostitu-

tion. A slap on the hand prevents nothing. If greater punishment, including *real* time in jail were a threat, I guarantee that our youth would be a little more reluctant.

And on and on, rehearsing in no uncertain terms the most common arguments leveled against the YOA in the media. Her partner, Tracey, began her restatement like this:

> You have expressed concern over the YOA. You are concerned that it actually encourages crime because of the lack of deterrence. You feel that a person under sixteen knows right from wrong and should be held responsible for his or her actions, regardless of the personal situation or background which might be used as an excuse for committing crimes. You believe that we should place the betterment of society above the protection of criminals, regardless of their age.

The important feature of this restatement is that it is not just a summary of the other's point of view, but, somewhat like Michael's, an attempt to get at underlying beliefs. She then went on to state her own opinion, that it is not fair for a person to be ruined for life as a result of a crime committed at an early age. But her response was moderate and had to deal with the delicate balance between protection of society and protection of individual youths that she had detected in Kathy's position. The effect of the restating process was not simply to soften up Kathy by putting her in the right frame of mind to receive Tracey's argument. Rather, it put Tracey in touch with the complexities of the matter, enabling her to see the matter from another's point of view rather than just her own.

Once students have begun to improve their ability to reflect the arguments of others who are physically present, I have them move on to Rogerian discussions of writers who are not present. One fruitful assignment is to have students reply to articles embodying worldviews that they do not share. Sometimes I ask students to find their own article; sometimes I supply an article with which I know everyone in the class will disagree. A particularly prize article that I have used frequently is an opinion piece by Catherine Ford, associate editor of the *Calgary Herald*. (The entire article is included as an appendix on pages 94-96.) Ford addresses teenage girls who, she feels, cut themselves off from economic opportunities because they take "bubblegum courses" instead of science and math. She cites chilling statistics about how much time most women spend in the workforce and how little most of them are paid, and equates science and math—which, she says, most girls have been "conned" into thinking are too difficult—with "one of the fastest ways to economic independence for women."

However, Ford begins by telling her audience that "the world is passing you by, while you're all out there spray-painting your hair purple and reading *People* magazine," and tries to get their attention by telling them, "You guys seem to have melted your brains with your stereo headphones." Ford clearly is not exactly a master of Rogerian rhetoric and the class usually has an entertaining few minutes raking her over the coals for her unsupported generalizations and unflattering portrayal of the very people she is supposedly trying to convert. Students taking a humanities course are particularly irritated by being accused, by implication, of having chosen a "bubblegum" course. Then I set my students a dyadic task: to write a letter *directly to Ford herself* that uses Rogerian techniques to convince her to moderate her position.

To do so, we discuss not only the areas of validity in Ford's argument, but also try to understand both the rhetorical situation—why she might decide to adopt such an aggressive tone to get her point across—and also who she is as a person. Nobody in the class ever knows much about her personally, but with a little exploratory discussion, we begin to think about the implications of being a woman in her forties—to judge by her picture—who has fought her way up to associate editor of the city's major newspaper. From this and years of experience with Ford's writing, we build up a picture of a woman who prides herself on pulling no punches, who is easily angered by behavior that she perceives as foolish, and whose feminism frequently takes the form of being disgusted by girls who cut themselves off from the opportunities that she herself fought so hard to make for herself. Her insistence on "economic independence" suggests someone with a fierce personal pride and a hard-nosed attitude to life, but not—judging by other columns in which she discusses government fiscal policy—someone who values money for its own sake. In short, the students are applying consciously the reader-response process of constructing both a text and the person behind the text. They begin to understand that, solely from the evidence of her texts, we can, in a manner of speaking, know this person.

None of these personal details need to find their way into the final written product, of course. There is not much to be served by presenting Ford with a detailed picture of herself that is not directly relevant to the issue and could very well be inaccurate. The object of this part of the exercise is simply to sensitize the students to the idea that arguments come from somewhere, and if you can understand where they are coming from, you can negotiate meaning more effectively.

Here is an example of the sort of texts students produce when they sit down to produce their actual written responses:

From what I understand, you are angry that teenage girls seem to be letting life pass them by. They are playing into the roles society seems to have laid out for them, even though the deficiency of women in math and science is an enormous myth. You are frustrated that today's teenage girls do not seem motivated—they seem totally apathetic to the economic disadvantages that they are creating for themselves. I see young girls in shopping malls who seem to be wasting their lives away, concerned more with buying the right kind of makeup than with insuring that they will have the resources to lead independent lives.

However, I have to ask you this—what about all the successful women in fields other than math and science? I think there are many opportunities in math and science—opportunities that many teenage girls overlook because they think that these fields are too difficult. But your own success in the field of journalism is a prime example of the fact that there are many other ways to achieve not only economic independence but also personal fulfillment.

I don't think we should make girls feel inferior because they have genuinely chosen to enter a non-science field. But I guess the point is that girls should not feel locked out of any profession, and they should take advantage of every strength they have and every opportunity life offers them. Otherwise they are going to end up being dependent on some guy because they don't have the skills they need to look after themselves.

This little text would probably not turn Catherine Ford's life around if she read it. But it would be more likely to engage her in honest debate than would a text that began "How dare you tell me that I'm lazy and ignorant because I'm majoring in the humanities!" More important, it reflects a new understanding on the student's part. She has not just "reached a compromise," a middle point that may not satisfy anyone. Rather, she has thought through what she and Catherine Ford might genuinely share on a subject that she has surely discussed before but perhaps not explored in this way.

The skills learned in this sort of reconstructive reading will, I hope, carry over from civil to academic discourse. As Booth long ago argued, and as rhetorics of science and rhetorics of academic disciplines increasingly make us aware, there is no field of knowledge in which "facts" emerge unencumbered by values. A history paper or even the literature review section of a laboratory report can be enhanced by a Rogerian belief that points of view come from somewhere, that the lenses other people choose to hold up to reality are worthy of honest, empathic understanding.[4]

One may ask, if Rogerian principles go so much beyond mere form, why is all of this Rogerian apparatus needed at all? My answer is that even if Rogerian rhetoric is best seen as fundamentally a matter of invention, this invention is driven by the Rogerian form. As Richard M. Coe contends ("Apology"), to choose any form, any pattern of arrangement, is automatically to impose an invention heuristic. If students are attempting to "fill in the form" of Rogerian rhetoric, they know that they must produce a statement of another's beliefs that the other person can recognize as his or her own and can take seriously. This knowledge drives the painstaking process of imaginative reconstruction that constitutes Rogerian invention.

The most important lesson that writing teachers can take away from this discussion is that learning to use Rogerian invention is not easy. This learning cannot be accomplished in a few classes as a coda to traditional argumentation, as one might think from textbooks that spare it only a few pages.

I don't mean to suggest that an entire composition course ought to be built around explicit instruction in Rogerian rhetoric from beginning to end. Dialogic communication is only one kind of communication, and Rogerian rhetoric is only one kind of dialogic communication. As a form of arrangement, Rogerian rhetoric may not always be appropriate; if communicative bridges are already in place, it may not be necessary to build them, and in some forms of triadic communication it may be desirable to underline only one's own point of view. Students therefore need to be taught a variety of rhetorical forms.

However, the general spirit of Rogerian invention should be woven into the fabric of the course through a variety of exercises that help students learn to understand others' points of view. Rogerian rhetoric is not so much a strategy as a habit of mind that must be built painstakingly over a period of months—or as I will argue, over a lifetime.

Criticisms of Rogerian Rhetoric

Rogerian rhetoric has been subject to a number of criticisms that shed light on its strengths and weaknesses. In particular, these criticisms illustrate the importance of treating Rogerian rhetoric as part of a larger system of knowing and valuing, not as an isolated "technique."

One criticism of Rogerian rhetoric is that it can be manipulative. In formal structure, it looks suspiciously like the often-described "indirect structure" in which a writer buffers unwelcome news or an unpalatable request by flattering the reader. (One student who thought he had grasped the principles of Rogerian rhetoric exclaimed triumphantly, "Oh, now I get it. First you get the reader on your side, then you hit 'em with your own ideas at the end.")

Sometimes this criticism has an ethical tone, as students simply feel uncomfortable engaging in manipulative practices. (In an interview with

Nathaniel Teich, Rogers himself states that using his techniques to win an argument or change another's mind is "a perversion of my thinking" [Teich "Conversation" 55].) Sometimes it has a more practical tone. Students frequently protest that Rogerian rhetoric is too idealistic to be used in day-to-day life. People are too hostile, they say, have too often been burned by smooth talkers, to be moved into a more cooperative mindset by Rogerian techniques.

Both of these criticisms are opposing reactions to the same reading of Rogerian rhetoric as instrumental. When seen purely as a *techne,* a specific tool that a student can pull out like a rhetorical torque wrench when a certain job needs doing, Rogerian rhetoric is always open to the charge that it doesn't always turn the nut or that it turns one that should not be turned. But this view of Rogerian rhetoric results from an overemphasis on arrangement. When Rogerian arrangement becomes divorced from the therapeutic roots of Rogers's philosophy, it becomes little more than an updated version of the *benivolentiae captatio* (securing of good will) recommended in medieval and modern letter-writing practice. That structure is as inane now as it was then, and I have written elsewhere about how easily most readers see through it ("Indirect Structure"). Aside from the ethical issues, foregrounded flattery just doesn't work very well in an age in which readers have been inoculated by a lifetime of exposure to sales techniques that would have made Gorgias envious.

However, when Rogerian techniques are taught more as a matter of invention than of arrangement, the emphasis falls more on the underlying attitude rather than the form, the mutual exploration rather than the attempt to convince an "opponent." The goal of Rogerian rhetoric is to identify genuine grounds of shared understanding not just as a precursor to an effective argument but as a means of engaging in effective knowledge making. Rogerian rhetoric is a way of activating the Kantian imperative to pay as much attention to others' ideas as you would have them pay to yours. If the result sometimes looks manipulative to a cynical audience, this is simply the price we pay for living in an imperfect world in which we can never be sure of each other's intentions.

A deeper criticism comes from feminist approaches to language. On the surface, Rogerian rhetoric might appear to be an ideal instantiation of feminist discourse. Studies of women's language suggest that women in conversation tend to engage in more transactional and cooperative than linear and competitive behavior. "Through question-asking and affirming utterances, women's speaking promotes understanding" (Spitzack and Carter 411). Rogerian rhetoric, because it privileges cooperative construction of meaning over goal-directed persuasion, the building of relationships over the winning of an argument, seems to fit neatly into the feminist perspective.

However, Phyllis Lassner, Catherine Lamb, and other feminist rhetoricians have reported that their students and they themselves have felt extremely uncomfortable with Rogerian rhetoric. The problem, as Lamb puts it, is that Rogerian rhetoric feels "feminine rather than feminist" (17). Although studies of women in conversation frequently show them working harder than men at promoting understanding and maintaining relationships, the typical method of doing so, especially in gender-mixed groups, is through self-effacement (Lakoff). Their tendency to interrupt less than men, to ask more questions, and to avoid direct confrontation, can be seen not just as a "maternal" desire to focus on relationships, but also as a willingness to give in, to let the conversation be directed by men. "It has always been women's work to understand others," claims Lamb. "Often that has been at the expense of understanding self" (17).

For men, who have been brought up to value the individualist, goal-directed construction of self, the challenge is to connect with others. For women, brought up to see themselves as socially constructed through their relationships with others, the challenge is to find ways of *having* a well-defined self without sacrificing that connectedness. Elizabeth Flynn's comparison of compositions by male and female students ("Composing as a Woman") dramatically illustrates these differences in orientation to self and other. In their important study *Women's Ways of Knowing*, Belenky, Clinchy, Goldberger, and Tarule also paint a powerful picture of women whose selves are not simply connected to, but all too often extinguished by, the more dominant selves (frequently but not always male) around them. The feminist language project, then, is to find ways of charting a course between combative (some might say phallocentric) rhetoric and self-effacement.

Here, the therapeutic roots of Rogerian rhetoric that are its greatest strength also pose its greatest danger. The role of the Rogerian therapist is precisely to efface the self to enable the client to use language as a tool of self-exploration. Even for the therapist, this is risky. Because the client in a therapeutic relationship is by definition dysfunctional in some way, the possibility of the therapist's personality being significantly changed by the client's is not necessarily an attractive prospect. "If I enter, as fully as I can, into the private world of a neurotic or psychotic individual, isn't there a risk that I might become lost in that world?" (Rogers "Communication" 333) The same danger confronts any student, male or female, who tries to use Rogerian exploration to enter another's world.

Moreover, as Lassner points out, the detached, unemotional tone recommended by standard Rogerian rhetoric goes against the grain of most women's preferred ways of knowing. As developed by Young, Becker, and Pike under the influence of General Semantics (by way of Anatol Rapoport's studies in conflict resolution), Rogerian rhetoric insists on a nonevaluative, neutral language of pure description that modern language theory, even without reference to feminist insights, rejects as impossible (Brent "Reassessment"). This privileging of rationalist objectivity, with its concomitant assumption that emotional involvement destroys the purity of reason, can be seen as yet another variant on the old theme that women make poor scientists, poor speakers, and poor leaders of society because they are inclined to be emotional.

Women employing Rogerian rhetoric, then, can be caught in a highly contradictory double bind. One tenet of Rogerian rhetoric, empathy, looks too much like feminine subservience; the other, suspension of judgment, looks too much like masculine detachment.

To deal with the first problem, it is important to keep in mind the differences and also the similarities between Rogerian rhetoric and Rogerian therapy. Rogerian rhetoric requires that rhetors suspend their tendency to judge *temporarily,* to make contact with other points of view. But the process does not end there; Rogerian rhetors, unlike Rogerian therapists, have their own point of view as well and put it forward in concert with the picture they have constructed of the other's view. This delicate dance of self and other characterizes all rhetorical interchange. If Rogerian rhetoric is to take its place as a means of participating in this dance, it must be a whole rhetoric, a rhetoric in which the rhetor's views and those of others collaborate in a dialectical process of meaning-making.

When students use Rogerian reflection to understand other points of view, then, it is important that they use the glimpses of other selves not just to understand those other selves but also to gain a fuller understanding of their own beliefs and what has caused them to think differently from the others they take in. In classroom practice, this means that the teacher needs to direct discussion toward differences in addition to similarities, and toward understanding the roots of those differences. The students coming to grips with their first defensive reaction to Ford's article, for instance, explored not only what might have made Ford such an outspoken advocate of math and science but also their own experience of gender differences, the reasons for their varied choices of specialization, and their relationship with different forms of knowledge in their high-school years. As part of this process they use not only Rogerian reflection but group conversation, storytelling and freewriting—all methods of exploration that can be and have been used without a Rogerian context but that take on new depth in a Rogerian frame.

Possibly male students profit most from the connection with others entailed by this process whereas female students profit most by the strengthening of their understanding of self. I do not, however, wish to buy into the politics of separation by setting up Rogerian exercises differently for male and female students. Rather, I try to allow space for all differences in meaning-making by emphasizing the connections between the two parts of the process—the exploration of self and the exploration of other.

To deal with the second problem, "neutral" language must be valued not as a pure good in itself, but in a dialectical relationship with emotional language and the connection with self that emotion entails. As previously noted, students get a chance to try out their first reactions to an opposing point of view, responding for instance to Ford's caricature of teenage girls with the derision that an overstated viewpoint deserves. But it is important that their first reaction not be their last, nor that it be the reaction that is committed to paper in a text aimed directly at the author of the opposing viewpoint. And even when they are passing through the most overt stage of Rogerian reflection, in which hostile language is to be avoided at all costs, I do not make them feel that avoiding overt hostility means adopting a tone of total detachment. We can strive for empathy, understanding, and the completest possible construction of the other, without supposing that language can ever be a fully neutral descriptor.

In short, most of the more problematic aspects of Rogerian rhetoric result from insufficiently complex uses of the technique and a failure to bring it into line with views of language, gender and politics appropriate to the nineties. Neither Rogers nor Young, Becker, and Pike ever pretended that their ideas were anything but a stage in the development of new paradigms of communication. To teach Rogerian rhetoric as if Young, Becker, and Pike's twenty-year-old formulation were the last word is to ignore the promptings of teacherly common sense and the work of Bator, Teich, Coe, and many others in constantly updating the spirit of nonadversarial rhetoric.

Rogers and the Ethics of Rhetoric

Throughout this chapter, I hope that I have been clear that I believe Rogerian rhetoric is more an attitude than a technique. The specific form of Rogerian discourse in which one must be able to reflect another's point of view before stating one's own is not just a technique to get someone else to listen to you. This form is a technique that helps students learn to connect with other points of view, explore them fully, and place them in a dialectical relationship with their own as part of a process of mutual discovery.

I believe, in consequence, that the benefits of Rogerian rhetoric go far beyond teaching students an alternative model of argument. An important goal of a liberal education is to create citizens who are fully equipped to take their place in society. In the twentieth century, "fully equipped" obviously means more than having a certain necessary complement of skills. "Fully equipped" should mean not only training in how to communicate, but also training in what communication is *for*.

Once people have fully internalized the process of inquiry into another's beliefs—not just the surface of those beliefs but the underlying experiences and values from which they spring—it will be proportionally more difficult for them to treat others as mere instruments for the fulfillment of their own desires. They will be in a better position to find, as Booth puts it, "grounds for confidence in a multiplicity of ways of knowing" (see also Bator "Teaching of Rhetoric").

This growth in understanding of others is frequently placed under the heading of "cognitive" growth by developmental researchers such as William Perry. This name is certainly not inappropriate, for the ability to think through one's own position relative to those of others and to find grounds for at least provisional confidence in an intellectual position is certainly a cognitive act. But it is also an ethical act. Cognition is concerned with understanding and ethics is concerned with valuing, but the one presupposes the other. We do not have to value positively all those whom we understand—we may "understand" a Nazi prison guard, as Bruno Bettelheim does in one of Young, Becker, and Pike's examples, without adopting the guard's views. But we certainly cannot make informed ethical choices without being able to explore other points of view.

Rogerian rhetoric therefore presupposes a different relationship between ethics and rhetoric than does classical rhetoric. Quintilian, for instance, insists on virtue as a *precondition* to good rhetoric: Rhetoric is "a good man speaking well." If "virtue" includes being able to achieve understanding of other people, not only those with whom we must argue directly but also those countless others, alive and long dead, who contribute to the rhetorical building of our selves, then Rogerian rhetoric reverses the equation. Rogerian training in speaking well helps to create a "good" person by contributing to ethical and cognitive growth. Good rhetoric is a precondition to virtue.

This is a heavy burden and of course Rogerian rhetoric cannot be expected to carry it alone. The world will not become populated by caring and mutually supportive citizens simply because students are taught one particular method (even if it is, as I believe, a particularly powerful method) of exploring others' points of view. But we could certainly do worse than to take up Rogers's challenge to "take this small scale answer, investigate it further, refine it, develop it and apply it to the tragic and well-nigh fatal failures of communication that threaten the very existence of our modern world" ("Communication" 337).

Coda: Beyond Rogerian Rhetoric

Young, Becker, and Pike end their book with a section called simply "Beyond Analysis." With almost no comment they reproduce A. M. Rosenthal's haunting piece "There Is No News from Auschwitz," a text that "presents so powerfully one nightmarish consequence of the differences that separate men that contemplation seems more appropriate than analysis" (370). This text is an eloquent testimony to the need to develop and teach any textual practices, however imperfect and in need of continued development, that we can find which might help our students bridge such tragic differences.

I would like to end, with equally little comment, with an incident that suggests a more optimistic counterpart to Rosenthal's dark vision: a renewed faith in the healing power of language.

I had paired several sets of students for an oral Rogerian discussion as previously described. One pair decided to discuss drunk driving. They are not exactly on "opposing sides"—who would be *for* drunk driving?—but they had very different views of the problem and its consequences. Was that all right? I told them that it was; in reality, differences of opinion seldom divide along neat bipolar lines of cleavage that allow pat "yes/no" sides.

Lisa went first. Her initial "statement of position" was much fuller than usual. In somewhat abbreviated form, it went like this:

> The year I was born, my grandmother was killed by a drunk driver.
> She was the stabilizing force in my grandpa's life, so when she died he became a bitter and miserable man. The only time I've ever spent with my grandpa is when he lived with our family after he was seriously injured in another drinking and driving incident. This time he was the drunk. This accident left him crippled and even more miserable.
> I see my grandpa once a year. He is usually in his wheelchair complaining. All I think is, "You did this to yourself." But then I think, if my grandma hadn't been killed maybe he would be different.

The driver that killed her robbed me. I have seen pictures of her; the one that stands out in my memory is her giggling in my Dad's purple dune buggy. She was wearing a short skirt, had a beehive and was 50 years old. I never got to meet her.

My family does not dwell on what happened so many years ago. We never talk about what happened to the other driver. But we never drink and drive.

Gayleen went through the motions of reflecting back Lisa's statement, appreciating the pain and the anger contained within it. But there really wasn't much to uncover. Lisa's eloquent narrative hid little that needed to be dug out by Rogerian techniques, and they reached agreement very quickly that Gayleen had "got it."

Gayleen's opening statement was equally full:

I also learned a very hard lesson, but from a different perspective than you, Lisa. I too was the victim of a drunk driver, and I too lost something that day that I will never be able to regain. The difference is that a member of my family was not killed by a drunk driver—a member of my family *was* the drunk driver.

When I was nineteen years old, my fiancé went to a stag party one night. They all drank and then drove home. On the way home, he went through a stop sign and broadsided a car, killing a woman in the back seat.

From that day on, my life was never the same. While the court case dragged on, I was trying to plan a future. But since my fiancé was charged with four counts of criminal negligence causing death, jail was a real possibility. Several people who didn't feel comfortable confronting my fiancé said terrible, hurtful things to me, as if I condoned this act he had chosen. "Friends" dropped us as if we had a contagious disease, including the same guys my fiancé had grown up with and partied with that night, and who also drank and drove themselves home. I also grieved for the family of the woman who was killed, a woman about my mother's age—I kept thinking that it could have been her.

My fiancé was never able to talk about his feelings about that night. Though we got married and were together for twenty years, it set a pattern for him of avoiding difficult situations and emotions. He continued to drink and drive—perhaps ten times in twenty years, but it was ten times too many, and it was the one thing we argued about until our marriage fell apart.

I always wanted to tell the woman's family how truly sorry I was for their loss. I thought of her every day for many years, so that now the incident is a part of the fabric of my being. I don't drink and drive, yet I feel the same shame as if I had been behind the wheel that day.

What more could be said? What could be "reflected back"? Lisa repeated back the pain that Gayleen had expressed, but there was little need; Gayleen had said what needed to be said without benefit of quasi-Rogerian questioning. And as for working through propositions to isolate areas of mutual validity—well, as you might imagine, we never got that far.

At the end of their "Rogerian discussion," they shared the background of their topic. Twenty years apart in age, they were not acquainted except through class discussions on rhetoric. Gayleen had recognized Lisa's name at the beginning of term, but they had not discussed the incident until they were paired by random number draw. At that time they decided to try discussing their beliefs on drunk driving because they shared far more than a general interest in the subject. The accidents they had discussed were actually the same accident. Gayleen's fiancé had killed Lisa's grandmother.

The class was left speechless by the courage they displayed in talking about this incident in front of people who until two months ago had been total strangers. They also had the courage to revisit the long-standing grief and anger with each other and with their families. Lisa, who had never really talked with her parents about the incident and what it had meant to her family, talked now, and gave a copy of Gayleen's speaking notes to her father. A renewed process of healing through language was begun.

Rogerian rhetoric is lauded for its power to build bridges. But in this instance, the elaborate scaffolding of Rogerian rhetoric was unnecessary because Gayleen and Lisa, through the most impossible of chances, had already found the opportunity to work through their long-separated feelings in both private and public rhetoric. The bridges were already in place when they stood to speak.

There is no news from Auschwitz, but there is news from Communications Studies 461. One news item is that Rogerian rhetoric is not always necessary if the conversants have the will to communicate. But the more important news is that the power of rhetoric, Rogerian or not, to heal is as powerful as its ability to persuade. It has a power that is beyond analysis.

Notes

1. To watch Rogers in action in films such as *Three Approaches to Psychotherapy, II: Dr. Rogers* is instructive. I do not necessarily suggest showing these films to a composition class, as they set up such a powerful image of Rogers's methods as therapy that it may be difficult for students to make the transition to written rhetoric. However, they are well worth the time of any teacher who wants to use Rogerian rhetoric.

2. For a more thorough critical analysis of the strengths and weaknesses of Young, Becker and Pike's entire project and a more complete discussion of the criticisms that have been leveled at Rogerian Rhetoric over the years, see my article "Young, Becker and Pike's 'Rogerian' Rhetoric: A Twenty-Year Reassessment."

3. Nathaniel Teich recommends exactly the opposite. Because controversial arguments tend to produce intractable positions, Teich suggests avoiding them and concentrating on less emotionally taxing ones ("Rogerian Problem Solving" 57-58). I take his point, but because emotional

situations are precisely the ones in which Rogerian rhetoric is most necessary, I tend to damn the torpedoes and let students argue about gun control, nuclear disarmament and such. Perhaps the main criterion for choosing between these paths is how long the course is—that is, how much time the instructor is able to spend on damage control.

4. In *Reading as Rhetorical Invention* (Urbana: NCTE 1992), I extend this argument to claim that all research, even into the most apparently "factual" information, is strongest when it consists of this sort of imaginative reconstruction of the person behind the text. That we can never do so perfectly—that all reading is fundamentally indeterminate—ought not to dissuade us from teaching our students to come as close as they can.

Works Cited

Bator, Paul. "Aristotelian and Rogerian Rhetoric." *College Composition and Communication* 31 (Dec. 1980): 427-32.

———. "Rogers and the Teaching of Rhetoric and Composition." *Rogerian Perspectives: Collaborative Rhetoric for Oral and Written Communication*. Ed. Nathaniel Teich. Northwood, NJ: Ablex, 1992. 83-100.

Belenky, Mary Field, Blythe McVicker Clinchy, Nancy Rule Goldberger, and Jill Mattuck Tarule. *Women's Ways of Knowing: the Development of Self, Voice, and Mind*. New York: Basic Books, 1986.

Booth, Wayne C. *Modern Dogma and the Rhetoric of Assent*. Chicago: University of Chicago Press, 1974.

Brent, Doug. "Indirect Structure and Reader Response." *Journal of the American Business Communication Association* 22 (Spring 1985): 5-8.

———. "Young, Becker and Pike's 'Rogerian' Rhetoric: A Twenty-Year Reassessment." *College English* 53 (Apr. 1991): 452-66.

———. "Reading as Rhetorical Invention. Urbana, IL: NCTE, 1992.

Coe, Richard M. "An Apology for Form, or, Who Took the Form Out of the Process?" *College English* 49 (Jan. 1987): 13-28.

———. *Process, Form, and Substance: A Rhetoric for Advanced Writers*. Englewood Cliffs, NJ: Prentice Hall, 1990.

———. "Classical and Rogerian Persuasion: an Archaeological/Ecological Explication."*Rogerian Perspectives: Collaborative Rhetoric for Oral and Written Communication*. Ed. Nathaniel Teich. Northwood, NJ: Albex, 1992. 83-100.

Ede, Lisa S."Is Rogerian Rhetoric Really Rogerian?" *Rhetoric Review* 3 (Sept. 1984): 40-48.

Flower, Linda. *Problem-Solving Strategies for Writers*. 4th ed. Fort Worth, TX: Harcourt Brace Jovanovich, 1993.

Flynn, Elizabeth. "Composing as a Woman." *College Composition and Communication* 39 (Dec. 1988): 423-35.

Ford, Catherine. "Science Courses Key to Future Jobs." *Calgary Herald* 20 Oct. 1983, A4.

Hairston, Maxine. "Carl Rogers' Alternative to Traditional Rhetoric." *College Composition and Communication* 27 (Dec. 1976): 373-77.

Lakoff, Robin. *Language and Women's Place*. New York: Harper and Row, 1975.

Lamb, Catherine E. "Beyond Argument in Feminist Composition." *College Composition and Communication* 42 (Feb. 1991): 11-24.

Lassner, Phyllis. "Feminist Responses to Rogerian Argument."*Rhetoric Review* 8 (Spring 1990): 220-31.

Lunsford, Andrea A. "Aristotelian vs. Rogerian Argument: A Reassessment." *College Composition and Communication* 30 (May 1979): 146-51.

Lunsford, Andrea A., and Lisa S. Ede. "On Distinctions Between Classical and Modern Rhetoric." *Essays of Classical and Modern Discourse.* Ed. Robert J. Connors, Lisa S. Ede, and Andrea A. Lunsford. Carbondale and Edwardsville: Southern Illinois University Press, 1984. 37-49.

Mader, Diane C. "What Are They Doing to Carl Rogers?" *Et Cetera* 37 (Winter 1980): 314-20.

Plato. *Gorgias.* Trans. W. C. Helmbold. Indianapolis, IN: Bobbs-Merrill, 1951.

———. *Phaedrus.* Trans. W. C. Helmhold and W. G. Rabinowitz. Indianapolis, IN: Bobbs-Merrill, 1956.

Rogers, Carl R. "Communication: Its Blocking and its Facilitation." 1951 Rpt. in *On Becoming a Person.* Boston: Houghton Mifflin, 1961. 329-37

———. "This Is Me." Chapter 1 of *On Becoming a Person.* Boston: Houghton Mifflin, 1961.

———. *Client-Centered Therapy.* Boston: Houghton Mifflin, 1965.

Rogers, Carl R., and David Ryback. "One Alternative to Nuclear Planetary Suicide." *The Consulting Psychologist.* 12(1984): 3-12. Rpt. in *Rogerian Perspectives: Collaborative Rhetoric for Oral and Written Communication.* Ed. Nathaniel Teich. Northwood, NJ: Ablex, 1992. 83-100.

Spitzack, Carole, and Kathryn Carter. "Women in Communication Studies: A Typology for Revision." *Quarterly Journal of Speech* 73 (Nov. 1987): 401-23.

Teich, Nathaniel, Ed. *Rogerian Perspectives: Collaborative Rhetoric for Oral and Written Communication.* Northwood, NJ: Ablex, 1992.

———, Ed. "Conversation with Carl Rogers." *Rogerian Perspectives: Collaborative Rhetoric for Oral and Written Communication.* Northwood, NJ: Ablex, 1992. 55-64.

———. "Rogerian Problem Solving and Rhetoric of Argumentation." *Journal of Advanced Compostition* 7 (1987): 52-61.

Three Approaches to Psychotherapy, II: Dr. Rogers. Psychological Films 1977. 50 min., sd., col., 16 mm.

Young, Richard E., Alton L. Becker, and Kenneth L. Pike. *Rhetoric: Discovery and Change.* New York: Harcourt, 1970.

APPENDIX:
SCIENCE COURSES KEY TO FUTURE JOBS

Catherine Ford
Calgary Herald

Okay out there—all you teenage girls—listen up and don't turn the page. This is specifically for you.

You won't believe your parents, you won't pay any attention to your teachers and counsellors, so I'll try. (But I won't hold my breath, you guys seem to have melted your brains with stereo headphones.)

The world is passing you by, while you're all out there spray-painting your hair purple and reading *People* magazine. About 10 or 15 years from now, you are going to be working at some menial, low-paying, miserable job and wondering what happened.

Allow me to tell you what is happening while it's happening and maybe you can do something about it. There's a whole great world out here waiting for you, if you have enough sense to prepare for it. Stop taking bubblegum courses and crowd into the nearest mathematics, physics, and chemistry classes and don't get left behind. Because you are being left behind even as you think that math and physics are too tough for you to take, and what difference will it make anyway?

It could make all the difference in the world to your future. Yes, you may well be married at 18. You may well meet Mr. Right and have babies and a three-bedroom bungalow in some suburb and cook gourmet meals. But please, for once in your life, listen: you will also work. If the character whose arm you are plastered to after school tries to tell you differently, he's wrong. He may say he will love and support you and let you stay at home and bring up babies, but the cold hard statistics call him a liar.

These days, having a career is not a choice, it's a necessity. You will work for about 30 years of your life and if you think that school is boring, you ain't seen nothing yet. When you graduate from high school, these are the facts you will face.

Over 80 percent of women spend up to 30 years in the workforce.

On average, women earn 40 percent less than men.

Half of Canada's families with two wage earners bring home less than $15,000 a year.

Most women work in clerical, secretarial or unskilled jobs.

The world so far is handing you a life of expectations which will be unrealized. We are in the midst of a technological revolution, and the science courses which are the foundation for jobs in that revolution are overwhelmingly populated with your boyfriends.

Why? Because you think that science and math are too difficult. You have been conned into thinking that. There is no difference between the brains of men and women. You think they're difficult because a society which tries to keep you in your place has led you to believe that.

You think that science and math are unfeminine. That is unadulterated nonsense. If you buy the "unfeminine" label you are condemning yourself to that ghetto reserved for women who still believe it's cute to be stupid. There is only one thing less attractive than stupidity, and that's being stuck in a boring job—or being unemployed, on welfare and seeking job retraining when you're 30.

Within a few years, many of the "traditional" jobs for uneducated women will not exist, as the computer takes over. By dropping science and mathematics, girls eliminate at least half of their job opportunities for the future, and if that isn't frightening, consider the economic implications.

Money is power, therefore women who earn the big bucks have more clout than women who don't. As Senator Bud Olson said last weekend at a conference on Women, The Law and The Economy: "Opportunities and freedoms flow from economic independence." Almost in the same breath he said that women are "discouraged" from entering science and math courses, yet those fields provide one of the fastest ways to economic independence for women.

It seems unfair to have to make lifetime decisions when you're only 14 years old and the most important thing is to have a date for the Grade 9 dance. But it's even more unfair to condemn yourself to always being treated as a 14-year-old, which is about the level of treatment that uneducated, unskilled workers are afforded.

5

Classical Rhetoric

The Art of Argumentation

Jeanne Fahnestock
University of Maryland

Marie Secor
Pennsylvania State University

In 1993, the Student Government Association at a large state university wanted all incoming students to read the same book. The idea behind this single requirement was to give first-year students a common experience on a large campus, something to encourage both planned discussion and spontaneous interaction. The book chosen was Garry Wills's Pulitzer Prize-winning study *Lincoln at Gettysburg,* a text that places Lincoln's famous funeral oration in its political, historical, cultural and generic contexts. The book proved a daunting choice for the incoming students. If it gave them anything in common, it was a common cause for complaint. Courses across the curriculum connected with the book, and one interesting observation surfaced several times. Students could not figure out what kind of book *Lincoln at*

Gettysburg was. Many, including the student reporter who wrote about the project for the campus newspaper, called Wills's book a novel. A speech teacher finding great resistance to the book finally asked the students what was troubling them. One student quizzically observed, "Well, it isn't a novel." If not a novel, what was it? In a response written in a freshman English class, one student decided, "It's not a novel because it has an index, so it's a reference book." In fact, Wills's book advances an argument, one that many scholars disagree with.

As the students' encounter with *Lincoln at Gettysburg* suggests, many freshmen have little conception of what it means to argue, to maintain a position with reasons that do not necessarily compel agreement but that nevertheless establish a good and likely case. Their educational experience includes textbooks, unassailable repositories of knowledge demanding sentence-by-sentence absorption, and works of literature, equally unassailable fortresses of excellence maintained by those in authority. Unless they had an exceptional history course, they probably never analyzed the momentous arguments that have shaped history, and unless they participated in a forensics club as an extracurricular activity, they never learned any skills of debate. Of course no one who has ever known an eighteen-year-old would say that people in that age group don't know how to argue. They are members of families, groups of friends, and clubs; they make decisions for themselves and persuade others, and a few are even involved in the political lives of their communities. They have certainly watched what passes for public debate on Oprah and Geraldo. Ad hoc verbal dispute, joshing and give-and-take are familiar. But many are unaware that the "knowledge" contained in textbooks is the product of inquiry expressed in arguments by researchers and scholars, that reasonable people can disagree without anyone being "wrong," that there are better and worse ways to make a case, or that when something is at stake competing arguments should be compared and weighed.

When these students arrive in freshman English, what do they find? A course that has long been a target of scorn, neglect, criticism, indifference, dismissal, and now, increasingly, of calls for abolition. Just recently, Walter Beale has argued that the resources invested in freshman composition should be rerouted to a senior-level course in civic rhetoric delivered to students in a better position to appreciate its importance. Sharon Crowley has blasted the institution of required freshman writing, accurately skewering its many weaknesses: the chaos of curricular models, the lack of evidence of effectiveness, and the cynicism with which the course is staffed and maintained. And Richard Larson, after sampling freshman writing programs across the country, has called for wiping the slate clean and beginning anew, citing in particular the neglect of training and supervision for the armies of graduate students and instructors who teach the course. These and other critics pose a hard question for all of us involved in composition: How can a course collect the lowest class of teachers in the academy—or rather create and exploit the lowest class of teachers in the academy—and expect to have good come of it? No wonder that the cleanest solution often seems to be to abolish writing courses. Sometimes it seems that only the funding requirements of English departments for their graduate students prevents this from happening. Although we find it impossible to dismiss the criticisms of these powerful voices, we still want to argue that freshman composition should not be eradicated. It should be changed.

Among the hopeful signs of possible change is the current turn, demonstrated by this anthology, to argumentation as the focus of the composition classroom. If the puzzlement of students trying to read *Lincoln at Gettysburg* is at all typical, more rather than less teaching of argumentation may be exactly what is needed to address their problem. The 1992 "Writing Report Card" of the NAEP concludes that students in fourth, eighth and twelfth grades perform most poorly on persuasive writing tasks ("Writing Skills Improve"). Students clearly need more exposure to argumentative texts, need to learn how to read and evaluate them, and need to learn how to write them.

If we wish to center our writing classrooms on the teaching of argument, how do we go about it? We want to argue that the best way to go about it is to acquire again the holistic vision, the "big picture" provided by classical rhetoric. Currently, there are many proposals and models in place for the teaching of argument, each emphasizing only selected aspects of the complete art and each applying to some of many possible rhetorical situations. What students may gain in facility from these approaches, they lose in wide applicability. Only classical rhetoric offers a complete, general art of argumentation that takes in the whole activity of discourse making, from the first stages of inquiry to the final stages of dissemination. Though it might be possible to reinvent this wheel for the classrooms of the twenty-first century, it seems wiser and certainly more efficient to adapt an art developed over twenty-five centuries, one that has been continually reshaped by different cultures and circumstances and one that remains relevant to our contemporary pedagogical context.

It is not the case that classical rhetoric and the teaching of argumentation have disappeared entirely from the contemporary curriculum. Fragments of the classical tradition can be found in various places. One popular approach has been developed by the critical thinking or informal logic movement that concentrates only on the logos, the logical plausibility of arguments. This movement, originating in philosophy departments and exported under the label *critical thinking,* emphasizes the analysis of arguments and the detection of fallacies. These are important skills, but teachers of writing know that they do not carry over directly into the construction of arguments. Proponents of informal logic resemble dialecticians, inheritors of the arts of disputation and the skills of refutation but not the skills of invention and audience accommodation. When their analytic approach migrates from the introductory philosophy course into the composition classroom, it may borrow the Toulmin model, the twentieth century's version of the classical *epicheireme* or, as some critics have labeled it, the syllogism turned on its side and expanded. As Richard Fulkerson points out in this volume, the Toulmin model may be an excellent analytical probe but less successful as a stimulus to constructing arguments. In addition, the informal logic movement's emphasis on fallacies raises more questions than it can answer, questions about the legitimacy of appeals given different audiences, genres, purposes, and contexts. These questions are more cogently addressed from the perspective of rhetoric than of logic.

The Writing Across the Curriculum movement could be said to embody another popular approach to the teaching of argument. Academics and administrators have found it expedient to promote WAC programs and writing-intensive courses on the presumption that the invention of arguments is best taught as a discipline-specific activity. There are, in this view, only arguments unique to evolutionary biology, to history, to economics, and so on, and these should be taught within their disciplines by people who are experts in these fields. One consequence of exclusive attention to arguments within fields has been the loss of a general vocabulary for talking about writing and argumentation. Another indirect effect has been the removal from the freshman classroom of the invention of arguments as a serious and central activity. What then is left to do in the lower-level course but to cultivate some reading, to discuss issues that the instructor hopes will be of interest, and to practice peer critiquing?

Certainly critical thinking and writing-intensive courses are legitimate parts of the full rhetorical *paideia,* but they belong later in the curriculum. The existence of critical thinking or WAC courses is not the problem; the problem is a lack of confidence in teaching generic skills of argumentation at the freshman level. The premise of classical rhetoric—itself developed by a particular group and culture in a particular time—is that there are such generic skills of argumentation that persist across situations, groups, cultures, and times, and that these skills produce, to use Quintilian's term, *facilitas,* an ability to improvise in a new situation. We believe that these skills, outlined on the pages following, could be the focus of our teaching in first-year writing courses. Furthermore, a knowledge of these generic skills of argument—acquired early in the college experience—helps students appreciate local selections and emphases both in the public discourse that they will encounter throughout their lives and in the particular fields they choose to study.

Our approach is based on the conviction that classical rhetoric is an art of argument in a state of completeness and elaboration that no other current rationale approximates. As an art of using language and of communication, it represents a whole act from the first act of inquiry to the final acts of decision and closure. When Corbett's *Classical Rhetoric for the Modern Student* (itself an incomplete redaction) appeared in the 1960s, it offered the most complete tour of the classical system then available, and a generation of teachers has mined it—selectively—for their classroom practice. A revived art of argument on the classical model of the sort we are proposing would make a different selection of the essentials and would emphasize different elements of the classical system. The fuller embodiment of the classical tradition that we suggest includes the following seven elements: the need for exigence, the stases as a way of sorting issues, the blending of the three appeals, a further explication of the topoi, the need to switch levels of argument, the restoration of narrative as a tactic of persuasion, and a deeper appreciation of the inventional possibilities offered by the figures of speech. We propose a composition curriculum featuring these generic skills, a somewhat differently shaded vision of classical rhetoric than the usual selection of emphases.

Exigence

In the lead article of the first issue of *Philosophy and Rhetoric* in 1968, Lloyd Bitzer introduced a new term to describe an essential feature of a rhetorical situation. Truly rhetorical situations, according to Bitzer, are characterized by *exigence,* an "imperfection marked by urgency" that rhetorical discourse addresses. In Bitzer's model, rhetors respond to external conditions and events, like the assassination of a president, addressing discourse that attempts to solve problems to audiences that can be agents of change. In naming this notion of exigence, Bitzer does not depart from the classical rhetorical model; rather, he foregrounds a concept inherent in Aristotle's situational definition of rhetoric as the art of finding the "available means of persuasion" on any given issue.

Bitzer's essay has had a profound and lasting influence on twentieth-century rhetoric even though his restrictive notions of rhetorical situation and rhetorical discourse have inspired some significant qualifications. Most notable among such responses have been Richard Vatz's point that it is not situations that make rhetoric but rhetoric that makes situations, and Richard Larson's broadening of what rhetors can take as "imperfections" requiring solutions to include issues that interest scholars. But whether political or scholarly, external, or constructed, Bitzer's key concept of exigence remains. Arguers need to consider not only the "what" of their discourse but also the "why"—why bother to speak or write on this point at this moment to this audience?

The power of this rhetorical insight is confirmed by the number of times it has been rediscovered in parallel fields, often, as Flower and Hayes have done, under the rubric of a problem/solution paradigm. Linguistically trained scholars like Joseph Williams and Greg Colomb, and John Swales, for example, intent on identifying formal models of the genre of scholarly or knowledge-forming arguments, have noticed that the opening paragraphs of such arguments require the setting up of a "problem" that is then addressed or solved in the article. Most recently Ellen Barton, in a linguistically oriented study of "evidentials" in argumentative discourse, identified what she called "problematization" in the arguments appearing on the back page of the *Chronicle of Higher Education.* What she discovered was the linguistic trace of the need to establish exigence, the demand for an explicit answer to "Why?" before launching a written argument. Barton points out that only 60 percent of students on placement tests used the explicit markers of exigence that she identified, not a surprising result given the problematic nature of the rhetorical situation of such tests.

Emphasis on the need to establish exigence has an important effect on writing courses. Establishing exigence turns the course outward toward an audience, including rather than excluding others, because the need to establish exigence requires that writers frame issues in terms that engage others, not just themselves. Thus, the student who wants to argue for show-all-work math exams has to demonstrate how the present Scantron scoring creates a problem not just for that student but for the intended audience as well; and the student who wants to extol the benefits of bodybuilding has to anticipate how readers might regard the activity and address their preconceptions about it. Such outward-turned writing courses deemphasize (though they certainly do not eliminate) personal, exploratory writing, the domain of what Berlin calls the expressivist tradition in composition. Argument-centered courses require that students establish exigence in their texts by defining or creating issues that can be of interest to others. These "others" should not be imagined as passive recipients of a writer's persuasive efforts; they have to be formed into an attentive audience and they are free to resist the invitation. Thus the need for exigence teaches that argument is a social act and the means by which a community forms and reforms itself. An arguer can tap into interests that already exist in a community (classroom, town, discipline, nation) or find a way to create those interests and perhaps even the community to acknowledge them.

Not surprisingly, there are both general and discipline-specific topics for establishing exigence. Classical rhetoric offers such topoi in the traditional advice given for the exordium, the opening part of an oration the function of which was to secure the attention and favorable disposition of the audience. According to Cicero's *De Inventione,* "We shall make our audience attentive if we show them that the matters which we are about to discuss are important, novel, or incredible, or that they concern all humanity or those in the audience or some illustrious men or the immortal gods or the general interest of the state" (I, xvi, 23). With deceptive brevity this passage covers the routine topoi for establishing exigence; virtually any published argument, academic or popular, will satisfy one of these requirements.

As important as exigence is, writing assignments made in academic settings seldom encourage students to think about the "why" of their arguments, because the fact that the teacher has made the assignment is sufficient exigence for the writing, and the immediate need to satisfy the teacher as audience may obscure consideration of other exigencies for other audiences. Nevertheless, even though the need to establish exigence is rarely taught explicitly, successful students often grasp intuitively the tactic of creating an opening problem and then solving it in their papers. If the teacher frames the assignment as a question, there is a step toward teaching exigence, but it can still fall short. Why is that particular question interesting and to whom? From the instructor's point of view, an assigned question may be important because the instructor has set it, but that does not teach the student to justify the question being asked. One of the generic skills of argumentation is this basic one of connecting a subject to an audience by establishing exigence. Writers should be able to anticipate the reader's question, "So what?"

The Stases: What's at Issue?

In addition to finding subjects with a constructable exigence for a constructable audience, an arguer must also be able to frame or identify one or more points at issue in order to open an inquiry or enter a controversy. The ability to frame an issue is another of the essential generic skills of argumentation that may go unnoticed and unpracticed in writing courses where the instructor sets the subject, exigence implicit, or where the student relies on personal experience as the subject matter. But any arguer who wants to enter an ongoing public or academic debate needs first to identify what points have been agreed upon, what points have been in contention, and which of them to address. The standard but often bewildering advice to "narrow the topic" reflects this need to specify an issue. What is needed is not so much "narrowness" as an addressable issue that can be made significant (given exigence) for an addressable audience. This significance for others can be significance for the self. Furthermore, this process of sorting through issues is a thinking skill in itself, whether it leads to a fully constructed argument or not. In classical rhetoric, this sorting process was formalized.

In one of its less accessible elaborations of terminology, the classical rhetorical handbooks taught this skill of issue identification under the rubric of the stases. In a forensic or courtroom setting, the opposing sides test each other to find the point of disagreement in a case, the point at which they can maintain contradictory claims. This point of balanced counterpressures—or *stasis*—gives rise to the question for the audience or judge to decide.

The famous trial of the Menendez brothers, accused of murdering their parents, illustrates how issues develop around a single topic. The defense in this case argued during the first trial that the brothers killed their parents because they had been abused, and feared for their lives. If the prosecution could successfully argue that the brothers had not been not abused, the defense could in turn switch the issue to their perception of abuse and consequent fear. The prosecution could then counter that their fear was not a sufficient justification for the murders. The issue was never "Did the brothers kill their parents?"—a point readily conceded—but "Were they abused?" "Were they afraid?" or "Was their fear a sufficient motive?" Arguments frequently require such a negotiation or testing of issues in this way, and there is nothing predictable about where they end up.

Students in literature-based writing assignments often do a similar sorting through issues leading to briefs in defense or condemnation of a fictional character: Should Captain Vere have condemned Billy Budd? How ought Hamlet to have responded to his father's ghost? Should Mookie, in *Do the Right Thing*, be convicted of starting a riot? Some such sorting out of arguable issues occurs whenever a writer investigates sources and reads around in a subject to map it out. What are the points at issue? Are there identifiable parties making counterclaims, each with support? What other claims could be made even if no one has made them yet? Most arguments conducted in public will form into positions offering reasons to support countering claims, thus creating a potential question for resolution: China should be an Olympic host (claim) because hosting the games will encourage its democratization (premise)/ China should not host the Olympic games (claim) because the Chinese government has been guilty of human rights violations (premise). Should China host the Olympic games?

Many teachers of argument use some system to lead students to identify issues and develop alternative positions. How formal should this system be? In classical rhetoric the kinds of questions or issues an argument could address were organized according to a system known as the stases: "Every subject which contains in itself a controversy to be resolved by speech and debate involves a question about a fact, or about a definition, or about the nature of an act, or about legal processes" (*De Inventione,* I, viii, 10, 21). This system was a fixed feature of classical pedagogy. An arguer considered whether a disagreement involved one of four kinds of controversy:

1. A matter of fact (Do spotted owls nest in second growth forests or don't they?)
2. A matter of definition (In the famous trial of the Menendez brothers, was their murder of their parents an act of malice or of premeditation?)
3. A matter of quality or value (Was the attack on Nancy Kerrigan the figure skater worse because she was an athlete about to compete for international honors?)
4. A matter of process or transaction (Does NATO have the right to intervene in Bosnia?)

We suggest that any course in argument on the classical model should include instruction in the formal system of issue or question formation; classifying the kinds of issues that can be in contention is one of the generic skills of argumentation. If writers learn to do this, they will always have a way of sorting out the new controversies that arise each day.

An immediate objection to the stasis system, with its emphasis on contention, will be that not all the subjects students write about generate or can be mapped as conflicting claims. First, when a view or proposal is new, it may not have a developed opposition: The first person to put forward the dinosaur/bird connection was not responding to a fixed claim that dinosaurs and birds had nothing to do with each other. But this nonexistent opposition, perhaps best described as an unarticulated assumption, needs to be given a voice. Second, the issues student writers take up will often have more than two easily identifiable sides. There are many competing positions on health care, gun control, crime prevention, or any of the crises that confront the public. But eventually, even on these more complex subjects, arguers have to support or oppose specific smaller-scale issues, one after the other. Third, and even more likely, some of the claims that students choose to support will seem too predictable to generate opposition. Who, after all, is going to counter an argument about how enjoyable skiing is with an opposing claim? But a perspective that values argumentation will encourage the trial creation of conflicting claims. Even the most avid skier must be asked whether the fun is worth the expense and the risk. In other words, the arguer pushes at or tests any claim as a mental exercise. When we teach the stases we are teaching students a generic skill that should become a habit of reading and thinking, so that nothing of consequence passes the courtroom of the mind without a prosecution and defense.

Other objections may be made against forming conflicting propositions. The very notion of conflict is offensive to some, and argumentation has been compared to aggression and violence, as Annas and Tenney point out in this volume. Certainly images of competition and even combat lurk in rhetorical terminology and in overt comparisons in rhetorical texts: The courtroom is the *palaestra,* the ring in which wrestlers contend; the devices of rhetoric, particularly the figures, are referred to as the rhetor's armament as well as ornament. Critics made uncomfortable by this agonistic element in rhetoric point out that conflicting claims are not always the product of the mental exercise of one person. They often have human locations and these locations rarely enter a debate equally empowered. Thus the very possibility of rhetorical efficacy has been questioned. Is it not the case that superior power wins after all, and that the exercise of argument and counterargument merely masks a foregone conclusion, temporizing while the issue is actually being decided on other grounds? Such questions are only the latest version of the ancient debate on the morality and efficacy of rhetoric.

This debate is important to continue. One might point out that power itself is a rhetorical construct and that its quantitative distribution or misdistribution a prevailing rhetorical figure. One might argue over whether there is any point in engaging in an argument. Or one might point out that the indictment of argumentation is itself an example of rhetorical argument, a version of the centuries-old tradition of using elaborately amplified rhetorical arguments against the power of rhetoric. Still another answer might be that any claim to avoid all arguing is impossible because there can be no location in language free of all a priori formal rhetorical devices. Even silence is a rhetorical gesture. It is rhetoric all the way down. We teach rhetoric to give people power against rhetoric.

But undoubtedly some power inequities are more than the creation of rhetorical amplification. There are material and perceived differences of power among rhetors; the Branch Davidians and the Bureau of Alcohol, Tobacco, and Firearms were in a face-off of more than words. Yet paradoxically, it is—and has always been—the purpose of rhetorical education to address and even attempt to redress differences in social and material status. One cannot read advice from handbooks like the *De Inventione* or the *Ad Herennium* and not realize that these are manuals for negotiating power inequities. We teach rhetoric to give people power against social and material differences. This is not to say that such education has been equally accessible to all throughout history; it has been monopolized by the powerful. But the response to that imperfect condition—that exigence—may be to make rhetorical competence more available to more people.

In this section we have tried to take our own advice seriously and imagine possible claims against the practice of defining issues and creating competing propositions. We have offered potential refutations of the "argument as agonistic position" made as though its worst-case characterization were valid. Actually we do not believe it is. A pervasive assumption of this criticism is that most argumentation casts its audience as the opponent. Perhaps the source of this impression is the construct of argument that many people imagine, the dialectical situation of verbal combat in the pursuit of truth, the sparring of Socrates with interlocutors who always lose. Confrontational "dyadic" situations, as Doug Brent points out in the preceding chapter, certainly do exist and call for the Rogerian techniques he describes so convincingly. But in the classical or "triadic" characterization of rhetorical argument, the audience is the judge, not the opponent; the citizens are the observers who decide the merits of the case and evaluate the skill of the arguers. The audience is courted, not vanquished, by superior eloquence. Why else all the advice about ingratiation of the audience in the exordium and elsewhere? There are certainly instances where written arguments are addressed directly to those who disagree, but how common are they? The Declaration of Independence certainly did not aim at changing George III's mind; Martin Luther King's Letter from Birmingham Jail is addressed to a larger audience than the eight clergymen who disagreed with him. Like advertising and election campaigns, most argumentation addresses the uncommitted, those who are disposed to agree, or those who agree already but can have their adherence strengthened. Few arguments try to dislodge the entrenched.

The Blending of Appeals: Ethos, Pathos, Logos

Two tendencies look at argumentation on the one hand as invalid unless it meets certain formal standards or at least bypasses most fallacies, and on the other hand as ineffectual in the face of the emotional and symbolic conditioning that modern society inflicts on its citizens. To be sure, it is difficult to discern a rational appeal in the use of Michael Jordan to sell sneakers or the concern for human emotion in a geometric proof. Proponents of these competing views—formal argument versus psychological conditioning—have competing visions of the world. From the perspective of rhetorical argumentation, both these views are insufficient. That is, it is not the case that legal or scholarly argument follows (or should follow) only the canons of rationality while advertising ignores logic and uses only the broad colors of conditioning. Advertising uses logic and scholarly argument uses conditioning or covert psychological appeals, and both together exploit the credibility and glamour of their sources. What we are calling for here, of course, is a pedagogy that blends the three Aristotelian appeals of *ethos, pathos,* and *logos.*

TV ads provide convenient texts for illustrating the appeals. A recent Volvo ad depicts two women walking along a surf-pounded beach, communing through laughter and entwined arms. At the end of this scene, a voice-over explains that these two sisters share a common belief that they owe their lives to a car. The final image is a black screen with the single word "Volvo." The emotional appeal is obvious; walking on a beach is our standard cultural symbol for a liminal or border experience. The sisters were near death but fortunately didn't enter the ocean. But logical appeals are also present. The two women are living examples and, as in classical rhetorical style where the audience is invited to complete the argument, we supply the premises for the conclusion that a Volvo was an agency of their salvation. Was it the air bags, the extra strong construction, the collapsible front end? Because the audience familiar with Volvo safety claims can supply potential reasons, the authoritative voice-over need not. The commercial gains more credibility by not specifying. Thus, although the ad appears to be primarily emotional, all three appeals work together.

In contrast, Darwin's *On the Origin of Species* might seem to be a safe example of an argument relying for its persuasiveness on logos alone. But Darwin's text is saturated with images of an ideal reader—a progressive biologist of the younger generation—and Darwin frequently demands the reader's trust because he claims again and again that he has evidence but not enough space to provide it. The evidence that is provided leads to trust in the evidence that isn't, and the image of a reader that Darwin provides leads to mimicking that image on the part of the reader. Thus logos serves ethos serves pathos. All scholarly texts depend on such a combination of appeals for their persuasiveness.

In analysis, students learning the appeals often want to scissor up an argumentative text and place the pieces in separate bins labeled "ethos," "pathos," and "logos," and indeed this is a useful first step. But as even the most rudimentary assignment in rhetorical analysis will reveal, the appeals can never be separated so easily. They are always blended and intertwined, and people will come to different conclusions about their efficacy and legitimacy in every instance. That is precisely why the appeals remain interesting and significant; there are no easy answers as to what constitutes an adequately constructed logos, a legitimate appeal to pathos, or an excessive reliance on ethos. But that all three are always working is the generic skill that students must grasp.

A major difficulty remains: how to teach these appeals not just analytically but constructively. Our tendency will be to favor logos but it would be a mistake to concentrate only on logos, especially at the expense of pathos, when we recenter on argumentation in our writing classrooms. The student Linda whose journal entry is quoted by Annas and Tenney (see page 144) shows how a belief in a radical disjunction between logic and emotion can be disabling. What we want to avoid is an allegiance to any one of the appeals or the notion that only one is legitimate (logos) while the others (ethos and pathos) are immoral. Does that mean that we want to show students how to create anger in an audience? The answer is yes. But we should also ask them to consider what can happen when audiences are roused to anger. How self-conscious do we want students to become about their own ethos? The answer is very self-conscious. But we should also have them question the difference between seeming and being. Such concerns about the morality of rhetorical choices never go away, nor should they.

Generation of Premises: The Topics

Perhaps in no area will a focus on classical argumentation meet with more resistance than this one: An arguer should be aware of general sources of argument and command a formal procedure for generating premises. When the classical system was lost in nineteenth-century education, it was because the notion of invention by topoi seemed to offer nothing in the face of the promptings of the imagination on the one hand and the results of empirical method on the other. The prevailing attitude now seems to be that students invent material merely by saturation in their research on a topic. Barbara Emmel has, however, shown us an explicit topical system used in art criticism. Without such a system, we might have a course that only facilitated the student's confrontation with a unique subject without providing any general analytical tools. The *reductio* almost *ad absurdam* of this approach is the course that emphasizes only the means for such saturation, namely the acquisition of library and computer skills. Again, a crucial balance has been lost: The interanimation between special and common topoi is what concerns rhetorically based argumentation. The compilation of facts, observation and detail has had all the good press, and there are obvious reasons for this preference for hard data even among teachers in English departments who disdain positivism and empiricism. But while rejecting these stances, they may nevertheless impose them as an aesthetic rather than an epistemological standard, the remnant of the showing versus telling regime of modernist fiction. In other words, whereas an empiricist "just give me the facts" approach is scoffed at on the one hand, it often gets reintroduced on the other as fresh, personal, authentic writing.

Anything like a topical approach to invention has also lost favor because it can resemble the modes, the empty formalisms of so-called current traditional rhetoric, the assignments that ask students to describe, analyze, classify, compare, and so forth, outside of any conceivable exigence or argumentative purpose. The topics, however, are not the modes, which can perhaps most easily be described as organizational patterns that incorporate some significant elements in the rhetorical tradition. A topic is not an organizational pattern but a prompt. A topic is a formalized warrant one "tries out" on a point at issue. Examples of topical prompting can be found in Book I, chapter seven of Aristotle's *Rhetoric,* where he lists ways of arguing in deliberative cases. How, Aristotle asks, do we argue that one good is greater than another? One answer is that a thing is better if it is sought for its own sake rather than for the sake of something else (recreation); another is that it is better if it has less need of other things, if it is more independent (growing your own vegetables). These all-purpose arguments go on: The more difficult thing is greater than the easier because it is rarer (climbing Mount Everest), and what all people prefer is better than what all do not (health).

Two observations about Aristotle's value topoi are in order. First, they include opposites, or arguments that could cancel each other. One could just as easily argue that what the few prefer is better than what the many prefer.

(Are Harlequin romances better because more people buy them? Is Shakespeare better because few people understand him?) Depending on the case, we use appeals to both mass and elite tastes. Second, they include arguments we might find problematic to teach: "And what belongs to better people [is greater] either absolutely or in so far as they are better" (Kennedy 71). What if an arguer defines "better" as "richer"? Once more, the answer is that teaching rhetoric draws attention to ethical issues; it does not solve them. Writers need to be made aware of their own ethical assumptions, and to that end, the only truly ethical procedure is to go through the act of making arguments as compelling as possible on all sides.

Topics such as those listed in the *Rhetoric* or in even more detail in Aristotle's *Topics* inspire little current interest. We simply do not teach the systematic discovery of premises at this level of precision because we find them odd and don't know how to use them. The only systematic attempt to revive the common topics seems to have been initiated almost half a century ago by the school of rhetoricians at the University of Chicago, who were largely responsible for reapplying the art of rhetoric to writing instruction in this century. They selected four large topics, roughly adapted from Aristotle and Cicero: genus, consequence, likeness/difference, and authority (Corbett 155-62). Anyone who has used these four topics to stimulate the invention of premises knows their power. A student with a thesis like "The two Koreas should reunite" can go through these topics systematically to invent arguments. Under the heading *genus* (or definition) she can create a premise that the two countries are by definition of culture, history, and language one; under consequence, that a merger will bring economic prosperity to both; under likeness/difference she can draw an analogy with the recent reunification of Germany, and under testimony/authority she can cite the results of opinion polls among Koreans or the judgments of expert commentators on Korean politics. Most important to the training of the developing rhetor, the same topics can be used to generate premises for the incompatible claim: "The two Koreas should remain separate." Here the definition argument might be that these two countries have been separate for half a century under radically different systems of government—in other words, that they do not belong to the same genus. Under consequence, the student can predict that the economy of the south or the order of the north will suffer from reunification, and under likeness/difference, she can draw on the same analogy with the reunification of Germany, making the parallel case negative rather than positive. Under testimony and authority, she will also cite opinion polls, which evidently produce different results about the merits of reunification when the population drawn on is Koreans in South Korea instead of Korean Americans. Whichever side the student finally decides to support, procedures will be more ethical if she has first thought through the arguments on both sides.

The discipline of going through these four topics can, in our experience and that of many others, generate premises. But two caveats are in order. First, the student must have read around in the subject before applying the topics, and second, the premises generated may support each other rather than separately support the overall claim. In other words, the parallel case of the reunification of Germany can be an independent claim based on the warrant that what has been done can be done again, or it can function as a premise supporting the argument from consequence that the reunification of two countries with divergent economic philosophies can have negative consequences for the richer of the two.

Perhaps a more promising contemporary system of topical invention might draw on Perelman and Olbrechts-Tyteca's *The New Rhetoric,* which features the objects of agreement, the loci of the preferable used for arguing value, forms of quasi-logical argument, and arguments that build on or construct an audience's conception of the real. Although rhetoricians have expressed great admiration for *The New Rhetoric* and the potency of its analytic system, compositionists have done little to turn it into a productive art of invention. As John Gage suggests, the broad perspective of *The New Rhetoric* is available, along with Aristotelian and Ciceronian elaborations of the common topics. No matter what system is chosen, some system of topical invention is one of the necessary generic skills of argumentation.

Thesis/Hypothesis

As we have seen, classical rhetoricians paid a great deal of attention to determining the nature of the question they were asking or the claim they were supporting. But there is still another organizing principle, also inherited from the second-century BCE Hermagorean expansion of rhetoric (Conley 32), that Quintilian describes in the *Institutio Oratoria:*

> It is also agreed that questions are either *definite* or *indefinite* [infinitas aut finitas]. *Indefinite* questions are those which may be maintained or impugned without reference to persons, time or place and the like . . . *Definite* questions involve facts, persons, time and the like . . . . An *indefinite* question is always the more comprehensive, since it is from the indefinite question that the *definite* is derived. I will illustrate what I mean by an example. The question "Should a man marry?"

is indefinite; the question "Should Cato marry?" is *definite,* and consequently may be regarded as a subject for a deliberative theme. (I, iii, 399-401)

Quintilian invokes the authority of Cicero to support the value of extracting the general question, the thesis, from particular cases, the hypotheses, " 'because we can speak more fully on general than on special themes, and because what is proved of the whole must also be proved of the part' " (405).

Modern usage has blurred the distinction that Quintilian would have made between thesis and hypothesis but the importance of moving between the two levels of generality cannot be overemphasized in the history of rhetoric. Both forensic and deliberative cases concern judgments on actions, whether past or future, and all such judgments, as Cicero points out in *De Inventione,* raise larger questions of right conduct (226). Thus arguers who defend or condemn a course of action, past or present, will find themselves arguing general points of morality. In the composition exercises of the *Progymnasmata,* used for centuries, students of rhetoric practiced this skill of moving between the particular and general case in a whole variety of set pieces praising virtues and condemning tyrants (Matsen et al. 274-83).

Although our rhetorical vocabulary does not maintain the thesis/hypothesis distinction, we still maintain the practice. We have all watched courtroom dramas where the prosecutor inveighs against the kind of crime that has been committed, although the crime has not yet been firmly tied to the defendant. And we have probably all listened to arguments where the question "Should we hire x?" becomes transmuted into "Should we hire at all?" Because the same argument for a general, indefinite thesis can be used in several definite, particular cases, the *De Inventione* went so far as to recommend set pieces on general *theses,* movable prefab units that could be used in many particular cases. To store up material for these prefab units, Erasmus in the sixteenth century recommended as an aid to invention the keeping of a Commonplace Book with headings for the various virtues and vices, sorting bins for noteworthy exempla and *sententiae* from one's reading (89). Today teachers of writing often recommend that students keep writers' notebooks where they record their observations in much the same way Erasmus recommended. We have lost the verbal distinction between thesis and hypothesis, but we have retained some of the associated pedagogy.

The effects of this method of keeping a commonplace book and moving an argument from a particular to a general claim are particularly evident in the essays that Montaigne and Bacon wrote on general subjects—Of Envy, Of Love, Of Simulation and Dissimulation—essays that are the direct ancestors of the themes set for centuries in composition classrooms. This branch, however, has outgrown its place in the rhetorical tree. Arguments for general theses were never meant to usurp the system. In the classical system, one argued the particular case—Milo's guilt, the awarding of a crown to Demosthenes—and used the general as a supporting tactic. An art of argument on the classical model would restore the proportion between the general and the particular case, the thesis and the hypothesis, but give teleological preference to the situated case and the definite claim. The switch to the indefinite should be recommended as one—but not the only—tactic for an art whose end is action in the world. In the Declaration of Independence, Thomas Jefferson, who no doubt learned to condemn tyrants copiously in his rhetorical training, argued the definite thesis against George III, and only after cataloging the King's very particular crimes did he turn to his indefinite claim to clinch his indictment: "A Prince, whose character is thus marked by every act which may define a Tyrant, is unfit to be the ruler of a free people." Being aware of the potential for moving from the particular to the general issue is one of the generic skills of argumentation.

The Restoration of Narrative

In most current discourse theories and pedagogical sequences, narrative and argumentation are separate, even antagonistic domains. They are seen as, first of all, structurally different, and indeed as two irreducible genres: Either one tells a story or one argues a brief. Second, narrative presumably accesses the personal, and in some value hierarchies, more genuine, perspective. Argumentation is somehow merely a simulacrum or mark, an impersonal structure created from second thoughts and therefore inevitably insincere. In addition, for those of us who live and work in English departments and who have been trained in literature, narrative and narrative theory are comfortable and recognizable categories; we delight in stories and disdain the crude functionalism of argument. In our institutional setting, narratives and narrative theory have a *cachet* argumentation lacks.

An opposition between argument and narrative does not exist in the classical system where narrative serves multiple functions. Whenever we recommend an action on the basis of comparison with a parallel case, for example, we offer a narrative—and an argument. Narrative appears even more explicitly in the standard six-part division of the oration; the *narratio,* the second part, follows the *exordium* that favorably disposes the audience, and precedes the *partitio* that sets up the parts of the discourse to come. In the forensic *narratio,* both sides in turn present the facts of the case: "On the night of the 21st," we might hear a modern lawyer begin a story. Presumably the *narratio* describes events as though they were objects of agreement to both sides, but classical rhetoric was under no illusion that the *narratio* was not part of the argument. Rhetors were advised to select every detail to slant the case in their direction.

As the pedagogical system that supported instruction in the arts of civic argument grew, so did the types of narration and practice of narration almost as an end in itself. The *Ad Herennium,* for example, proposes several kinds of narrative, including the following:

> The kind of narrative based on the exposition of the facts presents three forms: legendary, historical, and realistic. The legendary tale comprises events neither true nor probable, like those transmitted by tragedies. The historical narrative is an account of exploits actually performed, but removed in time from the recollection of our age. Realistic narrative recounts imaginary events, which yet could have occurred, like the plots of comedies. (I, viii, 23-25)

In addition to narrations of events the rhetorical tradition recognized stories or sketches the primary purpose of which was character delineation. The prosecutor in a criminal case had to convince the jury that the defendant was the kind of person who was likely to commit sacrilege or theft or murder; the defendant had to argue the opposite about his character. Then, as now, the best method for "hitting off" a character was a brief narrative sketch epitomizing an essential personal trait or type. So important was this skill that it appears not only as a potential element in the six-part structure of an argument but also as a figure of thought known as *notatio* or *ethopoeia* (*Ad Herennium,* IV, L. 63, 387-89). The most memorable examples of the art of character portrayal come from the *Moral Characters* of Aristotle's successor Theophrastus. These sketches of Flattery, Rusticity, False Compliance, the Shameless Man, the Profligate, and the Newsmonger capture the essential manners and speech of someone bearing each of these dominant qualities. These are not delineations of particular people but generic character types, or even stereotypes, written into particular events. They can be invoked for audiences who recognize the stereotype.

Of course, narrative has not been neglected in the typical composition course. Quite the contrary, it is frequently included as an assignment. But the narrative assignment is usually framed as if telling a story constituted one kind of discursive mode requiring one special kind of skill, while argumentation calls for completely different skills. We agree with Judith Summerfield that narrative as a mode of arguing needs to be taught in all its complexity. Students should not finish our writing courses with the assumption that narrative concerns itself with the personal and argumentation with the public, or that narratives should be judged according to aesthetic standards and arguments according to practical. Above all, they should not come away with the mistaken notion that narratives do not argue. Our experience tells us otherwise: The doctor's case studies, the lawyer's closing statements, the preacher's exempla, the historian's scenic recreations, the autobiographer's shaping of a life story—all are arguments and all narrate. Therefore, narrative deserves a position of prominence as one of the generic skills of argumentation.

Approaching Argument Through Style

The classical perspective on argumentation required facility in the use of language to integrate the appeals, to deliver layers and nuances of persuasion in single propositions. Classical rhetoricians understood that a bare-bones argument that fell short of demonstration would not persuade. No wonder that in Renaissance iconography logic is a fist but rhetoric is an open hand.

The notion that writing instruction aims at language facility is not controversial to most composition teachers, but the fragmentation of the elements of the classical curriculum has not enhanced the teaching of the third major canon of rhetoric, style. Composition courses tend to treat style in a way that deemphasizes its connection with rhetoric. But if students learn about style through sentence-combining exercises, they also need to learn how to select various forms for variety and emphasis; if students learn how to construct the Christensen cumulative sentence, they also need to learn what its special effects are and what genres use it most effectively. If style is treated as a concern during revision (as if invention, arrangement, and style were a linear process), its connection to argumentative substance may be diminished. In this volume, both Mariolina Salvatori and David Bartholomae emphasize such precise attention to language as a necessary constituent of critical and self-reflexive reading practices.

We believe that language skills are taught most effectively in a rhetorical setting. When writers know the who, why, and what of an argument, they have a reason to make one language decision over another. Furthermore, language skills need to be approached systematically, not in a hit-or-miss fashion that features the error of the weak. Every writing course should include a language curriculum that would teach students to identify and employ linguistic choices that promote rhetorical effectiveness. An outline of a full language curriculum would take far more space than we have in this essay, but here are the most important goals; the means are variable.

Students should learn the basics of topic/comment organization and the principle of end focus, that new and emphasized matter can be shifted to the ends of sentences, paragraphs or sections of discourse, and that other stylistic manipulations, like transformations from active to passive voice, depend in part on the more important (and very teachable) principle of end focus. They should also learn that conserving topic from sentence to sentence, or allowing the comment of one sentence to become the topic of the next, are two possible modes of local organization, along with using words that indicate logical relationships and transitions and relying on readers to supply relevant schema. They should know how to build and expand sentences, and combine them, learning the names and understanding the functions of various sentence elements. They should learn the concept of "register" and "register shifts." Many of these "sentence technologies" come to us more immediately from linguistics rather than from classical rhetoric, but a rhetorical perspective need not be rigidly antiquarian. Rhetoric is capacious enough to accommodate the insights of contemporary language study.

Is there anything in classical stylistics that we should revive for the teaching of argument? The first and most obvious answer is the figures of speech, which are already familiar territory to most teachers and many students. We propose teaching the figures of speech not to decorate but to create premises. This use of the figures is bound to strike us as artificial and strange; it is definitely a roll back to pre-seventeenth-century theories of invention and cognition. Consider, for example, an arguer with a claim to support about school voucher systems. Suppose that in either defense or in refutation, the arguer comes across or creates the following proposition, drawing on the topic of consequence: "Under a school voucher system, the quality of the public schools will decrease." In both the *Topics* and the *Rhetoric,* Aristotle advises the use of opposites, the creation of antitheses, as a means of testing out possible lines of argument. He points out that antitheses can be either single (with one pair of antonyms) or double (with two pairs of antonyms). Using this stylistic machinery, he recommends creating possible premises. If a premise made from the same subject linked to an opposite predicate can be supported, then the side supporting vouchers may have a point : "Under the school voucher system, the quality of public schools will increase." But if a premise formed from an opposite subject and an opposite predicate can be supported, then the side against the voucher system may have a premise: "Under the school voucher system, the quality of private schools will increase and the quality of public schools will decrease."

The formation of such statements can prompt a further search for evidence and a further exploration of the value dimensions of such a consequence. To be sure, an arguer might stumble onto such a line of reasoning, but the more conscious rhetorical approach goes after such potential premises systematically, either by topical probes (asking oneself for contrasts), or, as in this example, by language manipulation. Both linguistic invention and the topical invention discussed in the preceding section (Generation of Premises: The Topics) create a habit of mind that enables the arguer to suspend judgment and consider ideas regardless of their fit to any preconceived bias. This intellectual suppleness, using language features to generate arguments, characterizes the classical approach and is one of the generic skills we should revive. Our students should be more willing to entertain ideas—and themselves.

Most unusual, perhaps, of our proposals is our recommendation to resuscitate the figures of thought. From the *Ad Herennium* to Erasmus, the two main divisions of figures were not tropes and schemes but figures of thought and figures of diction. (The figures of diction were then divided into the tropes and schemes.) The figures of thought, as a category, have disappeared from our consciousness, perhaps because it is difficult for us to maintain any meaningful distinction between word and thought. Yet a reexamination of the catalogs of the figures shows how this distinction made a difference.

What are these devices? Quintilian, following the lead of Cicero in *De Oratore,* characterizes them as those devices that express emotions, commend the arguer to the audience, relieve monotony, and express meaning (III, 359). Such a list almost looks like a complete accounting of the functions of discourse itself, and Quintilian does indeed acknowledge that these purposes can be achieved without figuration, but he begins by listing those devices that "increase the force and cogency of proof." Many of these figures will be immediately familiar: They include *prolepsis,* the forestalling of objections; *concession,* granting some things to the audience or the opposition; *erotema* (the rhetorical question), asking a question and leaving the answer unstated, to be supplied by the audience; and *hypophora,* the asking and answering of questions on the arguer's part. Though we do not often teach these devices or moves specifically, we often point out their effects in readings, and we regard an awareness of such techniques as fundamental to literary and rhetorical awareness.

Beyond these is a large list of now less-familiar devices such as *reply,* responding to a question that has been asked by answering a different question (we see this one all the time in political news conferences); *putting a question as though asked* by an imaginary questioner ("But someone will ask, 'What would happen if . . . ?' "); *hesitation,* being at a loss over where to begin or over what to say or not to say (an audience would never know if such a gesture were faked or not); *communication,* taking an opponent or judge into consultation, as though asking them how to proceed; *suspension,* keeping the audience guessing about one's approach by discussing with them what they think they will hear but won't. In this same class belong *aposiopesis,* the sudden breaking off in mid-sentence, and *prosopopoeia* in all its many forms (e.g., imagining an absent or dead person speaking, or the gods, or animals, or inanimate objects, or even abstractions). Quintilian even recommends that rhetors behave as though they had images of people or scenes before their eyes or sounds and speeches in their ears. To point out these gestures in literary texts is the standard stuff of the literature classroom; it is not the practice of the writing classroom to recommend them—perhaps out of fear that they may seem *too* dramatic, *too* artificial for the writing that students do.

In Book IX of the *Institutio Oratoria,* Quintilian discusses another figure of thought for approaching the powerful with matter that will offend or threaten them. Using "frankness of speech," the rhetor directly addresses an inequality in power but makes a claim, tacit or explicit, on the superior virtue of the powerful to be able to listen to criticism, saying in effect, "I know you don't want to hear this, but you are such a noble person, you can take it." A very clever tactic and a familiar one. But Quintilian not only recommends this relatively straightforward device; he goes so far as to recommend *pretended frankness of speech* in which the rhetor begins in the same way, claiming the forbearance of the powerful to take criticism, but then continues by giving praise as though it were criticism: "I know you don't want to hear this, but your generosity is going to get you into trouble." Here he treads on ground where rhetoric starts to look suspicious, and we might well be uneasy about teaching such manipulativeness.

What are we to make of this proliferation of figures in the classical tradition? First, these "figures of thought" are not susceptible to syntactic or semantic definition like the more straightforward tropes or schemes. A speaker or writer can accomplish surrender or frankness of speech in any of a number of verbal ways and overextended swatches of text. Thus, instead of cataloging formal, easy-to-illustrate linguistic devices, the ancient rhetoricians seem to be cataloging something much more diffuse: the many shifting stances and *gestures* that arguers can develop toward their audiences and their material. *Gesture* is our word of choice here because we can imagine many of these devices accomplished by a speaker's body language or intonation, a shrug of the shoulders, a sigh of exasperation, a brief aside conveying attitude. In writing, such stances are of course harder to capture, although the work of much textual analysis is really an effort to recover and describe them.

This territory of gesture is no longer marked in modern composition pedagogy. We do not say to our students, "Here is your subject, your audience, and here are some possible gestures you could adopt toward each. And these gestures should modulate during your discourse to produce overtones in a theme with variations." One possible exception to our habitual silence about gestures is the device of irony. Yet even irony, well marked in literary studies and, under the old New Criticism, detected everywhere, is seldom recommended or practiced in any writing curricula. Imagine the marginal comment, "Why not be ironic here to suggest your disdain or mockery of anyone who does not hold this belief?"

There are several reasons for this absence. First, the identification and cultivation of gestural figures leads down the road to rhetorical immorality, the land where all rhetoric is mere rhetoric and the popular pejorative use of the term is the only one. We may well be uncomfortable recommending many of the gestures that Quintilian describes—though we may be much less uncomfortable teaching students how to recognize them, and we certainly would have little difficulty identifying such gestures in contemporary discourse. Whatever the criticisms of a rhetorical approach may be, they are not that this part of the rhetorical curriculum is dead and of interest only to antiquarians. Second, we assume that these gestures are not supposed to exist in disciplinary argumentation of the sort we teach our students. Of course, not all gestures abound in all the genres of writing we teach. Irony is hard to imagine in a set of instructions for sequencing DNA. But it is not difficult to identify many of these gestures in contemporary academic discourse. The debate over the literary canon, for example, has been an exercise in frankness of speech on both sides, each conveying this gesture of simultaneous defiance and flattery that says, "I know it is dangerous for me to speak out this way, but I will do it anyway, appealing to higher values of intellectual integrity."

Under a recovered model of classical argumentation, this territory of gesture would be noticed, marked, cited, scrutinized in its multiplicity. In the writing classroom students would learn a critical stance that labels rhetorical gestures in all their variety, that acknowledges that they are practiced and can be practiced, and that discriminates carefully in its recommendations for their use, just as it discriminates about deploying the appeals of ethos, pathos, and logos combined in these devices. The result will be a very uncomfortable consciousness, a double vision, an end of rhetorical innocence. (Students will discover that the sides they favor use the same devices as the sides they disagree with.) There is enormous resistance to the apparent insincerity of conscious gestural stances. But there is some enlightenment as well.

Conclusion

The classical rhetorical model, with its emphasis on generic skills of argumentation, provides an overall goal and a large-scale architecture for a writing course, capacious enough to accommodate diverse emphases and teaching methods. Just over ten years ago, the historian of rhetoric, James J. Murphy, edited a collection of essays for MLA, *The Rhetorical Tradition and Modern Writing,* calling for a restoration of the rhetorical perspective and tradition to the American college classroom in much the same way that we have argued in this essay. To all such calls there has been a respectful response but no radical restructuring of the composition curriculum. Considering the many substantial voices that have been calling for the same perspective we recommend here, we have to ask what are the impediments to a recovery of the classical model and a focus on argumentation?

First—and perhaps most formidable—is the amount of training teachers would require. The economic dynamics of most English departments favor putting graduate assistants or instructors into classrooms with very little training. Continuing this practice requires a concomitant belief—or an assumption that it is not in an English department's interest to challenge—that there is no discipline here to practice. The arguments we have made certainly show that there is a discipline to practice and, yes, it would take training in this discipline to place instructors in the classroom who are competent to teach argumentation, or it would require the preferential selection of instructors already so trained. Thus, to implement the model recommended in this article requires some changes in graduate education in addition to changes in the freshman curriculum. But just as many parts of the curriculum we recommend are already in place, so too are many parts of this academic training already in place in the courses and support systems we offer for teachers of composition.

Another impediment is the suspicion of deliberate, indulgent archaism in the return to a classical perspective on argumentation. To put this doubt in James Murphy's words, "Is this all just impractical antiquarian hogwash?" (10).

Couldn't we achieve the same effects without invoking those foundational texts of Western thought so suspect to so many? Do teachers really need to learn a lot of Greek terminology to teach writing? Isn't our present-day situation different enough from the teaching of Roman schoolboys to require a different pedagogy? Another version of this criticism might ask, "Can't we come up with a good writing curriculum given all our new knowledge about language and the proliferation of our theoretical approaches?"

Writing teachers need not become Latin or Greek scholars; they can learn what they need to learn in a graduate course. The terminology need not be oppressive. After all, graduate students in English—apprentice teachers all—acquire a language of literary theory much more arcane than the technical terms we have been using here, and they also learn how to teach students without overwhelming them with the argot of their own professionalism. Certainly we should draw on more recent rhetoric and language theory for supplemental vocabulary for the teaching of writing. We should not abandon any approach that helps students to be better writers. Whatever we have learned from linguistics and process research and disciplinary rhetoric should be incorporated. Nor is there anything antagonistic between an emphasis on rhetorical argumentation and an interactive, collaborative classroom. In fact, the elements previously recommended are best conveyed in an environment that promotes exchange, the testing or arguments, the playful development of stances on issues. The deliberate search for counterpropositions, for example, encourages hearing from all perspectives. The classical rhetorical model, then, need not dislodge any of the hard-earned pedagogical insights of the recent past.

The classical rhetorical model would include but not be limited to much that is now being offered. Take, for example, the course that concentrates on personal self-expression. From a rhetorical perspective, foregrounded personal expression is only one possible rhetorical tactic, a gesture that offers the arguer's personal experience as a warrant for the agreement of others. This tactic has its uses and historical successes—as suggested by texts ranging from Descartes's *Discourse on Method* to the autobiographical essays of E. B. White or Hunter Thompson or Maxine Hong Kingston. But why teach students how to play in only one key? Those who master the elaborate gestures of an exposed self-expression, locating and naming the personal and sociocultural sources of their beliefs, may be without defense when they meet with a different rhetoric that values impersonality or the agreement of many. We need to teach our students many keys to play in, both major and minor; improvisation can only occur when the performer is in the possession of a confident facility.

Works Cited

Aristotle. *Topics.* Trans. W. A. Pickard-Cambridge. *The Complete Works of Aristotle,* Vol. 1. Ed. Jonathan Barnes. Princeton: Bollingen Series LXXI.2, Princeton University Press, 1984.

Barton, Ellen. "Evidentials, Argumentation, and Epistemological Stance." *College English* 55 (Nov. 1993): 745-69.

Beale, Walter. "The Case Against Freshman Composition." Plenary Talk. Penn State Conference on Rhetoric and Composition, July 1991.

Bitzer, Lloyd. "The Rhetorical Situation." *Philosophy and Rhetoric* 1 (Jan. 1968): 1-14.

Cicero. *De Inventione.* Trans. H. M. Hubbell. The Loeb Classical Library. Cambridge, MA: Harvard University Press, 1949.

———. *Ad Herennium.* Trans. H. Caplan. The Loeb Classical Library. Cambridge, MA: Harvard University Press, 1954.

Conley, Thomas M. *Rhetoric in the European Tradition.* New York: Longman, 1990.

Corbett, Edward P. J. *Classical Rhetoric for the Modern Student.* 2nd ed. New York: Oxford University Press, 1971.

Crowley, Sharon. "Personal Essay on Freshman English." *Pre/Text* 12 (Fall 1991): 155-69.

Erasmus. *On Copia of Words and Ideas.* Trans. Donald B. King and H. David Rix. Milwaukee, WI: Marquette University Press, 1986.

Fahnestock, Jeanne, and Marie Secor. "Toward a Modern Version of Stasis Theory." *Oldspeak/Newspeak.* Ed. Charles W. Kneupper. Arlington, TX: The Rhetoric Society of America and NCTE, 1985. 217-26.

Flower, Linda. *Problem-Solving Strategies for Writing.* 2nd ed. San Diego: Harcourt, Brace, Jovanovich, 1985.

Kennedy, George, Ed. *Aristotle, On Rhetoric: A Theory of Civic Discourse.* New York: Oxford University Press, 1991.

Larson, Richard. "Lloyd Bitzer's 'Rhetorical Situation' and the Classification of Discourse: Problems and Implications." *Philosophy and Rhetoric* 3 (1970): 165-70.

———. *Presentation on the Ford Foundation Grant: Review of Writing Programs.* Penn State Conference on Rhetoric and Composition, July 1992.

Matsen, Patricia P., Philip Rollinson, and Marion Sousa, Ed. *Readings from Classical Rhetoric.* Carbondale: Southern Illinois University Press, 1990.

Murphy, James J., Ed. *The Rhetorical Tradition and Modern Writing.* New York: Modern Language Association of America, 1982.

Perelman, Chaim, and Lucie Olbrechts-Tyteca. *The New Rhetoric.* Trans. Purcell and Wilkinson. South Bend, IN: University of Notre Dame Press, 1969.

Quintilian. *Institutio Oratoria.* Trans. H. E. Butler. Loeb Classical Library. Cambridge, MA: Harvard University Press, 1920-22.

Swales, John. *Genre Analysis: English in Academic and Research Settings.* Cambridge, England: Cambridge University Press, 1990.

Theophrastus. *Characters.* Trans. J. M. Edmonds. The Loeb Classical Library. Cambridge, MA: Harvard University Press, 1993.

Turner, G. W. *Stylistics.* London: Penguin Books, 1973.

Vatz, Richard E. "The Myth of the Rhetorical Situation." *Philosophy and Rhetoric* 6 (Summer 1973): 154-61.

Williams, Joseph, and Gregory Colomb. "Formulating Problems." (Software program.) Little Red Schoolhouse: University of Chicago, 1992.

Wills, Garry. *Lincoln at Gettysburg.* New York: Simon and Schuster, 1992.

"Writing Skills Improve, but Some Problems Linger." *The New York Times,* 8 June 1994, A21.

ARGUMENT
REDEFINED

6

Positioning Oneself

A Feminist Approach to Argument

Pamela J. Annas
University of Massachusetts/Boston

Deborah Tenney
Yale University

> To think like a woman in a man's world means thinking critically, refusing
> to accept the givens, making connections between facts and ideas which men
> have left unconnected. It means remembering that every mind resides in a
> body; remaining accountable to the female bodies in which we live; con-
> stantly retesting given hypotheses against lived experience. It means a
> constant critique of language.
>
> *Adrienne Rich*
> *"Taking Women Students Seriously"*

Introduction (Deborah Tenney)

When Oberlin College first opened its doors to women in 1837, women
were permitted to take all of the courses offered except rhetoric and debate—
those courses in which one learned the art of argumentation (Conway 237).
Learning how to argue was a privilege limited to men, perhaps on the grounds

that only men would need to learn the skills of articulating, explaining, and defending a position. The ministry—the profession for which most Oberlin men were being trained and a profession that required skill in argumentation—was closed to women of all races and religions. Women were permitted to learn but not permitted to display their learning in a public forum. Today, women are well represented in the ministry and other formerly male-dominated professions: Two women serve on the Supreme Court, the current Attorney General is a woman, and women now rank at the top in all areas of industry, government, and academia. The entry of large numbers of women into the professions is evidence that more women are confident about advancing their opinions and positions publicly in ways men have for decades. Still, argument as a discourse has been troublesome for those women who have found the adversarial method alienating and for those feminists who have spurned argumentation as part of a patriarchal system that has subjugated women. Not all feminists have rejected argument out of hand, however, and some of the most innovative work in argument pedagogy is being undertaken by feminist compositionists.

Here we focus on contributions women have made to our understanding of how we use language to construct knowledge and how we interact when using language. In particular, this article examines how we argue a particular position or insight, what cultural biases surround the way we carry out argument, and to what degree women students and feminist scholars have contributed to helping us argue more effectively—and even to change the definition of argument. We describe here a feminist composition classroom that has enlightened us, our colleagues, and our students, to the problems that arise when students try to write arguments without understanding the nature of argument as an epistemological activity, one in which we ask students to assert what they know, how they know it, and why such realizations are important to them. We have learned from the women students in this course that they sometimes feel disassociated from the positions they are taking; they may be uncomfortable with the act of positioning themselves and making assertions; and they may feel they are engaging in an unethical act if they argue for positions they do not believe in. This chapter explores how and why traditional representations of argument (representations first rejected by such feminist scholars as Sally Miller Gearhart) can lead to a dissociation of self from language.

We have found that many students (not only women) have difficulty connecting to their arguments and carrying them out with commitment. Feminists interested in composition have made significant contributions to composition pedagogy and theory by focusing specifically on women, their place in educational and cultural institutions, their difficulty with that place, and their effects on existing institutions as women become more and more assertive about their own ways of learning, knowing, and constructing knowledge. How women feel about arguing—and the problems of connecting the self to argument—has helped us to understand how argument may work differently, how it may become more of a mutual undertaking for shared knowledge rather than an adversarial activity.

Because feminist theory has become so complex and varied, it is not possible to speak of one feminist approach to argument and certainly there is no agreement among feminist compositionists on how to go about making changes in the teaching of composition and argument. In a recent article, Elizabeth Flynn ("Feminist Theories") describes four different kinds of feminist approaches to composition. At one end, liberal feminists emphasize the similarities between men and women, advocate equality in the workplace, and call for equal representation "within traditional institutions," rather than changing those institutions. Liberal feminists ask why can't a woman write more like a man? Such an approach is reflected in articles like Margaret Pigott's "Sexist Roadblocks in Inventing, Focusing and Writing," which identifies perceived inadequacies in women's writing and strengths in men's writing. This approach also assumes mastery of traditional argument. But as the Women's Collective (the authors of *Women's Ways of Knowing*) discovered, many women are not at ease with this style of argumentation. Even the women they identified as "constructed knowers"—those confident in their own voices and able to use sources with authority—were unhappy when they had to adapt to a style of argumentation that was impersonal and combative:

> At times, particularly in certain academic and work situations in which adversarial interactions are common, constructivist women may feel compelled to demonstrate that they can hold their own in a battle of ideas to prove to others that they, too, have the analytical powers and hard data to justify their claims. However, they usually resent the implicit pressure in male-dominated circles to toughen up and fight to get their ideas across. (146)

The Women's Collective and other feminist scholars see much to be gained by exploring gender-based differences in the way women and men use language and learn to think and write. These feminists, whom Elizabeth Flynn labels "cultural feminists," emphasize differences between men and women and explore the processes by which women construct their worlds differently. Jane Tompkins and Olivia Frey, for example, have come to question the adversarial approach to argument, a commonplace of academic papers. Frey suggests that disagreement can take place without put-down and that there are other ways of writing about literature: "personal revelatory and non-adversarial" essays that explore without advancing a thesis or reaching a conclusion (521). Sally Miller Gearhart goes one step further in claiming that any attempt to persuade a reader amounts to an act of violence (195) and that all persuasion is part of a patriarchal "conquest/conversion mentality" (196). Chris Bullock finds compatibility between a feminist and a Rogerian approach to argument. Catherine Lamb, like Phyllis Lassner, rejects Rogerian argument as too much like "giving in" (17) and advocates a strategy of mediation. (For a more extended discussion of Lamb and Lassner, see Doug Brent's chapter on Rogerian argument.) Julia Allen finds Lamb's approach too conventional and too embedded in patriarchal forms. She proposes a rhetoric of resistance that would create a whole new discourse. Borrowing from the French feminists, Clara Juncker also encourages liberating and playful forms of writing to open women students to new textual possibilities. Clearly, these feminist scholars are all trying to make room in the academy for an alternative approach to academic writing, an approach that takes account of women's ways of knowing. These feminist critiques of traditional argument illustrate how argument is perceived and carried out and point the way for changing how we teach argument.

Although such inquiries into the nature of learning and gender difference are not new, we are still pedagogically challenged by the findings of the last 15 years of feminist inquiry into composition. In 1979, Thomas Farrell anticipated, in "The Female and Male Modes of Rhetoric," the idea that women's approaches to argument may take a different form from the traditional adversarial and thesis-support approach. Farrell cites a letter from Sarah D'Eloia (of City College CUNY) who identifies female rhetoric as a method of "indirection" in which the writer leads her audience "through a line of reasoning and the felt nature of the experiences upon which [she has] based [her conclusion]" (qtd. in Farrell 909). Although certainly not devoid of logic or evidence, this approach also makes use of personal experience, narrative and rhetorical questions, often with an implied rather than stated thesis. Farrell distinguishes this open and indirect female model from the male model that opens with the "conclusion" (thesis) and works for closure. The suggestion is that women may explore more and be more tentative about conclusions they ultimately will reach. Their writing may be a journey into their beliefs rather than making assertions for the sake of assertion. Farrell finds the female model primarily useful in spoken discourse where it can lower "the temperature in heated, live deliberations" (920). Here the female model seems to be personi-fied as a handmaiden who applies a cool cloth on the overheated brows of the men engaged in a real argument. But we believe that this perspective may be useful for all students to learn as we seek to see argumentation as community- and ethically-based rather than adversarial in nature, directed to win-lose positions. Although Farrell sees female rhetoric as primarily a verbal form of communication, one that is difficult to teach and a secondary form of argu-ment, a "cultural feminist" approach to argument takes the position that female rhetoric is an equally valid form of discourse and is, in fact, a more inclusive form that allows a writer both to take a stand and to find a voice, to integrate knowledge from authority and from personal conviction. Moreover, as we hope to show, such an approach *is* eminently teachable, although it requires techniques different from traditional approaches to teaching argument.

The movement into women's ways of knowing began in the 1980s with such cultural feminists as Gilligan and Belenky whose studies opened up inquiry about how women access knowledge and called into question the assumed norms of male ways of knowing and writing. In fact, these feminists viewed gender differences as positive. This change in perspective is reflected by Ferguson in a review article on feminist theory, where she notes that the early emphasis on oppression of women scholars has given way to a recogni-tion of how feminist theory has contributed to scholarly disciplines and how it challenges long-held assumptions. In her discussion of *Feminist Scholar-ship: Kindling in the Groves of Academe* (Dubois et al.), Ferguson writes that "the feminist challenge . . . has already furnished 'kindling' for a major shift in perspective—toward valuing a subjective approach and rejecting as merely apparent the touted male objectivity" (729).

In an interview published some years after *Women's Ways of Knowing,* Belenky cautioned against essentializing differences between male and fe-male, a step that would result in defining a male style of learning as "true, hard and real" and female as "soft, fuzzy, and loving" (Ashton-Jones and Thomas 289). Such a definition, which links women with a subjective ap-proach, comes perilously close to old gender stereotypes. What Flynn calls a postmodernist feminism "problematizes the categories 'male' and 'female' and rejects constructions of gender that depend on a binary opposition" ("Feminist Theories" 203). Moreover, the simplistic differentiation of mas-culine and feminine fails to take into account differences among women in sexual orientation, ethnicity, class, and race. Some feminists of color argue that theories that speak of a woman's way of knowing or a woman's way of writing run the risk not only of "essentializing" women but of essentializing the white woman, and allowing the experience of heterosexual, white, educated women "to define the experience of all women" (Harris 590). On the other hand, feminists of color, according to Harris, have acknowledged that without some categories and some reliance on shared experience, the feminist movement would become so fragmented that there would be no movement at all, only individual tales of oppression.

Further complicating the notion of a single mode of knowing for women are Wendy Luttrell's findings from her comparative study of black and white working class women students. Like Harris, Luttrell argues that cognitive processes are embedded in race and class in addition to gender. Both white and black working class women, Luttrell finds, distinguish between common sense (intuitive and based on feelings) and intelligence (learned and based on rational thought processes). The women Luttrell interviewed all believed they possessed common sense but did not credit themselves with possessing intelligence, which they tended to associate with men. For these working class women in particular, writing a formal, logical argument unconnected to feelings or beliefs must, indeed, seem like an alienating exercise. The writing course described here serves this working class population (among others) and this approach to argument helps such women bridge this perceived gap between common sense and intelligence.

The conversations of women and feminist scholars about discourse, learning and cognition have changed the pedagogy of argument. We have come to understand argument as a rhetorical construct that is connected to self-inquiry, the freedom to question authority, and the location of the self in a public discourse. Through a cultural-feminist approach to argument we have learned that students want to be connected to their writing and their arguments rather than imitate institutional requirements.

Joan Bolker's story of two women writers at Harvard and Yale is illustrative of how much work in argument pedagogy needs to be done. The women she describes excelled in their college writing assignments but, like Griselda, the patient and obedient wife in Chaucer's *Canterbury Tales,* suffered from being "good girls." Pleasing others, these students felt alienated from their own arguments and texts, which were organized, polished, and dull. They were disassociated from their own voices, smothered beneath a surface of competence in traditional argument. They experienced in their writing "a lack of personality . . . a sense of non-ownership" and expressed "disappointment at not being able to make [themselves] heard" (Bolker 906). Unlike the first women at Oberlin, these women were admitted to courses in predominantly male institutions where they were required to write academic arguments. Yet although students like these women were adept at maneuvering in a traditional academic setting, they felt distanced from the educational process and particularly from their own texts.

The approach to argument that we describe on the following pages seeks not only to address the writing problems of these modern-day Griseldas and help them write with more authentic voices, but also the writing problems of women from less privileged backgrounds who need to learn how to speak and write in the academy. To give women a place to find their voices, to adopt a nonadversarial stance, to open up the argumentative format from a traditional thesis-support mode, to create a cooperative rather than a competitive atmosphere, to study systematically the patriarchal structures and norms that have informed argumentative writing, to offer women a way to resist those norms with women writers as models, to blur the distinction between public and private, to write from a sense of personal conviction—these constitute some of the concerns of feminist composition instructors. The course described here shows us how one feminist composition class writes argument. No Griseldas here. The voices are lively, questioning, and engaged. This feminist classroom employs techniques that have become standard since the process movement took hold: workshops, peer evaluations, conferences, collaborative learning, revision. Indeed, Faigley and others have noted the convergence between the feminist movement and process pedagogy, both of which share a "broad call for emancipation" (58).

In describing the kind of issues that arise in helping such women and the kinds of pedagogies that address those issues, we also believe that we learn much from these women about how we can teach all students to see argument as a dialectic process eminently connected to the self.

Teaching the Course:
"Writing as Women" (Pamela J. Annas)

The apotheosis of traditional argument is the debate: the combative mode, the reification of belief into technique, the assumption that anyone can argue any side of any issue. My own discomfort with this model of discourse began in high school, as I recall, continued through graduate school, and peaked in a team-taught course somewhere in the late Seventies and early in my teaching career at the University of Massachusetts/Boston. The 90 or so women and men in this experimental team-taught writing class called "Law & Justice" were mostly white and working-class first-year students, and they were fairly

conservative politically. The four faculty in this particular class ranged from
liberal to radical politically and in this particular semester included a philosopher and a historian, both male, and two literary/composition types, myself
from the English department and a woman from Academic Support.

As we worked through our interdisciplinary syllabus, which included
historical, sociological and psychological, philosophical, and literary materials, the other faculty continually structured debates in class between the
students and between ourselves as models for the students. Although the
students admired to some extent their professors' adeptness at taking any side
of an issue and making a case for it, they were also rendered uneasy by this
same virtuosity, especially when the argument centered on the ethical issues
central to the course. Although some students found the technique of defending arbitrary positions useful as a means of understanding an opposing
viewpoint, most students didn't "get" why people would argue for something
they didn't believe in, something that didn't come out of their own lives and
their own needs. When told that they needed to learn the techniques of
argument and that once they had the techniques, they would be able to argue
anything from any position, they emitted a puzzled, "Oh." Increasingly I
found myself agreeing with the students that argumentative techniques ungrounded in actual belief were cynical, dangerous, and vaguely immoral.

I tell this story because, more and more, I realize that how we teach
argument (or anything else) is an accommodation to or a struggle with what
we've been trained to do in the course of our own professional training as
symbolic analysts: win an argument, make points, thrust our opinions onto
the page, buttress our thesis with evidence, set up our opponents to take a fall,
and so on. Clinchy et al. point out in "Connected Education for Women" that

> the adversarial model has dominated institutions of higher education. . . . In order
> to stimulate cognitive growth, according to this model, the teacher should point
> out flaws in the students' thinking, put forth opposing notions, encourage debate,
> and challenge students to defend their ideas. One should attempt to induce
> cognitive conflict in students' minds. (44)

Although this combative style may work well for some students, Clinchy's
research suggests that students in general benefit from a more collaborative, less
competitive way of learning. Such collaborative inquiry is an antidote for the
dissociation that women in particular may feel when they try to argue positions
they do not genuinely hold, but all students, as the work of composition scholars
such as John Gage, C. H. Knoblauch and Lil Brannon has shown, benefit from
understanding precisely why they might argue for a position or belief.

Teaching writing at several levels to students variously "nontraditional" in age, gender, physical capability, race, culture, social class, and sexual preference has led me to develop what I hope is both a more familiar and a more ethical approach to argument: that is, to redefine argument as a conversation with people who know how to listen and whose opinion we care about, on a subject we know something about and in which we have a passionate interest. This approach invites students to ground argument in personal experience and belief, to be inclusive of and receptive to alternative viewpoints, to steer a middle way between silence and the assumption of expertise, to be self-reflective and honest about their own assumptions, to keep in mind the material conditions out of which opinions arise and in which they are heard, and to consider their audience as perhaps coworkers toward truth rather than as opponents, dupes, or a row of *tabulae rasae*. This approach to argument asks students to *position themselves* in relation to their own experience, to their subject, to their audience, and to language. Although such criteria for positioning are implicit in traditional representations of argument, they are often not given their due—*supporting* a position becomes paramount over the equally important, if not more important, problem of *exploring* one's thinking and *formulating positions* that represent, in the end, the whole range of inquiry that led to their articulation in the first place.

Finding a Voice

Because argument itself is such a loaded term and because students come to the class with many cultural misconceptions about how argument can and should be carried out, roughly the first half of the course studies the connections between language, power, and gender (along with culture, class, and race) and explores the students' prevailing notions about women's roles in society.

As Adrienne Rich observes in "Taking Women Students Seriously," many women behave as if they are disadvantaged or intellectually impaired when they are in a class with men—or even in a class with women who range from silenced to articulate:

> Look at a classroom. . . . Listen to the small, soft voices, often courageously trying to speak up, voices of women taught early that tones of confidence, challenge, anger, or assertiveness, are strident and unfeminine. Listen to the voices of the women and the voices of the men; observe the space men allow themselves, physically and verbally, the male assumption that people will listen, even when the majority of the group is female . . . . Listen to a woman groping for language in which to express what is on her mind, sensing that the terms of academic discourse are not her language. (243-44)

In exploring how women argue and what we can learn from them about the difficulties all students have with argument, a first step is to develop a metaconsciousness about ourselves as rhetors, as people who have something to say. Often these self-images are lacking, for whatever cultural or educational reason: Many students may feel as if the language of the university is beyond their reach (see Bartholomae, for example); students may feel as if those around them—their teachers and other more outspoken students—are more intelligent, more insightful and thus more powerful, more worthy of advancing their opinions. Because many women often have learned (through their cultures) to hold their voices inside them and *not* to speak out, women in particular may be able to tell us how it feels to be uncertain about one's self, one's opinions, one's beliefs—in short the very origins of having something to say, of taking part in discussion and dialectic in the first place. Consider this student's reaction to position-taking:

> When I first heard about the position paper, I gasped. After all, I felt I didn't have anything to stand for. I noticed that everyone at UMass (at least everyone in my classes) had something to stand for. People protested over the chancellor's raise, over the parking fee, over the minuteman . . . . I saw people carrying signs saying "Free Tibet". . . . I heard people conducting heated debates about politics, abortion, and religion. I was simply against smoking and drunk-driving. But then I thought, "Those are real issues." Then I thought about the abuse of children, and that infuriated me. Or the way our culture admires thin, beautiful models, making teenage girls hate their bodies and their images. I thought about violence towards women on television, even in cartoons. Suddenly I had a million topics to choose from. I did stand for something after all—lots of things! Not only am I receiving academic challenges at UMass, but personal ones as well. I'm finding out about what I believe in; what I want to fight for. The position paper was the perfect opportunity to get my mind focused on disturbing issues, and to convince others that the issues I was concerned with were truly valid. (Erin)[1]

At this point it can be productive for any group of students to learn why they have difficulty taking positions and to explore the possibilities that their voices have been silenced. Any number of readings from any number of cultural and social aspects can help students explore the issues of their own voice and silence, if that is what they face, and it often is in argumentation. Dale Spender's *Man-made Language* and Casey Miller and Kate Swift's *Handbook of Nonsexist Writing* provide feminist analyses of patriarchal discourse that women students, especially, can use to understand the origins of their exclusion. Tillie Olsen's "Silences" can help students to explore the ways women writers can be muted because of gender and economics, and

Gloria Anzaldua's "Speaking In Tongues: A Letter to Third World Women Writers" considers the dimensions of race, ethnicity, and sexual preference around the struggle to find the time, space, money, and mental freedom to write. We read Woolf's *A Room of One's Own* and poems by June Jordan, Susan Griffin, Audre Lorde, Sharon Olds, and others on the difficulties and the joys of writing. As we are reading these texts, I assign writing that asks students to explore, narrate, and analyze their own particular relation to language and to writing, and their own understanding of themselves as "constructed knowers."

All writers need to learn that their writing can be powerfully convincing when authentically voiced and grounded in their own specific reality. Although the conventions of argument—whether subjective or objective—are also worth mastering, because their mastery is so empowering to students, at this point in the course women are typically confronted with their own silence—and the reversal of that silence. A first step in learning to argue is learning to have something to say and learning to own positions. Over the years, I have come to spend less time in the classroom focusing on the negative (the reasons why we are silenced) and more on the positive (the reversal of that silence), less time on analyzing patriarchal power structures and more time providing strong women writer role models from a variety of perspectives—from the British upper middle class Virginia Woolf to Midwestern socialist Meridel LeSueur and ex-slave Sojourner Truth. Any genre (poetry and fiction in addition to nonfiction) can be used to show how powerfully convincing writing can be when authentically voiced and grounded in one's own specific reality. Such realities are apparent, for example, in the poems of Native American poet Joy Harjo (and through a PBS interview with her as well) and in Sandra Cisneros's episodic novel, *A House On Mango Street.* We view a film about women blues singers in the 1920s, "Wild Women Don't Have the Blues." I have also added Natalie Goldberg's Zen-like manifesto for silenced writers, *Writing Down the Bones,* which students find filled with techniques that inspire them to write.

Argument is typically defined in terms of *supporting* a position, but such an approach assumes the position is already in place. By contrast, *forming* a position often presents a significant hurdle for students, particularly when we ask them to argue from heartfelt belief. Students who have been silenced need first to learn to break that silence in ways that do not necessarily commit them to positions they may not be sure of. They need, as Natalie Goldberg makes eminently clear, the freedom to explore without being criticized, either by their own internalized critics or by critics external to them. Such critical assessment comes later and is an essential part of argument—but in the beginning it can silence a neophyte voice simply because the demands of argument (owning a position, understanding the requirements of taking a stance, being willing to speak in support of that stance) are so great. Thus we practice, after Elbow and a great many others, activities of writing in the early stage of the course that are designed to encourage exploration of voice and position. Unshared freewriting, journal writing, reader response—all of these activities provide important venues for students to comment on class readings, on their own writing, on what goes on in class—in short, to ground their initial observations and responses in language. I also ask students to write about language interactions they observe that can be analyzed from the perspective of what they are learning about the social and political nature of communication from this course. The overall purpose in this first part of the course is to establish exploration as an essential activity in having something to say, in understanding oneself as a constructed knower who has beliefs and opinions worth speaking out on.

Although the essay writing, and particularly the analytical and argumenta-tive writing as it culminates in the position paper, is the heart of the course, writing assignments adapted from the process movement foster important attitudes and skills. Exercises in writing poetry and fiction give the students practice in image making and story telling that will save their essays from being dry as dust. Ten-minute freewriting exercises provide bi- or triweekly writing practice, break the grip of the censor who sits on the shoulder of many of these women, and constitute what Peter Elbow calls an "evaluation-free zone" (197) with its attendant benefits of privacy and freedom from judgment. Journal writing gives students weekly informal writing practice that is not assignment driven, allows them free range to comment and to process, and provides the opportunity for synthesis and continuity.

This locating of the self, this beginning to write what they need to say rather than what others want to hear, needs to be worked on before students are faced with the position paper, their longest and most challenging writing assignment of the course. The various readings and writing exercises in the first third of the semester allow these students to focus on their personal relation to language and to writing, exercises that help them begin to locate or *situate* themselves in relation to culture and ethnicity, age, race, region, sexual preference, physical capability, religion, social class, or anything else that seems useful to them in examining their lives in relation to their writing or to their use of language.

For example, the following exercise is useful in helping students to explore the reality behind words such as "writer" and discover that for many aspects of women's experience there are no powerful and accurate names. In this exercise, I ask students to make up a new word or phrase and write a dictionary entry for an experience common to women that doesn't yet have a name. As Dale Spender remarks in *Man-made Language*:

> The male-defined hierarchical world view that we possess is so deeply engrained that, if we are to avoid replicating the injustices of classism, racism and sexism, we must deliberately seek to give recognition and validity to those areas of experience that have been expressly denied in the male version of literature and truth. (227)

This analytical exercise has produced such coinages as: systergy, motherfail, femisphere, sports fematic, shero, backlashhers, daughterguilt, frovermate, piece a man, familystress, imposia.

Although sometimes a struggle for them, this assignment points out to the women in the class how much of their own experience has been muted or silenced in a discourse primarily developed by and for the interests of men, and it grants to these women the creative power of naming, the power of creating their own realities in which they are firmly situated.

This notion of the situated or positioned self gets at the very heart of my approach to teaching argument. You need to know who you are to know what you stand for. This concept seems to me both obvious and venerably traditional (yet also radical, because it goes to the root). This notion of argument and of public discourse is one that this country seems to have veered far away from in recent years. The models of investigation and of argument that our students receive every day on the radio, on television, even in print, reduce complex issues to good or bad, win or lose, and if it weren't pitiful or tragic it would be amusing to listen to yet another person being herded, struggling, by a journalist or politician or lawyer in a courtroom into the bondage of binary thinking.

Creating a Community

Although some composition scholars have examined the pedagogy of teaching argumentative writing and others have examined the role of community in the composition classroom, few have examined how classroom communities function as they engage in argumentative inquiry. In "Rescuing the Discourse of Community," Gregory Clarkson examines the ways a "discourse of community [can locate] writing and reading, and its teaching, within the project of constituting and maintaining a collectivity of equals" who can then "make space for the assertions of others as a part of the process of composing their own" (72). He suggests that we have much to learn about how classroom communities can effectively engage in argumentative inquiry.

Rhetorically, the notion of *community* is a variation on *audience,* although the word *community* does not invoke the passivity that the word *audience* does. *Community* means a group of interested others who share a mutual concern for the issues at hand (or for a specific question at issue), individuals who themselves have something to say about a given subject. A community of interested others is one whose members can give feedback, ask questions, provide different perspectives—all essential to the working out of one's position. This kind of community is essential if we are to engage in an argumentation based on mutual inquiry and responsibility to others rather than one based on opposition and winning.

I have learned from my women students, however, that such a community cannot be limited to the intellectual exercise of argument but also must be committed to its dimensions as a social act. Any community of arguers can be divisive, especially when challenging a point of debate. But feminist classrooms have taught us that such divisiveness can be disastrous, especially for those students whose rhetorical style is based on mutuality and respect rather than on opposition. The rhetorical responsibility of a questioning other in the process of argument must be combined with a willingness to support the rhetor as she seeks, through the forum of discourse, to work out her various beliefs and positions. I see part of my role as a teacher/facilitator, especially for beginning writers, to establish a safe enough space for people to try out the various positions they might own and take the risks that will enable them to grow as thinkers and writers. The system that seems to work best is to build a sense of responsibility to others in each class: to create a community of people who have certain relational and ethical obligations—despite the differences among individuals in age, social class, culture and race, and personal belief systems—to each other and an expectation of what is reasonably due to them from others in that community. The dialectic and rhetorical requirements of argument in a community of others willing to discuss the issues at hand depend, first and foremost, on those others being willing to *listen* to what each has to say as well. This means a willingness to hear the other's opinions not just as fodder for peremptory challenge or outright rejection but as important ideas and statements to be thought over.

Dialogue with others and a sense of dialectic are important to the working out of one's own position. Through the use of dialogue, we are able to create a sense of connectedness to our writing: Small group workshops and classroom discussion provide the opportunity to try out ideas, to explore what one thinks, to "own" our positions.

Such a supportive and responsible community might work as follows. For each position paper, a student writes an informal proposal describing her subject, various thoughts about the subject, and the kinds of beliefs and positions she might like to assert about the issues involved. She presents this proposal to the class as a whole; the ensuing discussions thus provide an opportunity to try out these ideas, to explore what she thinks, to "own" the positions proposed. The response to such proposals can involve several stages. Classmates might respond, for example, by suggesting further materials (students will bring in articles or books to loan to each other, suggest someone the writer might interview, or might volunteer to be interviewed themselves). We help the student narrow or refine her topic by asking questions. I ask the class: What would *you* want to know about this position and this topic when you read this paper? Personalizing it in that way seems to allow people to become an engaged audience full of questions—about the scope of the topic, about the specifics of the position, about whether the proposed approach seems workable or whether the materials seem adequate. I ask them whether they have any arguments against the position. The discussions are typically substantial, lively, and respectful. The point is not to knock down the writer's proposal but to help her explore whether it is a feasible position, whether she is comfortable enough talking about it to carry her through three more weeks on the assignment and two versions of the paper, whether the questions open up new ground for her. After this intense but not combative questioning, students have in some instances discovered that this was not the topic they wanted to work on after all. The public presentation of the proposal may help them realize they are not as committed to the position as they initially thought or that they simply, when pressed, realize they don't have the resources to do as good a job as they might want to on that particular topic. Often a student changes her topic after the proposal presentation because the original topic was superficially related to her life and the topic she finally chooses is one she feels committed to on a deeper level. And, equally important, these women learn to respect one another's ideas.

Such an approach to the responsibilities inherent in the rhetorical situation of argumentation leads writers to feel a greater connection to their ideas, their positions, and their writing. The process of dialogue and dialectic has drawn them into a commitment to exploring their own ideas rather than imitating positions or writing what they perceive others and the teacher want to hear—a stage essential to but not identical to the working out of the position they will speak to in the writing of their drafts and final paper. One student, Sam, had this to say in her journal about this part of the process:

> The process of writing the position paper for this class is unlike any other paper I have ever written. I have never been in a classroom full of women sharing their ideas about what they believe to be truly important. The breadth and depth of the subjects raised blew my mind. I learned more in the classes resulting from this assignment than I have in any other classtime discussion. We moved from the subject of murder in the guise of the death penalty, to genital mutilation to the way society's views about women's body size affects the development of healthy, well adjusted women.
>
> What really excited me was the fact that each of the women in the class had something very serious to address and everyone was capable of generating a well thought out opinion of these issues and the way they influence women's lives. There were so many things talked about that I could have spent the entire semester only writing position papers.

Sam, like many students in the class, sounds like a "connected knower" who "can permit her own voice to venture forth and allow others that same freedom" (Tedesco 24).

Work is required, however, to create supportive communities that also sustain intellectual rigor. One problem that always emerges in the first half of the semester is that although people do want specific honest criticism for themselves, they hold back from giving it to other people, sometimes from lack of confidence in their own ability or authority, sometimes from fear of hurting others. The midterm evaluations invariably bring out the fact of this holding back, to everyone's surprise, and the class discussion of the data from the evaluations reasserts that indeed each of them can and does want a solid, caring, and tough constructively critical reading of her work; by that time there is generally enough trust for people to settle in and provide that gift of attention for each other. In this kind of supportive environment, when "the goal is not to win or prove one's intellectual superiority but to clarify ideas and to work collaboratively" (Belenky qtd. in Ashton-Jones and Thomas 284), women have little difficulty accepting and giving criticism or, as Peter Elbow says, in "playing 'the doubting game.'" At this point I see critical skills improve, particularly the ability to be specific and constructive in offering criticism and to discuss honestly what parts of a paper do not work and for what reasons.

Although many traditional and mixed-gender writing classes begin the semester having the entire class workshop each piece, my experience suggests that the vast majority of beginning writers, men and women alike, need time to establish a sense of trust, safety, and mutual respect through the development of a sense of community, if they are to write from positions of genuine belief and assurance in the act of inquiry rather than from any perfunctory notion of pleasing the teacher. The dangers of moving to large-scale public criticism of the writing too soon are that people will drop out of the class, will stay in the class but emotionally and intellectually withdraw, will become competitive, or will likely opt for what they already know how to do rather than take the risk to grow in ways that might initially make them look awkward and feel out of control. Such nurturing is essential for students to feel ready to "go public" with their writing.

Owning Positions

Choosing a topic is itself a vital part of the process of learning to write argument. At this point in the course, writing in journals gives students an opportunity to explore topics and as they write about these topics they learn what a good argument might require. In "The Exploratory Essay," William Zeiger makes a persuasive case for just such an approach. He finds that asking students to construct a logical argument with thesis and supports sets up the now-familiar battle metaphor and bypasses the "spirit of inquiry" (765) so crucial to argument. Linda, a member of Amnesty International, first considered writing against torture, but as she remarked in her journal: "It seems ridiculous to write a paper opposed to it, because WHO, that I could show this paper to, would not agree with me that torture is a bad thing?" Clearly she's made a discovery about argument: There must be a point of debate that permits the possibility of different perspectives in resolving a question at issue. As a rhetorical term, *question at issue* means that the issue can be phrased as a question that can be differently answered or resolved depending on perspective—and so recognizes the possibility of differences of opinion. This does not mean that writers should try to defeat those holding other opinions, but rather that they should listen to alternative opinions and take these fresh perspectives into account when constructing their own positions. Difference is essential, for otherwise there is no reason for discussion, no point to make. But unless the point is serving to mutually enlighten all interested parties, argument devolves into win-lose positioning.

Although Linda abandons the idea of writing a position paper on torture, thinking about this topic has opened her thinking in general on the problem of the abridgement of human rights. She then finds that she might be able to argue effectively about some aspect of the death penalty: She has a strong sense of its injustice, yet the death penalty has its proponents, those whom she would ask to hear her opinion and whose perspective she needs to become aware of in considering her own beliefs. Although she discovers, through her journal writing, that this topic, too, may have pitfalls, she also discovers a greater commitment to the issues involved. The problems are not whether the issue is worth arguing but how well she will be able to make her own insights and arguments known:

> The death penalty is one topic I have been thinking about and talking about a lot recently, so I probably should write it. My big problem with an issue that I feel strongly about is that I can go on and on for pages and pages about how I feel, but that isn't very convincing in the face of a logical argument, it just sounds really emotional. If I write a really cold logical paper, I feel as if I have done the paper justice, but I don't feel as if there is any of me inside of it. It feels style-less and the kind of research paper my grammar happy eighth grade jerk of an English teacher would have gone into ecstatic fits over. And I really don't know how to integrate the two well. Sometimes that can be done with humor, and that's really not a possibility when talking about the death penalty—or any really serious human rights violation. I can usually, no matter how blah I find a paper assignment to be, just sit down and write about it anyway, even if what I write is really bad. I can't do that with this assignment. I sit down to write and nothing at all comes out.

Here the student expresses the dilemma Bolker defines. Should she be a "good girl" and please her audience or should she allow herself to become emotionally invested and please herself? If she is passionate, will her paper lack logic and therefore fail to convince an audience? Linda's concern with audience at this state of her writing process has the potential to become a kind of writing block ("nothing comes out"). In "What Happens When Things Go Wrong: Women and Writing Blocks," Mary Kupiec Cayton observes that for women this kind of block is not uncommon. In her research she found that men and women differed in their concerns about writing. Whereas men became blocked when they failed to identify a satisfactory research strategy or when they could not sustain interest in a project, women may become blocked when they imagine a hostile audience. This could have happened to Linda ("in the face of a logical argument"), but in fact her initial block, which she overcame quickly, seemed due more to her passionate commitment to the issue. How to integrate emotion, conviction, and persuasive rational argument was the writing problem that confronted Linda in this assignment.

As we get closer to the position paper assignment, we begin to use in-class timed writings to generate ideas. I ask students to write, "What makes me angry is . . . " and "If I could change one thing in the world, it would be . . ." Even with these prompts, some students still have difficulty identifying an issue for their position paper. Yet as the following journal entry illustrates, journal writing can be a powerful means of self-discovery:

> The weekend before I had to write the proposal for my position paper I got very depressed because I couldn't find one thing that could characterize me or an issue which I could feel strongly about. It was worse than writer's block. It was existence block. It became a challenge for me to figure out where I stand. I felt as if I have created a very thick rubber wall around me in order to allow the amusement or anger of the outside information to just bounce back to where it came from. I didn't want to blame those men I meet who ask me if I can cook soon after they ask my name, or the teacher who said, "Physics are not for you, but if you sit in the front row with a shorter skirt I may let you pass the course." Or my sad job at the restaurant where I work, where I have to kiss ass all day long in order to pay my rent. Or the public transportation, and the trains which are never on time. The homeless in Harvard Square, how long are they going to be there before anyone does anything about it? The public schools in Boston, gun control, AIDS, cancer, domestic violence, financial aid, Bosnia, Somalia, South America, South Africa. . . . (Maria)

Although this journal entry may seem unfocused as the student ranges from personal gripes to global issues, this process of winnowing through topics finally enabled the student to settle on a topic close to her heart but not so close that she is blocked by anger (though she is angry), nor so distant that she is hampered by indifference. Maria wrote an argument titled "Searching For That Place Called Home" about the treatment of immigrants, based, in part, on her own experience as a recent immigrant to this country. Her engagement with the topic and her control over language are both evident in this excerpt: "We became a category. Before you could identify yourself as Juan, Maria, Chang or Whatever your natural name may be, you had to check the box that says, MINORITY. And there is where the struggle starts, in that box."

All along, this approach has underscored the connection between self-inquiry, the social contexts of argument, and the rhetorical processes of argument. Emphasizing these connections empowers students to merge their private and public languages: Their positions in public discourse derive from commitments to personal beliefs. What changes in this last stage is their ability to wield language effectively in public discourse: They are more confident, more assured, more clear about just what the responsibilities of the position are once they have formulated a public stance on an issue.

Thus at this point students begin to work with the conventions of argument more directly. These conventions involve the identification of issues, personal connections to those issues, the formulation of a position, the exploration of ideas that both lead to and derive from that position, some consideration of the kind of writing they might do in response to the position, a plan for researching further information they want to find out, and coming up with the kinds of questions they have about their subject and position that their subsequent revisions will address. They do this work through proposal exploration rather than through any mechanical or formulaic procedure of steps. The result is a more fluid, even intuitive style of inquiry, as the following first draft of a position paper proposal reveals:

> The notion of "beauty" is very much a women's issue in America. Despite our gains in the workplace, etc., it is still important for a woman to be considered attractive, on top of being successful, fulfilled, intelligent, etc. If anything, despite the women's movement, the physical requirements are even more narrow than they were 20 years ago. Now it is not enough to be the right weight, you must be tall, leggy, and have the right muscle tone as well. Please be thin AND aerobicized, thank you. Despite the catalogued cancer risks, women still get breast implants and broil in the sun. Once it became available, liposuction became the number one cosmetic surgery performed on women. A recent article I read pointed out the alarming fact that obsessive dieting, leading to anorexia and bulimia in many cases, is now appearing in younger and younger girls. What used to worry only young women as they became 15 and 16 is now worrying girls of 10 and 11. They are picking up the media message. To be a woman whom people want to be with, you had better be concerned with the outer you.
>
> I have two ways of focusing on this issue. Using statistics, books (most notably Naomi Wolf's "The Beauty Myth,") the media, etc. I can do a more traditional paper on the crippling effects of what this beauty obsession does to American women and what I think should be done to combat these images. Or, what I'd prefer, is to write almost a stream of consciousness paper on what goes on in an appearance-crippled woman's mind as she goes through her day and through her life, doing all those things that she feels help her to be "beautiful." The dieting, the hair cuts, dye jobs, permanent waves, the manicures, the pedicures, the leg waxing, the tanning salon, the tooth capping, the exercise classes, the facials, the makeup applications, the breast implants, the tummy tucks, the liposuction, the facelift, the nose job, the colored contact lenses, and so on and so forth. (Monica)

This student clearly does not feel bound by a propositional thesis-support argument. By listing and describing the number of beauty procedures any one woman could cram into a day, Monica proposes to present evidence that will lead most readers to reach her conclusion (her thesis): that the beauty culture has overtaken the minds and bodies of American women. Monica ends her proposal with this comment: " I would try to make it funny and yet chilling. How, if you buy into what MTV and the *Sports Illustrated* swimsuit issue tell you what to look like, you've straitjacketed your life." She anticipates using irony as part of her argument, a technique Julia Allen advocates in advising her women students to overturn social "pieties," as Kenneth Burke labeled social conventions.

Because argument is a public discourse, we continue the process of public readings, workshops, and discussion. Rather than teach traditional methods of developing arguments—writing a thesis, providing evidence—I find that workshopping papers achieves the same ends but with a continued emphasis on real dialogue, personal commitment, and support. Building on the discussion of the student proposals, which offer a hypothesis and an approach to the subject, I find that workshopping the first draft of the position paper tests the effectiveness of the argument against a tough but supportive audience.

In these workshops, we first discuss and point to what is effective writing and arguing in the paper: The writer's position is clear, the progression of the discussion is relatively coherent, the language is precise and interesting, and there's enough detail of evidence to support the argument. Because I have promised my students at the beginning of the semester that I will never read a weak paper of theirs and embarrass them in front of the class, I choose papers to read that, to some extent, already have accomplished such criteria. Then we look for potential changes that could improve the paper: Does the argument need more material to back it up? Is there a gap in the argument? Has a certain point been discussed enough? Is there too much material, or is the direction of the discussion getting sidetracked or diffused? Has the writer's emotional commitment become too direct and polemical, rather than working through the presentation of details? Could a story, an anecdote, or an image be effective and powerful? Will a bit of humor disarm an alarmed reader?

These peer reviews help students become conscious of what works in an argumentative paper. Martha wrote in her journal about the death penalty paper: "I had not thought before about it (the death penalty) the way I do now. Our words are so powerful; but many times we do not recognize that. I learned from Linda's paper that the amount of facts and details that you add to your paper can change and open people's minds about something."

Students whose papers were workshopped throughout the semester found the comments quite useful and were nurtured by the time and attention given them by the group (eventually everyone had at least one of their papers looked at by the entire group). They could see that certain techniques like piling up evidence or moving to an anecdote to illustrate and to give relief from a paragraph of abstract reasoning would be useful in their own papers. By this point in the course, students are able to engage in some metaanalysis of their own mastery of argument as a rhetorical act. They are becoming aware of their own rhetorical practices, such as position taking and evidence building. But these are not mechanical acts disassociated from their own thoughts and beliefs; rather, they are highly connected acts. They are interested in evidence now not because it is what the teacher requires but because it is what their own rhetorical act of positioning requires. They are developing a real awareness of the process of argument at the same time that they are learning how to talk effectively about subjects and positions important to them.

Students gain their awareness and competence by discussing their own papers and by continuing to read powerful pieces by women writers, ones that rely on the cumulative power of detail to move the reader to consider a new position. They come to see that argument typically depends on detail to be convincing. Virginia Woolf's creation of an imaginary sister of Shakespeare, in *A Room of One's Own,* for example, depends on her careful detailing of that character's imagined life. Meridel LeSueur's 1932 journalistic exposé of homeless and unemployed women during the worst years of the Great Depression, "Women on the Breadlines," in which she creates several characters, enables women to understand just how bad conditions were for women then. They study LeSueur's use of the participant/observer stance, the possibility of using a letter form as in Gloria Anzaldua's "Speaking in Tongues: A Letter to Third World Women Writers," the use of humor in argument in Judy Brady's "I Want a Wife," and the use of repetition and question in Sojourner Truth's speech "And Ain't I a Woman?" We consider Julia Penelope Stanley's and Susan J. Wolfe's study of the use of circular instead of linear reasoning in experimental writing by women from Gertrude Stein to Jill Johnston and Monique Wittig in their essay, "Consciousness as Style; Style as Aesthetic."

One student's journal entry reveals the growing awareness of a metadiscourse that students develop as they discuss both their own arguments and those of the readings:

> I liked hearing the first drafts of the position paper in class and being exposed to different approaches to persuasion writing.
>
> I was especially touched by Linda's paper on Capital Punishment. From the paper it was evident that she feels passionate about this subject, but she doesn't resort to "guilt tactics" to persuade. She didn't base her paper on emotional aspects of individual cases, but vividly and graphically described how various methods work and the tremendous pain and suffering involved. Like many people, I have always thought that the legalized methods of execution were instantaneous and painless. After hearing her paper, I felt slightly nauseous, not only by the brutal

facts, but of the emotional impact these executions must have on the convict's family.

I also found the approach of considering and responding to potential counter arguments to be very effective. After waffling for many years on the issue of Capital Punishment, Linda's paper succeeded in persuading me.

Regarding Martha's paper on the issue of diversity at UMass, I found her approach to be very effective as well. She continually asks questions of the reader, which forces the reader to consider their own definition of diversity and their personal attitudes and prejudices.

Listening to these position papers helped me when doing my revision. I took aspects which I felt made the papers persuasive: refuting possible opposition, asking questions, describing alternatives and presenting hard facts, to make my own paper have a stronger voice. (Samantha)

Samantha's use of such words as "persuasive," "refuting," and "opposition" suggest the kind of awareness these students have developed of the requirements of arguments, yet the motivation is to share one's voice, to make oneself heard, rather than to silence other voices. This kind of mutuality presents argument at its finest: Argument is an act of listening and of being heard, rather than an act of winning and defeating.

Such insight into the rhetorical effects of language—effects that are nonetheless genuine because these students are so earnest in their use of language—enables students to enter into a conversation with their own papers and to make changes based on the results. One student, Michelle, found that her paper on lesbian custody issues had become too bogged down in a recent court case—and that she was therefore losing sight of the very point this discussion was to make. Rewriting without referring to her earlier draft helped to unblock her: She could sidestep reengaging with what was already on the page and take a fresh view. Another student, Lori, was dissatisfied with her first draft of "Up Front: Breast Image and Women's Health Care," but unable to say exactly why. This is her response to her revision process:

I am in the process of rewriting my position paper. I feel like I vomited the first draft on to the page. I was so uptight about writing it and it shows. I didn't really understand why this happened. I thought it was due to the fact that so much emphasis had been placed on this particular paper. The two days of proposal presentation really set me off. I was suddenly transported back to grade school, where I felt a deep insecurity about my writing. The women in the class were talking about research, facts, convincing arguments and I began to get sweaty palms. I was prepared to write an editorial, not a research paper . . . .

I kept getting this nagging feeling about the piece, that there were deeper issues at work than my confusion regarding the genre and how to approach it.

. . . I asked my frothermate (person she lives with and has a partner relationship with) to do a critique, the most valuable phrase being, "Lori, it just doesn't sound like you, you are not in here." Aha, of course. It immediately made sense. Breast cancer, breast health are issues that are very close to me, that's why I chose them. I attempted to write about these issues without facing the pain of my mother's illness/death. I wrote as though I was a remote observer, I wrote a few couched facts, without really even stirring the argument because I was too afraid of what would come out.

This approach to argument seeks to bridge the gap between private (her pain concerning her mother's illness) and public (women's health care). Through her revision process, Lori is able, as Adrienne Rich suggests, to perform the act of "re-vision—the act of looking back, of seeing with fresh eyes, of entering an old text from a new critical direction," which, as Rich goes on to say, "is for women . . . an act of survival" (35). A strong reading of her own argument leads Lori to reevaluate her own text and in the final version to integrate her mother's story with her central argument. This is Lori's comment on her revision:

The rewrite is going well. It is not forced. It comes out of my head and on to the page with an ease I couldn't imagine a week ago. I have begun cutting through the tangled fear that had been holding me down. I feel quite liberated. It is good to be able to analyze the influences of your writing. It is better still to allow those influences to have their way.

To encourage our students to write well, we need to look beyond the text that the students produce to the meaning it has in their lives. I see the training in argument I do in this course as training in critical thinking that they will use not just in producing "A" papers in college or even good memos or reports in their work life, but training that will help them to live their lives in a more grounded and committed way: to slice through the overwhelming sludge of opinion and information that threatens to engulf us every day. To learn how to ask the right questions about an issue. To know well enough who they are to take in new information and analyze it from their own perspective. To be confident that what they believe in is worth saying and worth pursuing the facts and evidence to back up what they have to say. To recognize that others may feel and believe differently and so to provide bridges between their position and those of their audience. To listen to the voices of others. To trust their own capacity to find language, images, stories and details that express their position and have a chance of convincing others. A writing class structured on feminist principles can provide a nurturing community of writers who listen to each other with respect and offer the kind of constructive criticism that will help each person to grow as a writer.

Note

1. Quotes from student papers and journals are from spring semester 1992 and fall semester 1993 classes of "Writing as Women." I am grateful to all the students who have taken and helped shape the course over the years and particularly to those who have allowed me to quote from their journals and papers.

Works Cited

Allen, Julia. "Rhetorics of Resistance." Conference on College Composition and Communication. Boston, March 21-12, 1991. ERIC Document ED 332207.

Anzaldua, Gloria. "Speaking in Tongues." *The Bridge Called My Back: Writing by Radical Women of Color*. Ed. Sheree Moraga and Gloria Anzaldua. Watertown, MA: Persephone Press, 1981.

Ashton-Jones, Evelyn, and Dena Kay Thomas. "Composition, Collaboration and Women's Ways of Knowing: A Conversation with Mary Belenky." *Journal of Advanced Composition* 10 (Fall 1990): 275-92.

Belenky, Mary Field, Blythe McVicker Clinchy, Nancy Rule Goldberger, and Jill Mattuck Tarule. *Women's Ways of Knowing: The Development of Self, Voice, and Mind*. New York: Basic Books, 1986.

Bolker, Joan. "Teaching Griselda to Write." *College English* 40 (Apr. 1974): 906-8.

Brady, Judy. "I Want a Wife." *Literature and Society*. 2nd ed. Ed. Pamela J. Annas and Robert C. Rosen. Englewood Cliffs, NJ: Prentice Hall, 1994.

Bullock, Chris J. "Changing the Context: Applying Feminist Perspectives to the Writing Class." *English Quarterly* 22 (1990): 141-47.

Cayton, Mary Kupiec. "What Happens When Things Go Wrong: Women and Writing Blocks." *Journal of Advanced Composition* 10 (Fall 1990): 321-37.

Cisneros, Sandra. *A House on Mango Street*. New York: Vintage, 1989.

Clarkson, Gregory. "Rescuing the Discourse of Community." *College Composition and Communication* 45 (Feb. 1994): 61-74.

Clinchy, Blythe McVicker, Mary Field Belenky, Nancy Rule Goldberger, and Jill Mattuck Tarule. "Connected Education for Women." *Journal of Education* 167 (1985): 28-45.

Conway, Jill Ker. *True North*. New York: Alfred A. Knopf, 1994.

Elbow, Peter. "Ranking, Evaluating and Liking: Sorting Out Three Forms of Judgement." *College English* 55 (Feb. 1993): 187-206.

Faigley, Lester. *Fragments of Rationality: PostModernity and the Subject of Composition*. Pittsburgh, PA: University of Pittsburgh Press, 1992.

Farrell, Thomas. "The Female and Male Modes of Rhetoric." *College English* 40 (Nov. 1979): 909-21.

Ferguson, Mary Ann. "Review: 'Feminist Theory and Practice.' " *College English* 48 (Nov. 1986): 726-35.

Flynn, Elizabeth. "Composing as a Woman." *College Composition and Communication* 39 (Dec. 1988): 423-35.

————. "Compositing 'Composing as a Woman': A Perspective on Research." *College Composition and Communication* 41 (Feb. 1990): 83-89.

————. "Feminist Theories/Feminist Composition." *College English* 57 (Feb. 1995): 201-12.

Frey, Olivia. "Beyond Literary Darwinism: Women's Voices and Critical Discourse." *College English* 52 (Sept. 1990): 507-26.

Gearhart, Sally Miller. "The Womanization of Rhetoric." *Women's Studies International Quarterly* 2 (1979): 195-201.

Gilligan, Carol. *In a Different Voice: Psychological Theory and Women's Development.* Cambridge, MA: Harvard University Press, 1982.

Goldberg, Natalie. *Writing Down the Bones.* Boston: Shambhala, 1986.

Harris, Angela P. "Race and Essentialism in Feminist Legal Theory." *Stanford Law Review* 42 (Feb. 1990): 581-616.

Juncker, Clara. "Writing (with) Cixous." *College English* 50 (Apr. 1988): 424-36.

Lamb, Catherine. "Beyond Argument in Feminist Composition." *College Composition and Communication* 42 (Feb. 1991): 11-24.

Lassner, Phyllis. "Feminist Responses to Rogerian Argument." *Rhetoric Review* 8 (Spring 1990): 220-31.

LeSueur, Meridel. "Women on the Breadlines." *Ripening, Selected Work 1927-1980, Meridel LeSueur.* Old Westbury, NY: The Feminist Press, 1982.

Luttrell, Wendy. "Working-Class Women's Ways of Knowing: Effects of Gender, Race, and Class." *Sociology of Education* 62 (Jan. 1989): 33-46.

Miller, Casey, and Kate Swift. *Handbook of Nonsexist Writing.* 2nd ed. New York: Harper and Row, 1988.

Olsen, Tillie. *Silences.* New York: Delacourte/Seymour Lawrence, 1978.

Pigott, Margaret B. "Sexist Roadblocks in Inventing, Focusing and Writing." *College English* 40 (Apr. 1979): 922-27.

Rich, Adrienne. *On Lies, Secrets and Silence.* New York: W. W. Norton, 1979.

Spender, Dale. *Man-made Language.* London: Routledge and Paul, 1980.

(Stanley), Julia Penelope, and Susan J. Wolfe. "Consciousness as Style; Style as Aesthetic." *Language, Gender and Society.* Ed. Barrie Thorne, Cheris Kramarae, and Nancy Henley. Rowley, MA: Newbury House, 1983. 125-39.

Tedesco, Janis. "Women's Ways of Knowing/Women's Ways of Composing." *Rhetoric Review* 9 (Spring 1991): 246-56.

Tompkins, Jane. "Fighting Words: Unlearning to Write the Critical Essay." *Georgia Review* (Fall 1988): 585-90.

Truth, Sojourner. "And Ain't I a Woman?" *Literature and Society.* 2nd ed. Ed. Pamela J. Annas and Robert C. Rosen. Englewood Cliffs, NJ: Prentice Hall, 1994.

Wild Women Don't Have the Blues. Dir. Dall. 1989, 58 min.

Woolf, Virginia. *A Room of One's Own.* New York: Harcourt Brace and World, 1929.

Zeiger, William. "The Exploratory Essay." *College English* 47 (Sept. 1985): 454-66.

7

Principles for Propagation

On Narrative and Argument

Judith Summerfield
Queens College of the City University of New York

"My dear little lady," exclaimed the King good-humouredly, "your arguments have convinced me."

George Cruikshank
Fairy Library

In weakness, we create distinctions,
then Deem that our puny boundaries are things
Which we perceive, and not which we have made.

William Wordsworth
The Prelude

My first epigraph is taken from George Cruikshank's remarkable *Fairy Library*, 1853. In his prefatory remarks to the 1854 edition, which he entitles "To the Public," he defends his highly criticized versions of Cinderella, Jack and the Beanstalk, and Puss in Boots. He insists that there is not one version of any tale, that the "four editions of 'Cinderella' now before me, all [differ] most materially from each other," and that being so, he had every right, in fact he was obliged, to revise the tales, especially because he had "found *some* vulgarity, mixed up with so much that was useless and unfit for children." He found it necessary to "re-write the whole story; in doing so which I have introduced a few *Temperance Truths,* with a fervent hope that some good may result therefrom" (Cruikshank 31).

Charles Dickens had increasingly found his friend Cruikshank's rantings against drink—especially at dinner parties—rather tedious. With the publication of *Fairy Library,* however, Dickens launched a hostile review, "Frauds upon the Fairies," in *Household Words* of October 1, 1853. That attack, Dickens claimed, was *not* personal: He objected to what Cruikshank had done to Cinderella.

Cruikshank's Cinderella is the Perrault Cinderella, as beautiful as she is good; she had a nature "which cannot be spoiled by any praise or indulgence." After her good mother dies, her father marries a woman who squanders his wealth, his property, and "he was so much in debt that he was put into prison." The plot proceeds conventionally: The King announces a ball to find his son a bride; the stepsisters prepare themselves with Cinderella's "excellent taste" and good-natured assistance; the fairy godmother intervenes with her magic; and, hey presto, one ball, two balls, the glass slipper, and the finale—the wedding.

The King, "who is in the highest flow of spirits," declares that among all the "grand doings to celebrate this wedding . . . there should be running 'fountains of wine' in the court-yards of the palace, and also in the streets" (Cruikshank 174).

At this point, the Fairy Godmother objects and issues forth a long, detailed argument against drink. The King objects, insisting that his guests will "take it in moderation." No, the Godmother argues, the "history of the use of strong drink" tells us differently; it is "marked on every page by excess . . . by ill health, misery, and crime." She argues that Divine Providence did not intend for a man to be intoxicated; that so long as the King himself sets an example with "even half a glass of wine a-day," it follows that his subjects will be "constantly falling by excess into vice, wretchedness, and crime," and that to understand the virtue of temperance is to look at Cinderella, "who never has taken any in all her life, and who never will."

"My dear little lady," exclaimed the King, good-humouredly, "your arguments have convinced me." Immediately, he gave orders that all the wine, beer, and spirits in the palace should be collected together and piled upon the top of a rocky mound in the vicinity of the palace, and made a great bonfire of on the night of the wedding;—which was accordingly done, and a splendid blaze it made! (Cruikshank 178)

Dickens objected: "I mean to protest most strongly against alteration," he writes to his publisher, "for any purpose—of the beautiful little stories which are so tenderly and humanly useful to us, early and late; and then to rewrite Cinderella according to Total-abstinence, Peace Society, and Bloomer principles, and expressly for their propagation" (Dickens in Buchanan-Brown 31).

This, interestingly enough, from the most celebrated novelist of the day, who knew full well from his own childhood experience of hearing tales from his young baby-sitter that fairy tales—Bluebeard, for one, to which he was "indebted for my first personal experience of a shudder and cold beads on the forehead"—were not just beautiful. He knew, as well, as a moralist who wove his points of view, biases, convictions, his *causes* into the fabric of his stories, that tales, inescapably, carry "principles," that they can be threaded imperceptibly into character, plot, setting, or they can be rough hewn, blatant crusades, as in Cruikshank's *Cinderella,* where the tale is sacrificed to the moral to be taught.

My second epigraph—Wordsworth's lines from the Prelude manuscript, 1799—takes me to this invitation: to consider narrative and argument in the teaching of college composition.

The point is now commonplace in this postmodern moment: The boundaries we acknowledge are those we have made. In the teaching of writing, narrative and argument are often set apart as opposites in what Britton calls the "great divide." The plots of countless syllabi, curricula, textbooks, and programs in writing are still constructed by the myths that narrative is a "simple" mode and, as such, a good beginning point for the composition course or sequence and that argument, more cognitively complex, a fitting end. Begin with narrative and move to argument.

Having written elsewhere about the sway that the narrative-argument plot holds over us, I wish to urge here, again, that we scrutinize the boundaries, plots, and principles of our own discourse at the same time that we teach courses where language, as Jakobson says, "is investigated in all the variety of its functions" (353).

In such courses, we enable students multiple opportunities, public and private, for writing and for entering the conversations in the university in a variety of textual roles. Such play of language, as Halliday puts it, enables students "to create meanings of a social kind: to participate in all forms of verbal contest and verbal display, and in the elaborate rhetoric of ordinary daily conversation" (3) and, I would add, in the elaborate and extraordinary rhetoric of the academy.

Writing so variously embraces complexity and multiplicity. There are no simple modes, no simple utterances, no simple stories. Every move is a gesture, a complicated mess of motive, argument, persuasion, hope, commentary, desire, need, and invitation to be negotiated with. Such a course would recognize the pervasiveness, complexity, and variousness of narrative; recognize how we transform *what happens* into story in our ordinary lives and in our dreams in our attempts to order the past and prepare for the future. To *narrate,* from the Greek, is *to know.* Narrative is about making sense, through order and sequence, boundaries and emplotments, beginnings and endings, of what we do and what is done to us. Always, says Barbara Hardy, the environment beckons and assaults with its narratives.

> Walls, papers, mass-media, vehicles, entertainments, libraries, talks, slogans, politicians, prophets and Job's comforters persuade, encourage, depress, solicit, comfort and commiserate in narrative forms. Even when we try to escape narrative, as when we listen to music or do mathematics, we tend to lapse. Even logicians tell stories. Humankind cannot bear very much abstraction or discursive reasoning. The stories of our days and the stories in our days are joined in that autobiography we are all engaged in making and remaking, as long as we live, which we never complete, though we all know how it is going to end. (4)

I

The Complexities of Narrative

> So daily life, whatever it may be really, is practically composed of two lives—the life in time and the life by values—and our conduct reveals a double allegiance. 'I only saw her for five minutes, but it was worth it.' There you have both allegiances in a single sentence.
>
> *E. M. Forster*
> Aspects of the Novel

The problem with narrative is, quite simply, that it isn't considered a problem. I want here to lay out some of the complexities of narrative so as to enrich our theories of composition and contribute to a breaking down of the distinctions, the boundaries between narrative and argument; to suggest, as do Leith and Myerson in their *Power of Address,* that all narratives are arguments in that they are inevitably constructed, composed, within a conversation, characterized, as is every rhetorical move, by "the extent to which speaking *to* or writing *to* is a central idea in making sense of speech and writing" (88).

Every narrative act *is* a composition; it presumes an act of selection, a consciousness making the selection, a construction of a subjectivity, a voice—a role—that narrates, that tells the story. There is no beginning, middle, and end "in the world." And we can do nothing, says George Eliot, "without the make-believe of a beginning" (3). The briefest chronicle, representation, diary entry, or most minimal narrative is scripted.

Consider Caesar's minimalism: I came, I saw, I conquered. The words, according to Plutarch, are expressed in an account Caesar made to a friend in Rome, on his swift defeat of Pharnaces (577). The narrative clauses, not cojoined by conjunctions, with no explicit causal connections, are as minimalist a narrative as possible, but not so simple: Through *parataxis,* the setting out of the independent clauses side by side with no conjunctions or subordinators, the narrator steps over time, land, space, men, horses. This is his version of the story. How many years? How many horses? From the first "coming" to the final "conquering," he has eclipsed time and space. He yokes the events together as he chooses: He is the hero, the teller of the tale—and the historian. His role is one of absolute certainty, absolute authority. There is no equivocation here, no hedging, no battle: this is the way it was.

To transform parataxis into *hypotaxis,* that is, to foreground and background the parts of the discourse, to fill in the gaps by exposing causal, temporal, logical connections, delimits the powers of the narrative:

- When I came, I saw, and, therefore, conquered.
- After I came, I subsequently saw, and consequently conquered.
- To conquer, I saw before I came.
- I came because I had seen what to conquer.
- I came so that I could see to conquer.
- Although I had come before I saw, I, nevertheless, conquered.

The narrators' interpretations, judgments, commentaries, and evaluations of the events they represent are either embedded or made explicit in the telling. In either case, they argue for their version of the story, for their construction of the world, for their sealing of history, for their principles for propagation. Implicit in their rendering is their allegiance to "it was worth it." As Forster puts it in his durable *Aspects of the Novel,* our lives are "composed of two lives," and our conduct "reveals a double allegiance," an allegiance both to time and to values: "I only saw her for five minutes, but it was worth it" (*Aspects* 28-29). In "The Narrativization of Real Events," Hayden White puts it this way:

> I assume we agree that narrativization is what Frederic Jameson calls "the central function or instance of the human mind" or a form of human comprehension that is productive of meaning by its imposition of a certain formal coherence on a virtual chaos of "events" which in themselves (or as given to perception) cannot be said to possess any particular form at all, much less the kind that we associate with "stories." The question is with what kind of meaning does storying endow these events which are the products of human agency? . . . (795)

The allegiance to values, to meaning, to what every story carries, either explicitly or implicitly, William Labov the sociolinguist calls *evaluation*: Evaluation is that textual threading within the narrative that shapes the telling so as to anticipate the listener's or reader's insistence that the story have a point, that there is a reason for its being told. In our culture, says Labov, we expect a story to have a point. We have little patience for the story that goes on and on and on. Because pointless stories are marked, we only remark on the story with no point: To remark on the "naturalness" of our expectations of stories having points, we need only think of a joke—any joke—without a punch line. But stories are not simply told to make a point. Nor are ways of telling universal.

Anyone who has heard a Trinidadian tell a story in *shit-talk* knows that the story is told, as a matter of course, to keep the floor, to mesmerize the audience with such magic, hyperbole, and derring-do that they will forget that fictions are being made as quickly as the teller can breathe them. Verbal display is the name of the game. In Navajo stories, as folklorist Barre Toelken tells us, outsiders are given only a glimpse of why stories are told: Narratives, for the participants, are used for nothing less than arguing matters of life or death. Stories have that kind of power. The linear story to make a point is only one way to tell a tale. The Hopi, says Leslie Marmon Silko, never begin at "the beginning," or end with what is typically marked as an ending. The story ends not with "and they lived happily ever after," but with "well, it has gone this far for a while" (88-89).

No matter how the tale is told or written, values will be inscribed, explicitly or implicitly. They may be declared outright, as Cruikshank does in his Cinderella, where he holds the tale captive for his "Temperance Truths," where he takes the tale to propagate his principles. Or evaluation may be embedded, disguised, or concealed in the way the story is told, in whose mouth the words are put into. Labov offers a scheme for looking at explicit and implicit evaluative techniques—insisting that the white middle class story is often "lame": The storyteller (who doesn't know *how* to tell a good story, he argues) gives away the point as if it were a punch line—explicitly. He claims that African American storytellers do otherwise: They make use of *implicit* evaluative devices and show rather than tell. (Shirley Brice Heath furthers Labov's argument in her study of African American and white storytellers in *Ways With Words.*)

But this is not the whole story about evaluation—to chart formal features and to rate the best and worst storytellers. Evaluation is an invitation for an exchange of values, a venture into a complex, multileveled, and often unpredictable dialogue. Narrative is inherently dialogic. The narrator plays a particular version of the tale, always in relation to what is told and what is not told, to those who are there and not there. Every act of history that tells of the past calls up role relationships within the representation and role relationships within the dialectic of telling. Halliday insists that all narrative—oral narratives ("traditional or spontaneous") and written texts, fictive and non-fictive—are "about as complex as it is possible for [a text] to be" (145-46) precisely because of the multileveled and dialogic interplays of role relationships within the social contexts represented within the tale, and within the telling itself.

In the tradition of the "well-reasoned" argument, we might say that the argument is out on the table; the conventions, if we expose them, rely on expectations we have about claims, warrants, evidence, logical fallacies, and how principles are to be propagated. But what of a "well-reasoned" narrative—or is that oxymoronic? Are there (logical) conventions of narrative? Can we say that argument is primarily a language of assertion? That narrative, as Todorov argues, is characterized by a rhetoric not of certainty but of the possible—a rhetoric of the *subjunctive* (*Poetics*; Bruner; Summerfield "Life"). The values carried are, likewise, embedded in metaphor, in "summonings," rhetorical gestures, subversions, omissions, silences, gaps, repetitions—what Toni Morrison calls "narrative gearshifts" (*Playing in the Dark* x). Morrison argues forcefully for reading the gaps, omissions, and silences in "master narratives," particularly in slave narratives which, to be published, had to straddle fences of telling and not telling, selection and omission, for the tellers were "playing in the dark," in uncharted rhetorical fields. Those mid-nineteenth-century narratives, she says, were written to say principally two things. One: "This is my historical life—my singular, special example that is personal, but that also represents the race." Two: "I write this text to persuade other people—you, the reader, who is probably not black—that we are human beings worthy of God's grace and the immediate abandonment of slavery." ("Site of Memory" 104-05)

Here, the persuasion is hardly outright, hardly Caesar's voice of absolute certainty and bravado; the most successful slave narratives avoided emotional display, so that an 1836 review praised one account this way: "We rejoice in the book the more, because it is not a partisan work . . . It broaches no theory in regard to [slavery], nor proposes any mode or time of emancipation" ("Site" 106). No explicit principles for propagation—the story is left to speak for itself.

Karl Kroeber, in his remarks on storytelling in (post) modern times, insists that "narrative's preeminent accomplishment is the articulation for contingent events without gainsaying their contingency" (qtd. in Hipsky, 431). Kroeber's reviewer Martin Hipsky explains:

On the simplest level, it means that no authentic storytelling—oral, written, visual, performed, or other—can ever be contained by a totality of extrinsic meaning. The accidents, the strangeness, the newness, the freedom of genuine story cannot be wholly assimilated by any conceptual system of exegesis. No form of expository discourse can fully "expose" the meaning of narrative. (431)

The *syntagmatic,* the laying out of contingencies through emplotment and through sequencing events, is one way of talking about narrative. The other, the *paradigmatic,* constitutes the system of values, beliefs, judgments, morals, and ideology, what Kroeber calls "intellectual, emotional, and ethical patternings," what I am here loosely calling the narrative's *principles,* cannot be pinned down—or exhausted.

"To raise the question of the nature of narrative," says Hayden White, "is to invite reflection on the very nature of culture and, possibly, even on the nature of humanity itself." The problem with narrative, as I have been urging, is that it is not seen as a problem. "So natural is the impulse to narrate," says White, "so inevitable is the form of narrative for any report of the way things really happened, that narrativity could appear problematic only in a culture in which it was absent—absent or, in some domains of contemporary Western intellectual and artistic culture, programmatically refused" (5). The problem with narrative arises when we read it as natural and as representing events as they really happened. White makes an important distinction: There is no sense in speaking of "events per se," he says, only "events under description," of the "storying" of events that are the products of human agency (795).

II

"Personal Porn"

> Don't forget the cardinal rule of showing not telling.
>
> *composition lore*

> Who are we, who is each of us, if not a combinatoria of experiences, information, books we have read, things imagined? Each life is an encyclopedia, a library, a series of styles, and everything can be constantly shuffled and reordered in every way conceivable.
>
> *Italo Calvino*
> Six Memos for the Next Millenium

Here is a story about a composition course, told in a fairly recent book for teachers about teaching. *Scenarios for Teaching Writing: Contexts for Discussion and Reflective Practice* offers lessons for teaching writing in the form of stories to learn from: Each scenario represents a classroom practice featuring an instructor, students, an assignment, and a problem, set before old and veteran teachers for discussion. What follows is a summary of one scenario titled "Personal Porn." The instructor, Chris Eastman (a fictitious name given by the editors), an adjunct faculty member for six years at a large university,

> always begins his courses with a personal narrative assignment. He believes that narrative helps students to think about their writing processes, and he likes the way he can rely on memories as occasions for introducing methods for discovering ideas, elaborating or exploring them, and then articulating them in vivid, stylish prose. (Anson 14)

But this time, the editors tell us, Eastman wanted to try something new, and although "he knew that model readings used for imitation have been out of fashion for some time in composition, and he knew that such modeling cannot be solidly supported theoretically," he decided, nonetheless, to "experiment a little," by asking students, in a first assignment, to select a reading by an author they would "like to model your own narrative on." The assignment then called for this:

In your own narrative, be sure to follow our in-class techniques for elaborating specific events and memories. Use especially the technique of taking generalized events and then listing specific features beneath them to embellish your memories. Try to *feel* the event or action; try to *see* it; try to *hear* it; try to *re-create and reexperience* it. The life of a narrative is in *detail*—don't forget the cardinal rule of showing, not telling. Please bring four *extra* copies of your rough draft on Friday. (Anson 14)

Of the four members of a peer-response group, one had written "a bland account of his grandmother's death"; another was a "sophomoric description of a summer job"; and a third detailed an expedition to a national park. The fourth, written by the only woman in the group, began like this:

I was living in a house with three guys and two girls in the summer of my third year after high school. We were all doing 'cid and smoking dope until our brains were nowhere, and this is a story about how I was introduced to group sex and learned to go down on men and women at the same time. At first going down on women and guys together was scary but then it started to blow my mind. (Anson 15)

The editors tell us that Eastman, on reading the piece, "felt mixed emotions": He was "taken aback," but eager "in an almost voyeuristic way, to read on." He was concerned that "Anna" had "taken too many liberties with his assignment." He wondered how the other three members of the group ("shy young men") would respond. He was "shocked to find . . . that she had described not one but six different sexual encounters with men and women." Finally, "he felt completely conflicted—aroused by Anna's erotic descriptions, amazed by her meticulous detail, thoroughly engaged in her unusual story, guilty that he had succumbed in this way, worried about his teacherly role, and utterly confused about how to respond" (Anson 15-16).

The editors leave us *in medias res,* with Eastman meeting the group in the cafeteria, with tension in the air, with Anna, "in high spirits" waiting eagerly for a group response, with Eastman "dazed," looking "tentatively" around the table and asking, "Okay, who wants to begin?" (Anson 15).

The scenario is here cut—faded out. The editors now invite our response to their questions for discussion, inviting us to identify with Eastman in that situation, to consider what is appropriate to write about in a class, to consider how texts may or may not be used as models. They suggest that instructors distinguish between models for writing and subjects for writing, and wonder if it is "appropriate to use professional readings as subject models." (Anna apparently had modeled her text after one she had read by Henry Miller.) They wonder if "highly constraining assignments" might "stifle creativity." They suggest that Anna's piece had "in fact, demonstrated all of Chris's criteria for successful narratives, including expertly elaborated descriptions," and wonder if he has any right to critique her choice of event to "practice these techniques."

What's Wrong with This Marriage?

The little scenario "Personal Porn" marries the real and the representational, the teller and the tale, the tale and its principles. The scenario is narrative; it also plays at being ethnography, at representing "real" events. James Clifford is useful here in calling ethnography a "performance emplotted by powerful stories." "Embodied within written reports," he says, are stories that "simultaneously describe real cultural events and make additional, moral, ideological, and even cosmological statements" (99). "Personal Porn" is performance in Clifford's sense of the word; it is a written report representing an informant's (the instructor's) representation of a real cultural event—a real composition class replete with assignments, rationales for assignments, real student writing, and representations of real conversations with real students. The editors are the tellers of the tale. They even set forth their guidelines for telling: names and teachers are fictitious; the situations may have been "slightly modified or elaborated," but the authors, who describe themselves as "experienced administrators of university writing programs and preparers of new teachers," have assembled "these scenarios from actual events that occurred in our own writing programs." They assure us that "the sample syllabi, assignments, papers, journal entries, and transcripts of group conferences are all real" (Anson x-xi).

Within the text, we have at least three stories: Anna's story framed within Eastman's story framed within the editors' story: What I want to look at simultaneously in all three are (a) the rhetoric about rhetoric implicated in the story, (b) the modes of emplotment and (c) the principles for propagation—that moral, ideological, evaluative commentary that is implied, tacit, and unstated, as Kroeber insists, even in the apparently "simplest" scenario.

Eastman's Story

Eastman's story is about an experiment that failed, resulting in a big surprise for the instructor, a response to his assignment that he hadn't expected. Eastman's narrative assignment, we are told, is meant to enable students "to think about their own writing processes"; they can "rely on memories as occasions for introducing methods for discovering ideas, elaborating or exploring them, and then articulating them in vivid, stylish prose." His "experimenting a little" calls for students to "model" their writing on a "professional narrative" that "may even be a piece of fiction, as long as there is a narrator who is describing a specific experience that happened to him or her."

He invites students to "embellish your memories." "Try to *feel* the event or action; try to *see* it; try to *hear* it; try to *re-create and reexperience* it. The life of a narrative is in detail—don't forget the cardinal rule of showing, not telling." But the assignment results in the production of either the bland or the sensational. What has gone wrong? We're invited to consider.

In treating narrative unproblematically, Eastman conflates life and text: Even in a fiction, he apparently asks students to assume a real writer having a real experience. Orwell really shot a real elephant. He assumes that writing personal narrative is a transparent act, an act of mimesis. That art = life. He assumes the classical notion that art/writing holds up a mirror to "reflect" life and that the writer is transcriber. That the "I" writing is naturalized, assumed authentic.

Memory is called on to work as an act of recreation, reexperience: what is *assigned* is a Proustian moment, but without the madeleine—again reducing narrative to a simple act. Remember: Try to feel the event; try to see it, hear it, try to recreate and reexperience it. Memory, though, is not so simple, and to consider narrative is to consider the complexity, the ineffability, elusiveness, instability, and unpredictability of memory. Proust reminds us that memory is not that tamable; it cannot simply be called up on demand. In *Swann's Way,* after Marcel's first bite of the madeleine, something moves within him, but as he tries and tries again to capture the past moment that has stirred within, to hold onto it, to get it back, he can't—it eludes him. He tries to unearth the association for he has recognized that something powerful has happened in that moment but doesn't know what—and *trying* makes it all the more impossible:

> I feel that there is much to be said for the Celtic belief that the souls of those whom we have lost are held captive in some inferior being, in an animal, in a plant, in some inanimate object, and thus effectively lost to us until the day (which to many never comes) when we happen to pass by the tree or obtain possession of the object which forms their prison. Then they start and tremble, they call us by our name, and as soon as we have recognized their voice the spell is broken. Delivered by us, they have overcome death and return to share our life.
>
> And so it is with our own past. It is a labour in vain to attempt to recapture it: all the efforts of our intellect must prove futile. The past is hidden somewhere

outside the realm . . . and it all depends on chance whether or not we come upon this object before we ourselves die (47-48).

To reckon with memory, says Gillian Beer (*Arguing*), is to look to what we remember *and* what we forget. To recognize the complexities of narrative is to reckon with the possibilities and impossibilities of memory, to reflect on how, what, and why we remember, to consider memory and time, and how time changes memories—and, often, the events themselves. Virginia Woolf writes of the "same" events some thirty years apart to find the events themselves feel different. What happened? The past eludes us. All we have is belatedness, deferral, *differance,* as Derrida puts it: The memory is not the event. And Walter Benjamin wonders, "Is not the involuntary recollection, Proust's *memoire involontaire* much closer to forgetting . . .?" (204).

Recreation is impossible. We can "feel" as if we're back there, feel as if we are reexperiencing, out of the books we read, out of the narrative imagination, but each version itself is a new event and a reworking of the past, another impersonation. To attempt to write the life, says Kierkegaard, is inexorably to live it backwards. In "Repetition: An Essay in Experimental Psychology," in fact, he describes an experiment with a deliberate *déjà vu,* with trying to go back to the same spot, the same place, to get himself in the moment of the past—and failing.

The writing up of the memory is an act of representation and not recreation—the difference is epistemological; *representation,* the word itself, holding cachet in this postmodern moment, with all the implications of multiplicity, multiple versions, voices, and multiple principles inherent in any act of representation—history, biography, memoir, ethnography, or our little scenario. Recreation takes us to a preSaussurean, preFreudian, preDerridian, preFoucaultian naïveté: that writing is not written, not language, not rhetoric. That it *is* possible to show and not tell.

Showing-not-telling, "a cardinal rule," is commonplace in the teaching of writing at all levels in composition courses, "creative" writing courses, and the teaching of literature. In the fairy tale, we would most likely concur with Dickens that the argument against drink should be shown, not told: Let the prince drink too much at his bachelor party, fall over backwards, break the glass slipper, and incite the wrath of the fairy godmother; and, embedded in the act, we could then, with a little help from Cruikshank, just in case we didn't get it, hear a bit about the evils of drink. Cruikshank jams the narrative machinery with his insistence on telling his Temperance Truths.

In privileging "showing" in our lore it may very well be that we have silenced the second allegiance—the life of values in story—and the potentialities, the narrative gearshifts, that can enable us to recognize how arguments are carried within narrative. Both allegiances can be explored through "detail," through showing rather than telling. But here again the "rule" needs to be problematized rather than accepted as "cardinal," and seen, most likely, as a vestige from the symbolists and their insistence on the image.[1]

Eastman's story also brings to the fore his presumed innocence about intertextuality: He sets up an occasion for modeling, for inviting students to imitate a text, as if it were possible to write without influence. Inescapably, texts are authored plurally: Bakhtin reminds us that "words carry with them places where they have been." Every word, he says,

> gives off the scent of a profession, a genre, a current, a party, a particular work, a particular man, a generation, an era, a day, and an hour. Every word smells of the context and contexts in which it has lived its intense social life. (qtd. in Todorov, *Bakhtin* 56)

Where Anna's story may come from I will consider next.

Anna's Story

> Madonna says we are nothing but masks.
>
> *Camille Paglia*
> Sex, Art, and the American Culture

Anna's story raises questions about dialogism or intertextuality, about the intersections between the public and the private, about popular narratives, their emplotments, and the values they carry, about verbal display and performance, and about how in the curious, liminal space of the composition class arise the increasing possibilities that Anna's story will increasingly appear.

The personal has become public: at the moment, there are 15 weekly talk shows, where we hear life as soap opera, life as personal porn. The public spaces for telling are multimedia events: Princess Diana tearfully announces in the public arena that she is extricating herself from the public gaze. She had not realized, she said, how the public would swallow her private life. She recovers, though, and learns to use the cameras to her advantage, seizing photo opportunities to announce before the cameras her terms for the divorce. The Queen of England renounces Diana's agreement—in public. Evangelist Jimmy Baker tearfully confesses his extramarital transgressions before millions. O. J. Simpson tries to rehabilitate his image on videotape, to tell his side of the story. Hugh

Grant apologizes to Elizabeth Hurley on Letterman, Leno, and the *Today* show. The confessional, telling *my side of the story,* the psychoanalytic couch, are painted large. This is the age of washing one's dirty linen on television.

My students, many of whom live on Long Island, have followed the Amy Fisher/Joey Buttafuoco saga. Several of them spotted the Buttafuocos at a Broadway show last year, surrounded by eager fans. These same students watch, too, the latest on Michael Jackson and Lisa Marie, and on O. J., Nicole, Marsha Clark, Judge Ito, and Kato Kaelin. They watch the latest on the failures of the princes and princesses of the British Isle. Of ordinary citizens we hear of incest, child abuse, homosexuality, bisexuality, transsexuality, pedophilia, drug addiction, teenage pregnancies. Last week, incidentally, eleven people were killed in New York City, the most ever recorded killed on one night. Last week, a Long Island couple buried their infant daughter alive.

If we treat narrative as transparent, as life, and not text, then we shouldn't be surprised if students turn up more and more personal porn, personal confession: This is the age of the talk show, of spilling the beans, of pathography, as Joyce Carol Oates puts it—the term she gives to "a new literary genre," biographies whose "motifs are dysfunction and disaster, illnesses and pratfalls, failed marriages and failed careers, alcoholism and breakdowns and outrageous conduct" (Atlas 1). Taboos of polite bourgeois culture are broken down and televised daily: The secrets of the bedroom, perversion, deviancy, incest, and abuse are no longer secret. The "personal self" presented to us on the interviewer's couch, in the student paper, needs to be read as performance, as an event under a description. To understand such descriptions, such inscribings of personae in public spaces, we need to historicize, to turn to the "sources of the self," and the making of identity and to constructs of the natural, the authentic, and the sincere. For such explorations, which are beyond the scope of this paper, philosophers Ian Hacking and Charles Taylor are useful, as is Foucault in *The History of Sexuality,* and Lester Faigley in his applications of postmodern theory to the teaching of composition, particularly as he looks at the "practice of writing about the self in college composition . . . as part of a much larger technology of confession for the production of truth in Western societies" (23).

The problem, then, with Eastman's assignment is that it calls for the uncritical reading of the "personal" and of narrative. What I'm suggesting here is that the "personal," the private, has become public—in the popular narratives displayed before us. Our students don't need to read *The Tropic of Cancer* to know what it's about: Oprah, Geraldo, Sally, and Ricki Lake will do just fine. How do these negotiations between "personal stories" and media discourse take place? This is the question that Marjorie Perloff asks in *Radical*

Artifice, where she considers what happens to the writing of poetry in the "Age of the Media," when the natural speech model of Modernism comes up against the natural speech of the talk show, where no word can escape the scent from the media landscape in which we live. We can expect fewer and fewer Cinderella stories where our Cinderella is innocent and true, and where the prince knows precisely how to recognize the girl of his dreams. The stories our students hear propagate the already given, the packaged, the normative stories of the cultures they live in: If we want them to do more than to spout the already given—to give more than the it-will-all-work-out-all-right maxims of greeting cards that popular narratives carry, then we'll have to enable them to recognize, understand, study, historicize, and interpret the principles that popular narratives carry with them, and to critique, challenge, and resist them.

Perhaps that is precisely what Anna is doing—resisting.

We don't know at all what Anna is up to. We don't know if she is simply seeing what the boys will say, shaking things up a bit. We don't know if she is resisting the assignment on showing-not-telling by showing off; we don't know if she is writing parody, fantasy, or fiction. We don't know if she shot the elephant at all, if the events represented are "real." We don't know if she is engendering the subject, appropriating it for a feminist agenda, casting the narrator into a Madonna-like role. We don't know what role she is playing, what mask she is wearing. We don't know about her motives for constructing the "I" as she did. She may be "the feminist of the fin de siecle," as that academic rapper Camille Paglia would say: "bawdy, streetwise, and on-the-spot confrontational, in the prankish Sixties way" (7).

We do know, however, how she is read by the tellers of the tale—the editors—and it is to their story that I now turn.

The Editors' Story

Their story-telling voice, also represented unproblematically, is uncritical, nonself-reflexive. They do not recognize themselves as taking on an ethnographic role, as representing performance, even though they admit to representing a real class, real assignments, real instructors, real students, real events. They do not recognize the emplotment, the ways they have chosen to tell the story, that they are writers writing Eastman's story about Anna's story. Their role is omniscient narration, and that is the problem. Omniscient narration has slipped imperceptibly into the norm of contemporary journalism. Newspaper writing, even in the ostensible "report," has become all-knowing and all-judging, and we have come to accept, uncritically, these god-like moves as conventional.

"Personal Porn," at first glance, caught my eye—it is, after all, the editors' selection of a title, meant to what? Startle, provoke, arouse—as the teaser in the talk show: This is real life soap opera. Throughout, the editors impute motives to their characters. Eastman is simultaneously taken aback, shocked, aroused, amazed, engaged, guilty, worried, utterly confused.

Whose words? Knowledge or judgment?

The three young men are "all from rural settings and seemed rather young and naive." "None . . . had visited a large city more than once or twice." One, John Campo, had written the "bland account of his grandmother's death." Keith Jackson had written "an equally sophomoric description of a summer job," and Richard Wilson wrote of an expedition to a national park. As Eastman is reading Anna's paper in the cafeteria, "he also wonders how the three shy young men would respond." As they are waiting to begin the conference, "Chris noticed that the three men were making little eye contact with him, with each other, or with Anna" (15-16).

Anna, on the other hand, is a woman of the world: she "had lived all her life in the city and was worldly-wise and street-smart." The details she uses to describe her "six different sexual encounters with men and women," say the editors, "would make the most explicit pornographic magazines sound like Winnie-the-Pooh" (15).

When she arrives at the cafeteria, she "drops her books confidently on the table." All are stymied, unable to respond, but Anna "seemed in high spirits and had displayed the papers and revision guides around her in anticipation of a lively and fruitful discussion" (15).

And finally: "Still dazed, Chris looked tentatively around the table. 'Okay,' he asked, 'who wants to begin?' "

Whose words are these? Eastman's? The editors'? And what are the motives? (If Anna's piece is a "real piece of writing," did the editors seek permission to print her writing—or to tell the story they tell about her that they do?) What genre are we in? Fiction or nonfiction? Report or research? Where do the quotation marks belong?

Why tell the story this way? What principles—what values, innuendos, emplotments—does the large frame story carry?

Can Anna (we use first names for students—for *subjects*) speak for herself?

Why didn't the editors give as matter-of-fact a chronology as they could: Eastman gave this assignment and this is what he got?

What is clear from the editors' rendering of Anna is that she is no Cinderella, as Cruikshank would have fashioned her. Cruikshank's agenda for Cinderella is made explicit but our editors' agenda is not. What I find particularly troubling are the ways in which Anna and her text are appropriated for this story—the emplotment sets up a struggle between a confident, city-smart, worldly-wise woman—a temptress—and three helpless, rural, shy young men and their dazed instructor. We are left with the image of her lording her confidence over them in "high spirits," waiting for the three young men and their instructor to be revived. A tale of innocence and experience.

What also interests me is this: I wonder if a male student would have been so cast—or if his story would have been so shocking. Anna's story, apparently, is successful in its explicitness, its "showing," its arousing Eastman's voyeurism, confusion, and so forth. The piece appears to have been about hedonism, boundaries crossed, bisexuality, drugs—about the carnivalesque, in the best Rabelaisian sense of the word. Ribaldry, hilarity, the grotesque, fun, excess, danger.

Perhaps this is a story, then, about female sexuality; perhaps the text being imitated is not Henry Miller, per se, but a cultural female equivalent who, as John Fiske puts it, "consistently parodies conventional representations of women, and parody can be an effective device for interrogating the dominant ideology" (105). More important, for my purposes here, this version of a woman "enables girls [sic] to see that the meanings of feminine sexuality can be in their control, can be made in their interests, and that their subjectivities are not necessarily totally determined by the dominant patriarchy" (107).

The Buttafuocos and Amy Fisher (who is in prison) are embattled over the "real" version of their story: Last year during the same week, three versions of Amy Fisher appeared in three different television movies starring three different versions of Amy:

> On CBS, she is a delusional temptress inexplicably determined to kill the wife of the kindly auto mechanic who fixes her car . . . . On NBC she is a confused kid who accidentally shot her lover's wife. And on ABC, she is a spoiled brat who may or may not have intended to kill the wife of the possible heel she may or may not have been sleeping with. (Henneberger 27)

In each, she is in the hands of the teller of the tale, just as Anna and Eastman are in the hands of the tellers of their tale, and we are left with images and innuendo—with what has been shown rather than told of a dazed instructor, three shy young men, and a confident, worldly-wise temptress.

The composition classroom is a curious nexus of the public and the private, particularly in this moment when talk-show culture promotes telling all in lurid detail and we, in composition, promote show-not-tell or, worse, "self-disclosure," or promote personal writing because we believe that it will be healing or transformative or promote personal growth. We need to scrutinize our own complex values, motives, principles, and ideologies for asking students to write in this hybrid form under the description "personal narrative," which is mostly peculiar to the composition classroom. What are our own normative stories, our agendas, our values for our students' stories?[2] I wonder: If Anna had represented her exploits as transgressions, would she have been forgiven? If she had written confession and called for redemption, would Eastman have been so thrown? What I am suggesting is that the "story" was one thing; the fact that she enjoyed herself, quite another. Our normative stories for students writing personal narratives in the composition course insist on the values current in these narratives: learning through suffering, vowing to change, being transformed, learning a lesson, and promising never to do it again.

III

In a recent article in *The Chronicle of Higher Education,* an English instructor and two psychologists raise disturbing questions about the "ethics of requiring students to write about their personal lives." In an age where some psychologists report that nearly one third of all women students have been sexually assaulted at one point in their lives, where more and more students have suffered traumatic experiences—deaths of parents, suicides of friends, violent or random killings, car accidents, robbery, drug addictions, sexual crimes, eating disorders—we cannot assume that the content of such writings will be safe, idyllic, or pastoral. What are we doing as instructors when we ask students for self-disclosure, for self-revelation, Susan Swartzlander, Diana Pace, and Virginia Lee Stamler ask. "Everyday in college classrooms . . . across the country, students receive writing assignments requiring inappropriate self-revelation" (Swartzlander, Pace, and Stamler B1).

What are the ethics of grading writings that are "tied to self-revelation"? Do the most emotionally charged writings earn the best grades? How can students be expected in such assignments that blur the boundaries between the personal and the public to know "how much to say and to whom"? What happens if victims of abuse "allow themselves to be emotionally vulnerable with others"? Maybe "course assignments that demand self-disclosure can intensify a student's feelings of abuse and powerlessness." What positions of power might instructors enjoy when students' vulnerabilities are disclosed? Might men, given that they are presumably "social[ized] to disavow emotion," be at a decided disadvantage when given such assignments"? (Swartzlander, Pace, and Stamler B2). They also raise questions about using students' writings—with colleagues and in print—without permission and about requiring students to read their work aloud in the classroom. They claim that their counseling center regularly sees students who have been asked to write self-disclosures in classes.

These are alarming concerns—more and more pressing in this talk-show culture, in this age of pathography. This is an age, too, of debate about the possible damaging effects of disclosure, and about repressed childhood memories that are evoked, provoked, or suggested by therapists. Elizabeth Kolbert, in an article in the *New York Times,* "When Baring All to 4 Million Viewers Doesn't Help," describes the "aftercare" program that "Geraldo" set up for the "victims of post-talk show stress" (2). No stretch of the imagination is needed to see a lawsuit against a composition instructor for *requiring* a student to write a self-revealing piece that is then claimed to have caused emotional damage.

Should we insist, then, that "personal narrative," autobiography, or memoir, be banned from writing courses?

No, but as I have been saying throughout, the words we use to represent writing represent, ineluctably, the ways that we see writing; we, ourselves, need to find ways to read our own fixed assumptions, our own epistemological and ontological constructs, the ways we read the personal and the public, and the ways we read narrative for normative stories, for master narratives, for arguments, for the principles they carry, for the pronoun "I," for questions about *propria persona* and role and voice. We must be vigilant against the temptation to read life as text. Eastman would never have gotten himself into such a quandary had he not done so. Inevitably, in any assignment we are likely to find the text that attempts to shock: Anna's text apparently succeeded in shocking the instructor. A productive exploration might then be: What shocks?

This in an age where we are continually, daily, being bombarded with images of the shocking. Philip Roth laid the question before writers thirty years ago:

And what is the moral of the story? Simply this: that the American writer in the middle of the twentieth century has his hands full in trying to understand, describe, and then make credible much of American reality. It stupefies, it sickens, it infuriates, and finally it is even a kind of embarrassment to one's meager imagination. The actuality is continually outdoing our talents, and the culture tosses up figures almost daily that are the envy of any novelist. (176)

We need, then, to enable students to read these frames—to recognize patterns and principles, to read the fairy tales in our popular narratives, which very well may be tales of recovery against all odds, tales of acceptance, transformation, change, and hope against the backdrop of violence, randomness and the possibility of individual acts of heroism in an age where 250 million private citizens own handguns. Maybe, as one psychiatrist, Charles Krauthammer, has suggested, in this age of increasing violence we confess domestic crimes because, at least, we can have a sense of having some control by talking about *personal* crimes when we feel so helpless in the face of such pervasive violence.

Cruikshank kidnapped Cinderella for his own devices, to make his Temperance Truths. Maybe as the outer landscapes of our lives become more and more treacherous, the stories about our own struggles to gain control give us the sermons that we need. To dismiss the powers, pervasiveness, and problems of narrative would be unfortunate: We need to learn how to raise to the level of the metatextual, the metacritical, the ways we tacitly make stories, to reckon with the narratives in daily life, folklore, journalism, anthropology, psychoanalysis, history, geology, physics, art, linguistics, and psychology with the historical and transhistorical of narrative, the cultural and transcultural, the literary and the popular, and always with language—with how things happen on the page.

We need to reckon with the double allegiances of time and value, those two inextricably intertwined threads in every narrative, and with the principles threading every narrative—the arguments, either explicit or implicit. We can represent that "threading" through any variety of lenses. One of my colleagues, the novelist Bette Ann Moskowitz, talks about the messages in narrative as "spinach": the sermons that are supposed to be good for you. Cruikshank gives us his message—his spinach—raw, uncooked, fresh from the garden, and laid on the plate of his fairy tale. We can't miss it.

Nor can we miss it in Dickens or George Eliot. Moskowitz much prefers the modernist move—the showing, not telling; the spinach is pureed, we hardly know it's there, only a taste. Or the metafictive, from Sterne's *Tristam Shandy* to Calvino's *If on a Winter's Night a Traveler,* where we get the recipes for cooking narratives, the principles of cooking. We can put the writerly options before students, giving even to freshmen in a composition course literary history and theory so that they can understand the various moves writers can make. These become questions for writers that have nothing to do with self-disclosure, self-revelation, re-creation, or authenticity. These are questions about role and voice, about versions, about choices of evaluative techniques, about making arguments implicit or explicit, about reading, critiquing, resisting normative stories, about history and language.

Joan Didion, in a passage from her *White Album* that I keep returning to, insists on that double threading within narrative of time and value, story and argument, narrative clause and evaluation, raw and cooked spinach. She talks about the need for the sermon, for the social and the moral lesson, for interpretation:

> We tell ourselves stories in order to live. The princess is caged in the consulate. The man with the candy will lead the children into the sea. The naked woman on the ledge outside the window on the sixteenth floor is a victim of accidie, or the naked woman is an exhibitionist, and it would be "interesting" to know which. We tell ourselves that it makes some difference whether the naked woman is about to commit a mortal sin or is about to register a political protest or is about to be, in the Aristophanic view, snatched back to the human condition by the fireman in priest's clothing just visible in the window behind her, the one smiling at the telephoto lens. We look for the sermon in the suicide, for the social or moral lesson in the murder of five. We interpret what we see, select the most workable of the multiple choices. We live entirely, especially if we are writers, by the imposition of a narrative line upon disparate images, by the "ideas" with which we have learned to freeze the shifting phantasmagoria which is our actual experience. (11)

The narratives these days, though, do not present themselves for easy lessons, for easy sermons, or, as Moskowitz might put it, for frozen spinach: There are images, perplexing, horrific, catastrophic, unrelentless, that do not, says Didion, "fit any narrative I knew" (13). There are possibilities, unnumbered, for us to explore in the texts we and our students write.

Coda

In the writing of this piece, theory has been implicated into the practice of teaching an experimental course at Queens College, part of the Freshman Year Initiative (FYI) that I have been codirecting over the past several years. Faculty from all the divisions at the college are engaged in teaching experimental freshman courses and in considering what kind of job we are doing to "initiate" students into the university.

Two teaching assistants and I began the composition course with Hemingway's *In Our Time,* with questions about storytelling after World War I. I have been intrigued by Walter Benjamin's insistence that storytelling changed after the war, that tales of the hero on horseback became tales of mutism at the horrors of trench warfare. (Benjamin puts it this way: "Was it not noticeable at the end of the war that men returned from the battlefield grown silent . . . " [84].) Mutism during and after World War I is explored in extraordinary detail in Pat Barker's non-fictive novel, *Regeneration* and is also a subject of the 1995 period film, *The Englishman Who Went Up a Hill but Came Down a Mountain.*

How did the young Hemingway, not far removed in age from these freshmen, represent, in the aftermath of the war, his time? He is at the very same time wiring cables to the *Toronto Star* about what he sees in the wreckage of the war, in the chaos of the Greek-Turkish War. He is using that same material to write the interchapters in *In Our Time.* The course attends to questions about genre and about fiction and nonfiction, to the construction of the "I" in any piece of writing, to the weight of an adverb, to parataxis in advertisements, to metaphor and metonymy, to hypotaxis in the op-ed page, to representations in movies and films, to reading symbols, images, parody in popular culture, to talk-show talk, to relationships between the oral and the written, to poetry, to fairy tales, to normative stories, to role-relationships, to doing research, to writing as a participant or a spectator, and to memory and forgetting.

We end the course with a final assignment—an invitation to represent a bit of "your own life and times, in any genre—memoir, short fiction, research, critical analysis, etc.—you choose." Students are asked to include representation and interpretation—time and value, the double allegiance. These are some of the guidelines they are offered:

1. The representation is not the event.
2. The memory is not the event.
3. To be "personal," you don't have to "be" personal, that is, to lose control, to spill the beans, to confess, to say what you don't want to say.
4. The "I" of your piece will be an invention, a fiction.
5. You're always a writer choosing.
6. Writers write to readers: You might want to invent an audience, a letter, say, to a daughter, a son. Consider why you're telling: You're coming, say, to the end of your life and you're looking back, you want to amuse a friend in need, you're trying to understand the past so as to prepare for the future.
7. There is the fish and there is the stream. This is how Virginia Woolf puts it:

Consider what immense forces society brings to play upon each of us, how that society changes from decade to decade; and also from class to class; well, if we cannot analyze these invisible presences, we know very little of the subject of the memoir; and again how futile life-writing becomes. I see myself as a fish in a stream; deflected; held in place; but cannot describe the stream ("A Sketch of the Past" 80).

8. Beware of the pull of the easy narrative close: "and this is an event that changed my life." That's the typical how-I-spent-my-summer-vacation ending, isn't it? That isn't to say that some events aren't pretty big in our lives, but is it the event that changed a life? Yes, sometimes, of course, but isn't it also the ways we read, interpret, make sense of, what happens to us? Take into account the visible presences and the invisible presences. The life and the times. Time and value.

9. Consider this: How would you write about your life metaphorically? My life is a _____? A river? A journey? A what?

10. Consider this: The memoir is generally written by those who have lived a long time. Is it, therefore, ridiculous to ask you to write anything like an autobiographical sketch or a memoir?

11. Consider this: Writing about oneself is the most difficult of tasks—that's why we're ending the course with this challenge. You've had a chance to consider differences between fiction and nonfiction. Is the memoir a piece of fiction or nonfiction? Ostensibly, it is based on what happened, but remember, you are the bearer of the tale, and you can tell the story in whatever way you choose.

12. Our agreement as readers will be that we will not be allowed to ask: Did this *really* happen?

13. Consider this: E. M. Forster says, "Only connect" (*Howard's End* i). We can use writing to connect a shoelace and a rainbow, if we want to. Consider not only one but also several moments to link up, to tie together, to connect. One from the past, one from the present, etc. How do you relate them?

14. Consider this: Virginia Woolf says that when we write about ourselves, we call into play an "I now" with an "I then" (75).

15. Consider the roles of the participant and the spectator. One form might be to represent events in the role of participant and to step back and reflect on them via the role of the spectator. You can try parataxis in the role of the participant. Go hypotactic in the role of the spectator.

16. Remember spinach: It can be cooked or raw. The interpretation, argument, commentary, evaluation can be explicit—raw; or it can be cooked, pureed, sauteed, fried, sprinkled throughout the whole.

17. Remember Hemingway's iceberg theory: He wrote it all in, and then took out what he wanted the reader to sense, to feel "the underwater part of the iceberg" (*On Writing* 43).

18. Consider this: Hugh Brody, an Irish villager in Henry Glassie's book, *Passing the Time in Ballymenone,* says, "Stories, they're all fictions, they're always made up" (37).

19. You don't have to write about the extraordinary, about the big events: You can take a moment, an image, an insight, and try to represent it and reflect on it.

20. Consider this: Men, like poets, rush "into the middest," *in medias res,* when they are born; they also die *in mediis rebus,* and to make sense of their span they need

fictive concords with origins and ends, such as give meaning to lives and to poems (Kermode 7). Remember that you're writing a poem and not a life.

21. Consider this—you, the writer, can enter into the role of a frog, if you want to, or of Cinderella's fairy godmother; you can be "plastic," as Italo Calvino puts it:

> Who are we, who is each of us, if not a combinatoria of experiences, information, books we have read, things imagined? Each life is an encyclopedia, a library, a series of styles, and everything can be constantly shuffled and reordered in every way conceivable. [You can] escape the limited perspective of the individual ego, not only to enter into selves like our own but to give speech to that which has no language, to the bird perching on the edge of the gutter, to the tree in spring and the tree in fall, to stone, to cement, to plastic. (124)

To prepare for the final assignment, we told stories in class and then translated the oral to the written; we told and then wrote several versions of the "same" event, the same memory. We explored the ways that memory is triggered—I find that students are fascinated by explorations of memory and forgetting, the ways they attach language to events. We considered metaphors for a life. Several emerged that students then explored in their writings: a river, silence, cooking, a piano, an iceberg, sandpaper, cloud, fog.

We then read several versions of Cinderella, including the Perrault, Grimm, and Cruikshank.

Gillian Beer in *Arguing with the Past: Essays in Narrative from Woolf to Sidney,* talks about the hermeneutical power of narrative and the multiple possible futures of a story, about how stories do not stay inside their own covers, and the "hermeneutical network" in which the reader participates in a narrative, about the immensely detailed interconnecting systems of texts and (203) the speculative space the reader/writer can enter into, the "perpetual presence of narrative" (Todorov's term, in *Poetics* 132), the novelty of each telling, and the occasions for argument, for making the story our own, suiting our own needs. "Understanding begins," Beer quotes Gadamer, "when something addresses us" (*Arguing* 2). And narratives address us. Narratives

> do not have fixed limits. They reach us double freighted with debate; the argument, engagements, and estrangements, within which they are embedded at the time of the work's production, the arguments, estrangements, and engagements within which we read [and write] now. (*Arguing* 2-3)

And, finally, narratives entice us to hold them captive, to make them our own, for our own devices, our own principles. As Beer insists: "the perpetual presence of narrative allows fresh participation on each occasion of reading"—and of writing.

Notes

1. William Empson is useful here in his comments on "argufying," perhaps a "tiresomely playful word," he admits, but he distinguishes it as "the kind of arguing we do in ordinary life, usually to get our own way; I do not mean nagging by it, but just a not specially dignified sort of arguing." He agrees that "conscientious uses of logic could become a distraction from poetry," but in the symbolist movement, the rule—"that a poet must never say what he wants to say directly," must only hint at it "by metaphors, which are then called images," has now become an obstacle, a way, says Empson, "of fostering evasiveness and false suggestions," and of being "completely out of touch with another tradition, fair debate" (167-68).

2. Lacan in his "Intervention on Transference," points out that Freud had a very clear sense of what he hoped for Dora. Dora, one of his first cases, had been "approached" by an older man, who, as it turned out, was the husband of Dora's father's mistress. In a particularly pregnant footnote, Freud laments Dora's disinclination; after all, he says, "I happen to know Herr K . . . and he was still young and of prepossessing appearance" (Freud 44). Freud quite apparently had an agenda, a normative story for Dora—even after the breakdown of treatment, as Lacan says, "Freud persists in dreaming of a 'triumph of love' " (Lacan 69).

Works Cited

Anson, Chris, Joan Graham, David A. Jollife, Nancy S. Shapiro, Carolyn H. Smith, Eds. *Scenarios for Teaching Writing: Contexts for Discussion and Reflective Practice.* Urbana, IL: NCTE, 1993.

Atlas, James. *"Speaking Ill of the Dead." New York Times Book Review* 2 Oct. 1988, Sec. VII, ii; 1.

Barker, Pat. *Regeneration.* London: Penguin, 1991.

Beer, Gillian. *Darwin's Plots: Evolutionary Narrative in Darwin, George Eliot and Nineteenth-Century Fiction.* London: Routledge & Kegan Paul, 1983.

———. *Arguing with the Past: Essays in Narrative from Woolf to Sidney.* London: Routledge, 1989.

Benjamin, Walter. *Illuminations.* London: Fontana, 1970.

Britton, James. *Prospect and Retrospect.* Ed. Gordon Pradl. Montclair, New Jersey: Boynton/Cook, 1982.

Bruner, Jerome. *Actual Minds, Possible Worlds.* Cambridge: Harvard University Press, 1986.

Burke, Kenneth. *The Philosophy of Literary Form: Studies in Symbolic Action.* New York: Vintage, 1957.

Calvino, Italo. *Six Memos for the Next Millennium.* Cambridge, MA: Harvard University Press, 1988.

Clifford, James. "On Ethnographic Allegory." *Writing Culture: The Poetics and Politics of Ethnography.* Ed. James Clifford and George E. Marcus. Berkeley: University of California Press, 1986.

Cruikshank, George. *Fairy Library.* London: David Bogue, 1854.

Dickens, Charles. "Frauds Upon the Fairies." *Household Words* 184: 1 Oct. 1853, 97-100.

———. "Letter to W. H. Wills, July 27, 1853." *The Book Illustrations of George Cruikshank.* Ed. John Buchanan-Brown. London: David & Charles, 1980.

Didion, Joan. *The White Album.* New York: Simon & Schuster, 1979.

Eliot, George. "Daniel Deronda." *The Works of George Eliot.* Vol. I. London: Cabinet Edition, 1878-80.

Empson, William. *Argufying: Essays on Literature and Culture.* Ed. John Haffenden. Iowa City: University of Iowa Press, 1986.

Ewald, Helen Rothschild. "Waiting for Answerability: Bakhtin and Composition Studies." *College Composition and Communication* 44 (Oct. 1993): 331-49.

Faigley, Lester. *Fragments of Rationality: Postmodernity and the Subject of Composition.* Pittsburgh, PA: University of Pittsburgh Press, 1992.

Fiske, John. *Reading the Popular.* Boston: Unwin Hyman, 1989.

Forster, E. M. *Howard's End.* New York: Signet, 1910/1992.

———. *Aspects of the Novel.* New York: Harcourt Brace, 1954.

Foucault, Michel. *The History of Sexuality: An Introduction.* Vol. I. Trans. Robert Hurley. New York: Vintage, 1978.

Freud, Sigmund. *Dora: An Analysis of a Case of Hysteria.* New York: Collier, 1963.

Glassie, Henry. *Passing the Time in Ballymenone.* Philadelphia: University of Pennsylvania Press, 1982.

Hardy, Barbara. *Tellers and Listeners: The Narrative Imagination.* London: The Athlone Press, 1975.

Halliday, M. A. K. *Language as Social Semiotic: The Social Interpretation of Language and Meaning.* London: Edward Arnold, 1978.

Heath, Shirley Brice. *Ways With Words.* Cambridge, MA: Cambridge University Press, 1983.

Hemingway, Ernest. *In Our Time.* New York: Scribners, 1925.

———. *Ernest Hemingway on Writing.* Ed. Larry W. Phillips. New York: Grafton Books, 1984.

Henneberger, Melinda. "Like Ya Nev-ah Seen It Before: TV's Fisher Movies Create Amy-villes That Never Were." *New York Times* 3 Jan. 1993, Sec. L, 27.

Hipsky, Martin A. "Karl Kroeber, *Retelling/Rereading: The Fate of Storytelling in Modern Times.*" *Modern Language Quarterly* 54 (Sept. 1993): 431-34.

Jakobson, Roman. "Closing Statement: Linguistics and Poetics." *Style in Language.* Ed. Thomas A. Seboek. Cambridge, MA: M.I.T. Press, 1969.

Jameson, Frederic. *The Political Unconscious: Narrative as a Socially Symbolic Act.* Ithaca, NY: Cornell University Press, 1981.

Kermode, Frank. *The Sense of an Ending: Studies in the Theory of Fiction.* New York: Oxford, 1966.

Kierkegaard, Soren. "Repetition." *A Kierkegaard Anthology.* Ed. Robert Bretall. Princeton, NJ: Princeton University Press, 1946.

Kolbert, Elizabeth. "When Baring All to 4 Million Viewers Doesn't Help." *The New York Times* 18 July 1993, Sec. 4, 2.

Krauthammer, Charles. "Defining Deviancy Up." *The New Republic* 22 Nov. 1993: 20-25.

Labov, William. *Language in the Inner City.* Philadelphia: University of Pennsylvania Press, 1972.

Lacan, Jacques. "Intervention on Transference." In *Feminine Sexuality: Jacques Lacan and the ecole freudienne.* Ed. Juliet Mitchell and Jacqueline Rose. New York: Norton, 1982.

Leith, Dick, and George Myerson. *The Power of Address: Explorations in Rhetoric.* London: Routledge, 1989.

Morrison, Toni. "The Site of Memory." In *Inventing the Truth: The Art and Craft of Memory.* Ed. William Zinsser. Boston: Houghton Mifflin, 1987.

———. *Playing in the Dark: Whiteness and the Literary Imagination.* Cambridge, MA: Harvard, 1992.

Paglia, Camille. *Sex, Art, and American Culture.* New York: Vintage, 1992.

Perloff, Marjorie. *Radical Artifice: Writing Poetry in the Age of the Media.* Chicago: University of Chicago Press, 1992.

Plutarch. *The Lives of the Noble Grecians and Romans.* Trans. John Dryden and Rev. Arthur Hugh Clough. New York: Encyclopaedia Britannica, 1952.

Proust, Marcel. *Remembrances of Things Past.* Trans. C. K. Scott Moncrieff and Terence Kilmartin. New York: Vintage, 1981.

Roth, Philip. "Writing American Fiction." *Reading Myself and Others*. New York: Farrar, Straus & Giroux, 1975.

Silko, Leslie Marmon. "Language and Literature from a Pueblo Indian Perspective." *Critical Fictions: The Politics of Imaginative Writing*. Ed. Philomena Mariani. Seattle, WA: Bay Press, 1991.

Summerfield, Judith. "Framing Narratives." *Only Connect: Uniting Reading and Writing*. Ed. Thomas Newkirk. Montclair, New Jersey: Boynton/Cook, 1986. 227-240.

———. "Is There a Life in This Text?" in *Writing Theory and Critical Theory*. Ed. John Clifford and John Schilb. New York: Modern Language Association, 1994.

Summerfield, Judith, and Geoffrey Summerfield. *Frames of Mind: A Course in Composition*. New York: Random House, 1986.

———. *Texts and Contexts: A Contribution to the Theory and Practice of Composition*. New York: Random House, 1986.

———. "States of Mind, Acts of Mind, Forms of Discourse: Towards a Provisional Pragmatic Framework." *Territory of Language: Linguistics, Stylistics, and the Teaching of Composition*. Ed. Donald McQuade. Carbondale: Southern Illinois University Press, 1986. 238-50.

Swartzlander, Susan, Diana Pace, and Virginia Lee Stamler. "The Ethics of Requiring Students to Write about Their Personal Lives." *The Chronicle of Higher Education* 17 Feb. 1993, B1-B2.

Taylor, Charles. *Sources of the Self: The Making of the Modern Identity*. Cambridge, MA: Harvard, 1981.

———. *The Ethics of Authenticity*. Cambridge, MA: Harvard, 1991.

Todorov, Tzvetan. *The Poetics of Prose*. New York: Oxford, 1977.

———. *Mikhail Bakhtin: The Dialogical Principle*. Trans. Wlad. Godrich. Minneapolis: University of Minnesota Press, 1984.

Toelken, Barre. "Life and Death in the Navajo Coyote Tales." *Recovering the Word: Essays on Native American Literature*. Ed. Brian Swann and Arnold Krupat. Berkeley: University of California Press, 1987.

White, Hayden. "The Value of Narrativity in the Representation of Reality." *Critical Inquiry* 7 (Autumn 1980): 5-29.

———. "The Narrativization of Real Events." *Critical Inquiry* 8 (Summer 1981): 795.

Woolf, Virginia. *Moments of Being*. New York: Harcourt Brace, 1976.

Wordsworth, William. *The Prelude, 1799, 1805, 1850*. Ed. Jonathan Wordsworth, M. H. Abrams and Stephen Gill. New York: Norton Critical Edition, 1979.

8

The "Argument of Reading" in the Teaching of Composition

Mariolina Salvatori
University of Pittsburgh

The art of dialectic is not the art of being able to win every argument . . .
Dialectic, as the art of asking questions, proves itself only because the person
who knows how to ask questions is able to persist in his questioning . . . The
art of questioning . . . i.e. the art of thinking . . . is called "dialectic," for it
is the art of conducting a real conversation . . . . To conduct a conversation
means to allow oneself to be conducted by the object to which the partners
in the conversation are directed. It requires that one does not try to out-argue
the other person, but that one really considers the weight of the other's
position . . . .

Hans-Georg Gadamer
Truth and Method

AUTHOR'S NOTE: This essay is a revision of a lecture I delivered at the University of Oregon's
Annual Conference on Composition and Rhetoric (April 1992). That lecture was itself a revision
of a talk I had given at the Conference of College Composition and Communication the previous
year. I would like to take this opportunity to thank John Gage, Jim Crosswhite and their graduate
students for being interested in my work. I would also like to thank Dave Bartholomae for the
ways in which he "understands my texts," and the editors of this volume for their insightful
comments and suggestions.

■

Here Gadamer is writing about face-to-face conversations, but he does so to articulate the rules and the workings of other inaudible conversations, those that readers make happen as they read. Gadamer theorizes reading as a "hermeneutical conversation with a text"—a conversation that can only begin and be sustained if and when the reader/interlocutor reconstructs and critically engages the "question" or the argument that the text itself might have been occasioned by or be an answer to.[1] He writes, "Texts . . . have to be *understood,* and that means that one partner in the hermeneutical conversation, the text, is expressed only through the other partner, the interpreter" (349, emphasis added). This view of reading enables us to imagine a text's argument not as a position to be won and defended by one interlocutor at the expense of another, but rather as a "topic" about which interlocutors generate critical questions that put them in a position to think what it means to know, to understand, and to reflect on different processes of knowledge formation (of which the argument can be seen as an example). Thus, a text's argument can function as a fulcrum that brings parties (reader[s] and text) together. But for this to happen, a reader must accept and carry out the tremendous responsibility of giving a voice, and therefore a sort of life, to the text's argument. Although Gadamer does not point it out explicitly, a corollary to a reader's responsibility is a writer's responsibility, that is, the responsibility to write a text that asks (rather than answers) questions, that proposes (rather than imposes) arguments, and that therefore makes a conversation possible. And although Gadamer's subjects are expert readers and writers, what he has to offer to those of us who teach as yet inexperienced readers and writers is, I believe, very valuable. The preceding quotation, "Texts . . . have to be understood," for example, makes me think of the tremendous and delicate responsibility I have as reader of my students' arguments. But it also makes me think of the corollary to my responsibility, students' responsibility to write argument in ways that allow their readers to converse with it. To teach students to assume and to exercise this responsibility is indeed very difficult. Nevertheless, I will suggest, they can learn to exercise this sophisticated practice of writing while, if, and when they learn to understand and to appreciate the effects of this writing on themselves as readers.

What follows is an argument on behalf of the theoretical and practical appropriateness of using *reading* as a means of teaching *writing.*[2] Throughout this essay, I will be using the phrase *the argument of reading* to refer to the debate about the presence of reading in the composition classroom.[3] But I will also be using the phrase *the argument of reading* as a descriptor of the particular understanding of reading and the teaching of reading that I am proposing here.

* * * * *

In 1974, in *Teaching Composing: A Guide to Teaching Writing as a Self-Creating Process,* William E. Coles argued against the use of reading in the composition classroom. He wrote,

> So we decided to get rid of everything that teachers and students alike are tempted to look at writing from behind or through or under. The anthology went; so did the standard plays, novels, poems. (2)

I remember, when I read these lines for the first time in the early 1980s, how struck I was by what I considered a peculiar and arbitrary decision. In 1992, in the process of composing a paper to be delivered at 4Cs, I returned to Coles's text and for reasons that have to do with the kind of work I had done in the interim—mainly, my historical research in pedagogy and my work with hermeneutics and the phenomenology of reading—I was able to read and to respond to this quotation differently. In that paper I returned to a subject that, though central to my intellectual formation as a compositionist and central to my undergraduate and graduate teaching, I had not written about for some time. The paper was my attempt to understand which theoretical and institutional forces had led first to the separation and subsequently to the integration of the activities of reading and writing in the composition class-room. Focusing on the juncture of the theoretical and the institutional gave me a vantage point from which I was able to conjecture and to reconstruct the "argument" that had led Coles to make what had seemed to me such an iconoclastic gesture. This time, rather than judging Coles's statement as a blanket and arbitrary indictment of the presence of reading in composition classrooms, I began to see in Coles's gesture a specific denunciation of what reading had been reduced to within *the teaching of composition* (but also within the teaching of literature, which was and remains the model for much of the teaching of reading done in composition classrooms). I began to see that what Coles was indicting was a particularly enervated, atrophied kind of reading. A reading immobilized within textbooks and reduced therein to sets of disparate simplifying practices that, separated from the various theories that motivate them, turn into meaningless and arbitrary *exercises*: reading for *the main idea,* for *plot,* for *argument,* for *point of view,* for *meaning,* for *message*—interchangeably and without knowing why. Or reading texts as inscrutable and unquestionable "models" of style or rhetorical strategies. Or as "blueprints" for linguistic theories, political programmes, or philosophies of language. I began to see, *through* Coles, the effects of practices that restrain students and teachers from asking questions of a text other than the ones the textbooks have already "gridded." I began to see, *with* Coles, why the kind of writing that these texts and their "facilitating" questions would foster could be nothing but "canned" or "theme" writing. This I understood to be the "problem" of reading that Coles was attacking and for which he proposed, as a *pharmakon,* "get[ting] rid of" anthologies, plays, novels, and poems, and replacing them with the text of the assignments and of the writing that students did in response to them.

Considering the position of composition in the academy in 1974—both within and without departments of English; considering the available work force of teachers of composition at the time; considering that the services of composition were in ascending demand; considering the perceived need for compositionists to define their discipline on their own terms, Coles's apparent "disciplinarian" act can be read, perhaps, as a stern act of self-discipline. That act, set in motion by a confluence of institutional needs, theoretical positions, and programmatic divisions, had its lasting influence. That act, moreover, in a complex sort of way, led to, encouraged, hastened or catalyzed other compositionists' felt need for a theory and practice of the reading-writing relation that had the potential to construct a teacher's respectful attentiveness to a student's writing as an issue of theoretical responsibility and rigor.

In the 1980s, Coles's move seemed to be challenged, if not reversed, by some compositionists who shared his concern that student writing would not hold the center of attention in the composition classroom. Rather than turning away from reading, however, these compositionists turned to theories of reading that seemed to make it possible to obviate that problem.

A 1985 essay by John Clifford and John Schilb, "Composition Theory and Literary Theory," reviewed the work of literary theorists who made it possible to imagine and to justify the teaching of literature and composition, reading and writing, as interconnected disciplines and activities. In their article, Clifford and Schilb assessed the influence of reader-response theories, post-structuralist theories, and examined the work of those compositionists and literary critics (to name a few: Susan Miller, Richard Lanham, Ross Winterowd, Wayne Booth, Nancy Comley and Robert Scholes, and Terry Eagleton) who, they argued, offered ways of thinking about reading and writing that would elide programmatic and disciplinary separations. In the 1980s, then, it seems that the argument about the reading and writing connection was constructed in terms antithetical to those of the 1970s. Rather than seen as an impingement onto the field of composition or as a pretext and a justification for paying attention to something other than students' writing, reading, re-seen through some of the new theories and practices being disseminated, was now appealed to as a means of "bridging the gap" between the two activities and disciplines; a way of paying attention to "reading and writing *differently.*" But, I wish to argue, to set the two arguments side by side is to realize what either position unwittingly ended up obscuring and deflecting attention from: that "the argument of reading in the teaching of composition" is not merely an argument about whether reading should or should not be used in the composition classroom. The argument is about *which kind of reading* gets to be theorized and practiced. To be more precise, that argument cannot be critically and reflexively engaged apart from the following interconnected questions: (1) Which theories of reading are better suited to teaching reading and writing as interconnected activities? (2) What is the theoretical justification for privileging that interconnectedness? (3) How can one teach that interconnectedness?

Q.1 (a). In response to the first question, I will argue that *not all* theories of reading are suited to uncovering and enacting the interconnectedness of reading and writing. Among those least suited to doing so are those that construct writers as visionary shapers of meanings and their works as venerable repositories for those meanings;[4] theories that construct as mysterious and magical the complicated and farraginous processes of thinking on which writing imposes provisional order and stability;[5] and theories that subject texts to unquestioned and unquestionable interpretive frames thereby reducing texts to various thesis statements—cultural, political, religious, and so forth. What I find objectionable about these theories is that they make it possible to cover over the processes by which knowledge and understanding are produced. By invalidating the possibility of recapturing, recuperating, and learning from the complex processes that have given a written text its particular shape, these theories, in different ways and for different reasons, simultaneously glorify reading and proclaim its unteachability. In classrooms where these theories of reading are unreflexively performed *for* students, where reading materials are used as mere pretexts for writing exercises, a *student's* reading of those materials may become *secondary* in at least two ways: It may become less important than and not necessarily accountable for the writing it produces or it may be constructed as needing to rely on a series of simplifications which, although meant to help inexperienced readers understand the materials in question, inevitably expose the assumption that such understanding can only be promoted through somebody else's simplifying practices. In these cases, the use of reading as a means of teaching writing can indeed be arbitrary, questionable, and even counterproductive.

Q.1 (b). In contrast with these notions about reading, theories that posit the possibility and the advantages of exploring the complex processes by which "reading" gives a voice to an otherwise mute "writing"; theories that turn both texts and readers into "interlocutors" of each other; theories that interrogate rather than mystify the "naturalness" and the mystery and the interpretive "framing" both of the reading and of the writing processes, make it possible not only to claim that reading can be taught but also that it can be taught as an opportunity to reflect on, investigate, and intervene in at least some of the processes that produce the knowledge that shapes and is shaped by one's understanding of a text. Rather than divining a text's meaning or making a text subservient to preestablished significations, such theories construct reading as an activity by means of which readers potentially engage texts responsibly and critically.[6] Responsibly, that is, in ways that will as much as possible make *those* texts speak, rather than speak *for* them or make them speak *through* other texts. And *critically* in ways that demand that readers articulate a reflexive critique both of the argument they attribute to those texts and of the argument they compose as they respond to those texts. However, it does not follow from what I just said that these theories automatically and necessarily lead to their own rigorous enactment (see section Q.3). A case in point: Two of the texts that in the 1980s advocated a programmatic and theoretical rapprochement of reading and writing and their attendant domains of expertise and performance—literature and composition—demonstrate what I would call a perplexing inattentiveness to moving from theorizing the interconnectedness of reading and writing to making it visible and to teaching it. The texts I am referring to are *Bridging the Gap*, edited by Winifred Bryan Horner, and *Writing and Reading Differently*, edited by Douglas Atkins and Michael Johnson. With a few notable exceptions (the essays by Sharon Crowley, Barbara Johnson, and Jasper Neel) *the teaching* of reading and writing as interconnected activities, in these volumes, is constructed as something that teachers either do *to* and *for* their students or for themselves and for equally enlightened others, rather than something teachers do *with* their students to open up the areas of investigation that this particular focus makes possible. The interconnectedness of reading and writing (that virtual, provisional trans-action of two extremely complex, invisible, imperceptible processes that can nevertheless be used to test and to foreground each other's moves) tends to be constructed as something either obvious or authorized by such an illustri-ous tradition—from Plato to Derrida—as not to require much explanation or articulation. The advantages for the teaching of writing that this understanding of reading promises are ultimately invalidated. Teaching the reading/writing interconnectedness becomes another kind of hermetic performance, one that covers over, one that hides rather than reveals, the processes of cognition that ought to be the subject of investigation and reflection. Paradoxically, these two texts end up reconfiguring the very problem that Coles was trying to excise—approaching students' writing and reading "from behind or through or under" something else. In this case, the theory calls for the teaching of a "differently" conceived interconnectedness between reading and writing, literature and composition, critical theory and composition theory. Perhaps, though, what I perceive as a regrettable shortcoming of otherwise encomiable projects can serve an important function: to remind us that although certain theories of reading *are* more conducive than others to teaching reading and writing as interconnected activities, to foreground and to teach—rather than just to understand—that interconnectedness is a highly constructed, unnatural, obtrusive activity—one that requires a particular kind of training that, histori-cally, U.S. educational systems and traditions have neither made available nor valorized.

Q. 2. What is the theoretical justification for focusing on the interconnec-tedness of reading and writing?

I wish to suggest at least two reasons. (1) Insofar as reading is a form of thinking (Gadamer calls it "an analogue for thinking"), written accounts of it, however approximate, can provide us with valuable insights into the ways we think. (2) To learn to recapture in one's writing that invisible, imperceptible moment when our reading of a text began to attribute to it—began to pro-duce—a particular "meaning" makes possible to consider again, and to reconsider, what leads us to adopt and to deploy certain interpretive practices. In other words, although the processes that constitute our reading and writing are essentially invisible, those processes are, in principle, accessible to analy-sis, scrutiny, and reflection. The ways we think need neither be *kept*

imperceptible, *shrouded* in mystery, nor be *reduced*, in the interest of demys-
tifying the reading process, to a bunch of technocratic, predictive, or authori-
tarian formulas. To learn to gain access to these processes by no means implies
that they can be completely controlled, contained, or managed. Nor should
they. But to learn to gain access to these processes does mean, I believe, that
one might learn to account for, however approximately, and to understand,
however imperfectly, how certain meanings, certain stories, certain explanations, and certain interpretive frames get to be composed or adopted. Expert
readers/writers have developed and have learned to summon a kind of *introspective reading* of their own and of others' readings that allows them to
decide—as they read and as they write—when to pursue, when to revise, when
to abandon this or that line of argument, and when to start afresh. Part of the
challenge confronting us as teachers is to learn how to make it possible—
within the time and institutional constraints that bind us—for students to learn
to perform this kind of introspective reading. To think about reading and the
teaching of reading in these terms—to think of reading, that is, as an analogue
for thinking about one's own and others' thinking, about how one's thinking
ignites and is ignited by the thoughts of others, justifies the presence of
reading in composition classrooms not as a pretext but as a context for writing.

   Q. 3. How can we teach this interconnectedness?
   To say that, even to articulate how, reading and writing are interconnected
(as most of the authors featured in *Bridging the Gap* and *Writing and Reading
Differently* do) is one thing; and it is another to imagine and to develop
teaching practices that both enact and benefit from that interconnectedness.
This approach to teaching, one that requires teachers' and students' relentless
attention and reflexivity, is difficult both to initiate and to sustain.[7] Over the
years, both as a teacher of composition and of literature, I have learned to
deploy certain teaching strategies that simultaneously enable and force me
and my students to reflect on the moves we make as readers, writers, and
thinkers. I do not consider these strategies mere *applications* or *implementa-
tions* of somebody else's theories, and as I proceed to describe some of them,
I certainly do not intend to offer them as such. Rather I think of these strategies
as means teachers have of exposing (i.e., of making visible and of making
available to reflection and critique—their own and others') the *nexus* between
the theory they espouse and the practices that theory demands.[8] To foreground
and to exploit the interconnectedness of reading and writing, I make a point
of framing reading and writing activities (formal assignments, in-class writings, journals) that ask students to write their response to a text, to construct

a reflective commentary on the moves they made as readers and the possible reasons for them, and to formulate an assessment of the particular writing their reading produced. By means of this triadic (and recursive) sequence, I try to teach readers to become conscious of their mental moves, to see what such moves produce, and to learn to revise or to complicate those moves as they return to them in light of their newly constructed awareness of what those moves did or did not make possible.[9] Initially, my assignments generate considerable resistance on the part of students, mainly because they are not accustomed to performing this kind of introspective reading. When I ask of a point they made, "Why did you think so?" or "What made you think that?" or "How did you come to such a conclusion?" they often hear reproach in my questions despite my concerted efforts to explain, in the course description and repeatedly in class, my rationale for such an approach. Occasionally students do readily learn to hear my questions as I intend for them to be heard, but often they don't. In that case I try to be extremely sensitive to any clues they offer that might make it possible for me to develop a strategy that answers the need of the moment. Here is an example. Several years ago, one of the first times I taught "The Yellow Wallpaper," I was temporarily silenced by a female student's defense of the doctor. She was very articulate about all that the doctor had said and done and had come to the conclusion that the text made an argument for men's (versus women's) inclination for science (medicine), and for what women had to lose when they did not abide by men's counsels. As I tried to collect myself enough to formulate a question that might make her reflect on what she had just said and why, the book in front of her caught my attention. The text was highlighted, rather sparsely. I picked it up, flipped through it, and in a rare moment of extraordinary clarity, I noticed that what she had marked in the text, what she had chosen to pay attention to, was all that in the text had to do with the doctor. She had paid little or no attention to anything else. I asked to be shown how other students had marked the text. The rest of the period was spent first discussing the marks in the text as correlatives for what readers choose to be attentive to as they read a text and then focusing on three representative samples: one by the student who mainly paid attention to the character of the doctor; one by a student who chose to focus on the narrator; and one by a student who after an initial rather random system of marking the text focused on the various characters' responses to the wallpaper. That class made it possible for me to turn a rather mechanical study habit—the highlighting of a text—into a strategy, one that can make visible the number and the intricacy of strands in a text's argument that a reader (or an interlocutor) pays attention to and that can show how the selection, connection, and weaving of those strands affects the structuring of the argument a reader constructs as/in response to a text.[10] As any strategy, this strategy is not effective in and by itself—it is a tool to be used at the appropriate moment, more as a commentary on an incipient awareness of what it means to read a text's (or an interlocutor's) argument than as a means of instructing a reader about how to pay attention to somebody else's argument. A less local strategy, one less contingent on a particular context, is the assignment of what I call the "difficulty paper."[11] Before we discuss a text collectively, I ask students to write a detailed one-page description of any difficulty the text they have been assigned to read might have set up for them.[12] I select and photocopy what I consider a representative paper and I distribute it for class discussion. What I try to do is to guide the discussion toward an assessment of the kind of reading that names a particular feature of a text as "difficult"—is it because readers' expectations do not make them pay attention to a text's clues? Is it because inexperienced readers tend to assume that difficulties are an indictment of their abilities rather than characteristic features of a text? Is it because the method of reading a reader is accustomed to performing will not work with this particular text? I have repeatedly relied on this kind of assignment not as a means to expose my students' inadequacies but as a reflexive strategy that eventually allows them to recognize that what they perceive as "difficult" is a feature of the text demanding to be critically engaged rather than ignored. What is remarkable about this approach is that students' descriptions of difficulties almost inevitably identify a very crucial feature of the text they are reading and contain *in nuce* the interpretive move necessary to handle them. They might say for example that they had difficulty with a text because it presented different and irreconcilable positions on an issue—their difficulty being an accurate assessment of that text's argument.

The focus on difficulty can also be profitably used as a means of fostering students' attention to the assignments by means of which many teachers suggest a possible reading of a text. In this case, students can be asked to reflect on the kind of argument that the assignment's frame simultaneously makes and does not make possible to construct about the assigned text. Thus, the focus will be on the assignment simultaneously as an example of the difficulty of doing justice to a complex text and of the difficulty of adequately representing the complexity of one's response to a complex text. This exercise can be useful to foster habits of rigorous attention to one's reading of others' positions and to one's representations of them, and it can teach students to read (and to remind teachers to think of) assignments as more than sets of injunctions.

There are many ways of putting students in a position to practice recursive and self-monitoring readings, and they will vary according to different contexts, the rapport that different teachers can establish with their students, the configuration of the group, the "feel" of the classroom. The ones I am partial to are those that contribute to making what is imperceptible—thinking—at least dimly perceptible. Let's assume, for example, that student writers have begun to compose a reading of a text (whether in response to an assignment, to the "difficulty paper" instructions, or as a response of their own) that their teacher thinks might benefit from a second, more attentive reading. Let's assume, in other words, that the students have produced a hasty generalization, an inaccurate conclusion, or an overbearingly biased and unexamined preunderstanding that makes them oblivious to a text's argument. To ask those students to account for the steps they took to compose that reading, to ask them to actually *mark* which places in the text they "hooked up with" and which they merely skimmed, can serve as a dramatic visualization of how much of a text's argument can be ignored (erased) because of preestablished conclusions or inattentiveness to that argument's construction. Another way of putting students in a position to "see" the limits and the possibilities of how one chooses to structure an argument is to set up a comparative analysis of two or three different papers. Focusing on the papers' introductory moves as simultaneously points of entry into a text (reading) and tentative beginnings for the arguments they will formulate (writing) helps one consider what difference it makes for one's argument to begin a (written or oral) discussion of a text *there* rather than *elsewhere,* or to begin with a question rather than an evaluative comment. This exercise also helps to avoid interventions and discussions that focus on mistakes, on deficiencies, and on what is wrong with this or that way of thinking.

The strategies I have cursorily described here represent some of the ways I choose to participate in and to respond to my students' reading/thinking/writing activities. What should be noticed about these strategies is that they function simultaneously as heuristic devices (through them I teach my students how to perform certain reflexive moves) and as constant reminders to me that as a teacher I must demonstrate in my reading of my students' comments, questions, interventions, and arguments the responsiveness and the responsibility with which I expect them to engage texts. (Which does not mean, unfortunately, that I will always be successful in doing so.) What should also be noticed is that they deliberately go to "moments of reading" to foreground how those moments determine the writing they produce and that they tend to privilege—for the purpose of discussion—places or occasions in a student's text that can serve as points of critical reflection on the connection between reading and writing.

$$* \quad * \quad * \quad * \quad *$$

In the concluding section of this essay, I want to turn to and to acknowledge what in my experience are two of the most frequently articulated academic objections to the theory and practice of the reading/writing interconnectedness I have outlined. I find these objections compelling and challenging, so much so that I keep returning to them to assess how they can help me better to understand the assumptions about and the preunderstandings of reading that subtend them. Insofar as for the past ten years these objections have consistently complicated and forced me to reexamine my position on reading, on writing, on teaching, and on education, I cannot exclude them from an argument of which they are such an integral part.

Using the names of the programs in my department whose theoretical orientations and proclivities these objections could be said to represent, I will call them the "creative writing" and the "culture studies" positions. What follows is a composite sketch of these objections that I glean from three graduate courses I teach—the "Seminar in the Teaching of Composition," "Literacy and Pedagogy," and "Reception Theories." These are courses that lend themselves extremely well to engaging the issue of the intellectual and programmatic division of which the argument of reading in the teaching of composition, in the two senses I have discussed, is both a cause and a consequence. Some of the representatives of the "creative writing" position articulate their opposition to the rigorous introspection that the interconnectedness of reading and writing requires in the name of (a version of) creativity that is constructed as *being,* and *needing to remain,* beyond analysis. When as a group we discuss the need and we grope for ways of describing not only *what* happens when we read but also *how* it is that we tend to construct one and not another critical response to a text, some of the graduate students who align themselves with the "creativity" position seem willing to engage the first but not the second line of inquiry. Their descriptions of reading are often magical, mysterious. They recollect, lyrically and convincingly, scenes of instruction within which—as children or adolescents—they taught themselves to read with passion and imagination as their motives and guides. In response to questions about the context that favored their autodidacticism, some will describe households replete with books and talks about books—a kind of oasis of family discourse that "naturally" fostered a love of reading and writing. Others, however, will describe settings that are exactly the opposite, within which they performed a sort of heroic, individually willed—and therefore "natural" in quite a different sense of the word—form of self-education.

My aim in interrogating these poignant accounts of education is not to devalue or discredit their veracity. My aim is to point out that these notions of reading may lead to approaches to teaching that are potentially elitist and exclusionary.[13] What happens when students show little cultural, emotional, and intellectual predisposition to this mythical love for reading? What kinds of responses will they write to a text they did not *love* reading? How can teachers teach their students to perform a kind of reading that they have themselves learned to perform mysteriously and magically? I think it is significant that when some of the readers who describe their reading processes as dreamlike or intuitive are asked to read back those processes so as to gain insight into their habitual cognitive strategies, they often declare their anxiety about or suspicion of a process they call "critical dissecting."

The "culture studies" position, on the other hand, objects to the focus on critical self-reflexivity as a nostalgic, reactionary, humanistic, and ultimately ineffective educational practice. Such a focus, this position claims, can foster, on the one hand, the illusion of human beings as independent, self-relying subjectivities and it can, on the other hand, disseminate a pernicious account of knowledge formation that exploits self-reflexivity or a focus on method as a tactic of avoidance, derailment, or deflection. A teacher's commitment to enacting ways of reading that make it both possible and necessary for readers to reflect on and to be critically aware of how arguments—one's own and others'—are constructed becomes within this critique a structured avoidance of more substantial issues. According to this critique, to focus, for example, on *how* John Edgar Wideman in "Our Time," Alice Walker in "In Search of Our Mothers' Gardens," or Gloria Steinem in "Ruth's Song (Because She Could Not Sing It)" construct their narratives is potentially a way of avoiding an ideological argument of race, class, and gender issues.

Insofar as it does not reduce critical reflexivity to an intentionally depoliticizing attention to form or to deadening pigeonholing, the culture studies position provides a salutary warning. Insofar as it does not reduce it to a version of necrophilia, the creative writing position on critical self-reflexivity as a potential blockage to action—creative or political—is compelling. But why is it that at their most oppositional, these and other critiques of self-reflexivity are predicated on a construction of it that turns it into an unnecessary, arbitrary, or stultifying practice?

What is so disturbing and uncomfortable about critical reflexivity? Why do the critical questioning and the introspective analysis it requires generate such suspicion and anxiety? How are we to read these responses? Do they indicate that the project of teaching reading and writing as interconnected activities is unreasonable, utopian, and oblivious to the material circumstances within which it is to be carried out? Should we decide, as Coles did in the 1970s, that it might be opportune to scale down this project of reading in the composition classroom from reading the interconnectedness of reading and writing to reading the assignments and student papers? (What does this suggest about teachers' and students' ability to engage in this task?) Does my critique of the ways most "integrationists" carried out in the 1980s the project of eliding the schism between reading and writing, literature and composition, suggest, indeed underscore, the wisdom of Coles's solution?

I see how it might be possible to answer all these questions in the affirmative and I become despondent. My current historical work in pedagogy, work that I undertook to understand what as a foreigner I found here puzzling and disturbing, namely the separation of reading from writing, the proliferation of specialized programs within departments, the reduction of pedagogy from a philosophical science to a repertoire of "tips for teaching," shows that our educational system has consistently opted for simplifying solutions every time it has been confronted with the inherent and inescapable complexity of educational issues. What I find disturbing is that decisions often made for teachers, without the participation of teachers, are subsequently read as indictments of teachers' inadequate intellectual and professional preparation. (One of the most frequently voiced reservations to my project is that "it is too difficult" to carry it out without sacrificing writing to reading.) We cannot afford not to come to terms with the consequences of these streamlining interventions. We need to acknowledge that, for reasons the complexity of which we cannot deny but we can certainly call into question, our scheme of education has consistently and repeatedly skirted the responsibility of nurturing one of the most fundamental human activities—critical self-reflexivity.

Every time I teach reading and writing as interconnected activities I begin by declaring, by making visible, my teaching strategies and exposing their rationale. And yet every time it takes considerable time for students to see this approach to teaching not as a cynical tendency to tear apart and to discredit the ways they read and write, as an exercise in dissection or a paralyzing threat, but rather as it is meant, as an attempt to promote engagement in the kind of self-reflection and self-awareness that they are so often expected to demon-strate but are seldom given an opportunity to learn.

In *On Literacy,* Robert Pattison argues that the project of developing the critical mind requires "another kind of training not generally available in the American scheme of education" (176). I agree with him and I believe that we can and we must find ways of providing that kind of training even within institutional environments that are opposed to it. Let me suggest that teaching reading and writing as interconnected activities, teaching students how to perform critically and self-reflexively those recuperative acts by means of which they can conjecture a text's, a person's, argument and can establish a responsible critical dialogue with it, as well with the text they compose in response to it, might be an approach appropriate to developing the critical mind—an approach that might mark the difference between their partaking in, and their being passively led through their own education.

Notes

1. For the purpose of this essay, I use the term *argument* to replace, or interchangeably with *question,* which is Gadamer's word. Since I wrote this piece, I have found it useful to work with both terms in my continuing attempts to theorize and to practice a transactional understanding of reading with undergraduates. The two terms—used together, overlapped, or in a relation of adjacency—have made it easier for students to interrogate common preunderstandings of them as "cozy, fireside talk" and "high-pitched debate or quarrel."

2. The teaching of argumentative writing has a strong and respected tradition in composition that I have no intention to challenge. My understanding of argumentative writing is only indirectly related through Gadamer to classical rhetoric. But I am pleased to notice possible points of contact between, for example, John Gage's approach to argumentative writing as "reasoned inquiry" and mine.

3. For a revival of this debate, see Erika Lindemann ("Freshman Composition," "Three Views") and Gary Tate ("A Place for Literature," "Notes").

4. These theories of reading generally discourage or consider as inappropriate a reader's (particularly an inexperienced reader's) critical response to a text. See, for example, Wilson Knight's *The Wheel of Fire,* especially the difference he sets up between *interpretation* and *criticism.*

5. I am thinking here of critics and theorists as different from one another as Benedetto Croce and Georges Poulet.

6. Among the theorists of reading who, in different ways, provide such possibilities are Hans-Georg Gadamer (especially *Truth and Method* and *Philosophical Hermeneutics*); Wolfgang Iser (*The Act of Reading* and *The Fictive and the Imaginary: Charting Literary Anthropology*); M. M. Bakhtin (*The Dialogic Imagination*); and Paul De Man (*Allegories of Reading*).

7. One of the reasons why this approach to teaching is often met with considerable resistance and skepticism (by students, teachers, administrators, and the public) is that it can be said, and rightly so, that such an approach does not aim at producing a body of knowledge and is not efficient in terms of immediate and quantifiable results. Both resistance and skepticism need to be taken

into serious consideration. Clearly, they indicate a widespread appreciation of at least one version of the aims of education, that is, education as the accumulation of a cultural capital that can be weighed and used as currency. To mock these assumptions, to underestimate how they regulate much of our lives, would be unwise. But equally unwise would be to suggest that the two approaches to and understanding of knowledge formation are antithetical to one another. To do so might amount to denying students and teachers the possibility to acquire certain bodies of knowledge and at the same time to learn to assess and to critique the processes that make the formation of certain knowledge possible and to understand the rules that regulate how and which kind of knowledge gets to be included, valued, and circulated, and correspondingly, which kind of knowledge gets to be excluded, devalued, even ostracized.

8. Let me enter an important caveat. The strategies I describe here, as *all* strategies, make sense, that is, are plausible and justifiable, within the particular approach to teaching that my understanding of the act of reading and its connections with writing calls for. They cannot and they should not be lifted out of the theoretical framework that I have articulated here, and be offered as transportable tips or prescriptives.

9. This "frame" is my attempt to imagine strategies that enact what Gadamer sees as the three pivotal and interconnected phases of reading—*kennen, wiederkennen,* and *herauskennen.* Important to notice is that this frame is not a "grid." Insofar as readers bring to the texts they read, the situations they find themselves in, and the experiences they live, their own "presuppositions of knowledge," and insofar as those presuppositions of knowledge will vary from one person to another, readers' readings of a text will vary accordingly.

10. The strategy consists of asking students to reproduce two or three marked pages of their texts and to articulate the system that determines their marks as interventions in the text and the connections among them. This is one way of approximating, though very inadequately, the otherwise imperceptible moves that readers make as they read a text. This is one way to begin a conversation about and a critical assessment of reading practices.

11. In *Ways of Reading,* Dave Bartholomae and Anthony Petrosky have developed a sequence of assignments ("The Problems of Difficulty") around the generative force of difficulty.

12. In "Towards a Hermeneutics of Difficulty," Salvatori articulates a theoretical framework for such an assignment.

13. Salvatori develops this argument in "Pedagogy and the Academy: 'The Divine Skill of the Born Teacher's Instincts,' " and more fully in *Pedagogy: Disturbing History,* forthcoming.

Works Cited

Atkins, Douglas G., and Michael L. Johnson, Eds. *Writing and Reading Differently: Deconstruction and the Teaching of Composition and Literature.* Lawrence: University of Kansas Press, 1985.

Bakhtin, M. M. *The Dialogic Imagination: Four Essays by M. M. Bakhtin.* Ed. Michael Holquist. Trans. Caryl Emerson and Michael Holquist. Austin: University of Texas Press, 1981.

Bartholomae, David, and Anthony Petrosky. *Ways of Reading: An Anthology for Writers.* 2nd ed. Boston: Bedford Books of St. Martin's Press, 1990.

Clifford, John, and John Schilb. "Composition Theory and Literary Theory." *Perspectives on Research and Scholarship in Composition.* Ed. Ben W. McClelland and Timothy R. Donovan. New York: Modern Language Association, 1985.

Coles, William E. *Teaching Composing: A Guide to Teaching Writing as a Self-Creating Process.* Rochelle Park, NY: Hayden, 1974.

De Man, Paul. *Allegories of Reading: Figural Language in Rousseau, Nietzsche, Rilke, and Proust.* New Haven, CT: Yale University Press, 1979.

———. *Blindness and Insight: Essays in the Rhetoric of Contemporary Criticism.* Minneapolis: University of Minnesota Press, 1983.

Gadamer, Hans-Georg. *Truth and Method.* New York: Continuum, 1975.

———. *Philosphical Hermeneutics.* Trans. and Ed. David E. Linge. Berkeley: University of California Press, 1976.

Gilman, Charlotte Perkins. "The Yellow Wallpaper." *The Charlotte Perkins Gilman Reader.* Ed. Ann J. Lane. New York: Pantheon, 1950.

Horner, Winifred Bryan, Ed. *Composition and Literature: Bridging the Gap.* Chicago: University of Chicago Press, 1983.

Iser, Wolfgang. *The Act of Reading: A Theory of Aesthetic Response.* Baltimore, MD: Johns Hopkins University Press, 1978.

———. *The Fictive and the Imaginary: Charting Literary Anthropology.* Baltimore, MD: Johns Hopkins University Press, 1993.

Knight, Wilson. *The Wheel of Fire.* London: Methuen, 1930.

Lindemann, Erika. "Freshman Composition: No Place for Literature." *College English* 55 (Mar. 1993): 311-16.

———. "Three Views of English 101." *College English* 57 (Mar. 1995): 287-302.

Pattison, Robert. *On Literacy: The Politics of the Word From Homer to the Age of Rock.* New York: Oxford University Press, 1982.

Salvatori, Mariolina. "Towards a Hermeneutics of Difficulty." *Audits of Meaning: A Festschrift in Honor of Ann E. Berthoff.* Ed. Louise Z. Smith. Portsmouth, NH: Boynton/Cook, 1988.

———. "Pedagogy and the Academy: 'The Divine Skill of the Born Teacher's Instincts.' " *Pedagogy in the Age of Politics: Writing and Reading (in) the Academy.* Ed. Patricia A. Sullivan and Donna J. Qualley. Urbana, IL: NCTE, 1994.

———. *Pedagogy: Disturbing History.* University of Pittsburgh Press, forthcoming.

Steinem, Gloria. "Ruth's Song (Because She Could Not Sing It)." *Ways of Reading: An Anthology for Writers.* 2nd ed. Ed. David Bartholomae and Anthony Petrosky. Boston: Bedford, 1990.

Tate, Gary. "A Place for Literature in Freshman Composition." *College English* 55 (Mar. 1993): 319-21.

———. "Notes on the Dying of a Conversation." *College English* 57 (Mar. 1995): 303-09.

Walker, Alice. "In Search of Our Mothers' Gardens." *Ways of Reading: An Anthology for Writers.* 2nd ed. Ed. David Bartholomae and Anthony Petrosky. Boston: Bedford, 1990.

Wideman, John Edgar. "Our Time." *Ways of Reading: An Anthology for Writers.* 2nd ed. Ed. David Bartholomae and Anthony Petrosky. Boston: Bedford, 1990.

9

The Argument of Reading

David Bartholomae
University of Pittsburgh

I

It is almost impossible to find a recent account of English (or English as a school subject) that does not begin with a reference to the problem of the new criticism and its legacy in the American classroom. The new criticism is everywhere, we are told; its hold on practice seems firm in spite of the ways its key texts and key figures have been routed by recent developments in theory and critical practice. Here, for example, is Frank Lentricchia (in "Someone Reading") on the new criticism:

> The American New Criticism, the critical movement which made formalism famous in this country, and whose death has been periodically announced ever since the late 1950s, remains in force as the basis (what goes without saying) of undergraduate literary pedagogy, so that, having passed into the realm of common sense, the ideological effect of the New Criticism in the United States is to sustain, under conditions of mass higher education, the romantic cult of genius by dispossessing younger readers of their active participation in the shaping of a culture and a society "of and for the people"—by stripping those readers of their right to think of themselves as culturally central storytellers: an extraordinary

AUTHOR'S NOTE: Quoted material throughout this chapter from Richard Poirier, *The Performing Self,* copyright © 1992 by Richard Poirier. Reprinted by permission of Rutgers University Press.

irony for a critical method whose initial effect was entirely democratic—to make the reading of classics available to all, even to those of us whose early cultural formation did not equip us to read Shakespeare and Milton, but a predictable irony, in retrospect, when we remember that new critical formalist reading at the same time defined and valued itself as secondary reading of explication. So while the New Criticism taught us to read, it simultaneously taught us how to subordinate our reading powers and humble ourselves before the "creative" authority of superior primary writing. (323-34)

In this line of argument, the "new criticism" marked a potentially positive moment of intervention in the English curriculum, one that would redefine the relationship between the student and the text (and, through this realignment, between the student and literary or literate culture—"the initial effect was entirely democratic"—students might have been represented as "culturally central storytellers"), but the potential of the moment was lost when the classroom exercise became not only formalistic (focusing on the features in the text rather than on the relationship established between the text and its readers) but also elitist (a celebration of the "genius" of the author and a necessary subordination of students and their writing before "primary writing"). The subject in the curriculum became someone else's reading and writing, someone bigger, better, more famous, more powerful, and this is the subject we continue to teach today, over and over, in literature and in composition.

Anyone who works in the field can think of local exceptions to this generalization, but it still has great explanatory power. Composition, in spite of its celebration of democracy, still marks the place in the curriculum (according to Susan Miller) where bad or immature or amateur student writing proves the value of the great writing taught down the hall. And when composition thinks and talks about reading, it is usually in terms of levels: beginning, intermediate, and expert. The goal is to improve students' reading by improving the level at which they can read and work, hence the speed reading/study skills add-ons to many courses of instruction; or to control the reading (with the assumption that students are beginning readers) so that the difficulty of the text, its complexity, is not allowed to get in the way of writing, hence the many readers that offer short, easy-to-read selections as the material for student essays.

This is a quick and convenient account of the place of reading in contemporary American composition, but let me use it for a minute as a point of reference. The problem in either case is defined as developmental rather than, say, ideological. This representation of the problem of reading finesses the wide view in Lentricchia's argument, that the problem is a general cultural problem, one that is reproduced in but not specific to learners. Good reading is not, in other words, simply a matter of development or maturity or experience. Behind Lentricchia's despair over the state of reading is the sense that schooled readers, even at their best, have learned a form of mastery ("the secondary reading of explication") that is itself the problem (defined at least partially as a humility before or subordination to the primary text of schooling).

I want to use this essay to think about the competing desires to deny and to recover reading in the introductory course in the English curriculum. The issue for me, at least for the moment, is not whether or what students should read, but *how*. I want to argue that the introductory course should be a course in "close reading," the fundamental method of the New Criticism. I want to argue that this reading is neither retrograde nor politically naive, and I want to think about close reading as a form of argumentation, the techniques and goals of which are disappearing from the undergraduate curriculum. There are composition courses and programs that make close reading part of the necessary preparation of a writer, but they are few and far between and they are becoming more and more invisible when composition talks to itself about key people, programs, ideas and issues.

I would say, for example, that the course represented in Bill Coles's book, *The Plural I,* is a course in close reading. As, with some important differences, is the course alluded to in Mariolina Salvatori's chapter in this collection. (This is a course I know well. I've sat in on it, even taught a version of it, as I have sat in on and taught a version of Bill Coles's course. This has been one of the great pleasures of working in my department. The work that Tony Petrosky and I have done similarly assumes a course where, for example, both assigned texts and student papers are used as occasions for lessons in close reading.)

In her chapter, Mariolina Salvatori begins with Bill Coles's concern that the presence of reading (or literature) in the writing classroom would make writing disappear as a subject and students' writing disappear as a text. She moves from this example to consider the ways reading might be (and has been) reconfigured as part of a writer's necessary preparation. Her account of reading, it seems to me, attempts to recover a form of close reading for the composition classroom—a reading that is recursive, that pays particular attention to the text, a reading that is argumentative and reflexive. Lentricchia refers to the problem of writing as the willed product of American literary culture, or literary culture as represented in schooling. The course Salvatori alludes to was designed to stand in opposition to the "common sense" of reading as it has prepared generations of students and teachers. The course asks students to pay particular attention to the text (including the text of their own reading, often the text they write), to make this the center of their attention, paying a particular and unnatural attention to the words on the page. The course puts a particular premium on irony—that is, the distance one can achieve from the very systems that produce one's reading. The goal is not the production of meanings nor a formal description of how a text works. The course teaches, rather, a way to pay a disciplined and difficult attention to one's own practice.

I would like to locate this kind of course in a history that links it with the New Criticism but differentiates it from those classroom practices enshrined in, say, *Understanding Poetry*. The impulses represented in the New Criticism, those acknowledged by Lentricchia—to center criticism in the work of students, to make all texts available to the largest number of people—these admirable desires are perhaps the positive legacy of the New Criticism and can be imagined separately from the less interesting products of the larger movement that carries its name.

II

One way I have of reading and understanding Mariolina Salvatori's work (and, I should add, one way I had of reading and understanding Bill Coles's work when I first came to Pitt) was through the work of Richard Poirier, both his written work and his teaching in graduate courses (where we worked not on great authors but on the problems of language as they were represented or worked out in certain literary texts, and worked on them through short written exercises designed to engage us most productively as readers with the works we were reading). I came to this sense of what it meant to work in English through Poirier's teaching and through what was then his recent book, *The Performing Self* (1971). In brief, the argument of that book was that one came into identity (or *presence*) as a language user through one's awareness of and struggle with the languages of the present and the past. These moments of contact were constant and continuous but could be realized most profoundly through the kinds of confrontation allowed by literature and brokered through the classroom. Poirier argued, for example,

> English studies cannot be the body of English literature but it can be at one with its spirit: of struggling, of wrestling with words and meaning. Otherwise English studies may go one of two ways: it can shrink, in a manner possibly as invigorating as that which accompanied the retrenchment of Classics departments; or it can

become distended by claims to a relevance merely topical. Alternatively, it can take a positive new step. It can further develop ways of treating *all* writing and *all* reading as analogous acts, as simultaneously developing performances, some of which deaden, some of which will quicken us. (84)

What I have since come to learn is that through Poirier and Coles I was also learning to think about English through the terms and practices of two teaching programs of great significance to English in America, the composition program at Amherst and a staff-taught introductory literature course at Harvard called Humanities 6 (or Hum 6). In Poirier's account, which I will turn to in a minute, Hum 6 was a course that linked close work with written language to Emerson, Frost, Wittgenstein, Leavis, Richards, and, as its negative counterpoint, to Brooks and Warren's *Understanding Poetry* and that form of teaching we have learned to identify with the New Criticism.

Let me take a moment to work out Poirier's account of the course in the final chapter of his most recent book, *Poetry and Pragmatism* ("Reading Pragmatically: The Example of Hum 6"). Poirier argues that the problem with the recent histories of criticism (or of English studies) is that they tend to leave out critical works of "stunning individuality." Among these omissions are works in the Anglo-American critical tradition that promoted the kind of "linguistic skepticism" later defined as deconstruction. With this lost work, he includes examples of teaching:

> Without necessarily depending on any of these writers [Peirce, James, Dewey, Santayana, Cavel, Stein, Stevens, Frost], certain kinds of intense close reading were being pedagogically advanced, well before the post-World War II period, which without defining themselves theoretically—at the time that would have been thought inappropriate in undergraduate classrooms—or calling themselves skeptical, managed to inculcate in more than a few teachers and students a habit of enjoying the way words undo and redo themselves to the benefit of social as well as literary practice. (173)

The course he takes as an example, one that he taught as part of a staff at Harvard in the mid-Fifties, was an introductory literature course, "The Interpretation of Literature," known to students and staff as Hum 6. This course began on a different campus as the sophomore follow-up to the Amherst freshman course, the course identified with Theodore Baird (for a discussion of Baird, see Gibson and Varnum, particularly Varnum's book on English 1-2). The sophomore course was created by Armour Craig, Baird, and Reuben Brower. Brower carried the course with him when he went to Harvard (as others like Bill Coles or Roger Sales carried an Amherst-like course to other campuses). Poirier was part of a staff that taught with Brower at Harvard, a staff that included Peter Brooks, Thomas Edwards, Neil Rudenstine, David Kalstone, Anne Ferry, Margery Sabin, and Paul De Man (who wrote in *TLS* that "my own awareness of the critical, even subversive, power of literary instruction does not stem from philosophical allegiances but from a very specific teaching experience [Hum 6]").

But it is the details, not the names, that make this story interesting. The sophomore course at Amherst, according to Poirier,

> appeared to be less daring than the Baird course, English 1-2, perhaps because it emphasized, as did courses then being given at other places, the close reading of texts or, in Brower's better phrase, "reading in slow motion." For him reading ideally remained *in* motion, not choosing to encapsulate itself, as New Critical readings nearly always ultimately aspire to do. It was different from Brooks and Warren, with their *Understanding Poetry*—importantly so. (180-81)

The differences are represented in their touchstones—Eliot for the new critics, Frost for the Harvard/Amherst group—and in their ideological commitments. New Criticism idealized religious, political, and poetic unity. For the Harvard/Amherst group, through Frost, the lesson to be taught was that order is linguistic, manmade, contingent, and temporary. And order was the product of work with language, with language that was already in play, and the goals of this work were not simply improved reading but an improved participation in the culture and in the world ("to the benefit of social as well as literary practice").

> Hum 6 was distinguished not so much by a commitment to a reading list as a commitment to assignments or "exercises." Any athlete or dancer or musician—or reader—must have learned *how* to exercise and when to get back to exercise in order always to know the rigors by which any degree of mastery is attained. Reading is an acquired talent with words, which is all that reading ever can be directly engaged with, and it involves the measured recognition that words can do unexpected and disturbing things to you . . . . Reading must be actively synchronized with the generative energies of writing itself. It is not enough to understand what is being said, since this is always less than what is being expressed. (Poirier 175-76)

And, Poirier adds,

> Obviously, reading/writing of this kind cannot occur in space; it occurs in time, word by word, sentence by sentence, responsive to opportunities as they open up, to resistances as they are encountered, to entrapments which must be dodged, all

of these latent in the words just previously laid down and in the forms, both large and small, that reading and writing often fall into. (176)

What distinguished the work in Hum 6 (and marked its separation from the Brooks and Warren brand of New Criticism) was its moral urgency, an urgency rooted in the sense that "words can do unexpected and disturbing things to you." Like the composition course represented in *The Plural I* (a course, we should remember, that makes immediate use of assigned readings, usually short passages, and that asks students to read their relation to the world and to knowledge and to language by learning to read their own essays closely), the literature course assumes that the stakes are very high indeed, that these introductory courses are places to work out in practice (to enact) what it might mean to be present in the world (or to be present as a language user in a discursive order not of one's own making). The course was ambitious and called for the best from both teachers and students, which is most likely why it is remembered so fondly and in such detail.

Hum 6 was, at the same time, unwilling to make grand claims for its significance. The course was "low-keyed" in comparison to the courses with which it competed, courses with titles like "Ideas of Good and Evil" or "The Individual and Society." (The course I took at Ohio Wesleyan in the Sixties was called "The Devil, Hero and God.") Here, for the last time, is Poirier:

> Meanwhile, the people I have associated with this course, from the Hum 6 staff all the way back to Emerson, harbored no such illusions as are now abroad about the power of reading or of writing, especially in criticism. Reading and writing are activities which for them require endless scruple. That is how the activity of reading begins, how it is carried on, and why, so long as the words are in front of you, it should never end. It need never be broken off out of some guilty feeling that the activity of reading is not sufficiently political or socially beneficial. It is to be understood as a lonely discipline that makes no great claims for itself. Reading conducted under such a regimen can be subversive only to the extent that it encourages us to get under and turn over not systems and institutions, but only words. (193)

The importance of this qualification still holds. Those who work on reading and writing in introductory courses can easily be seen to be working with very little in comparison to colleagues whose students, at least putatively, are dealing with the "big" questions (say) of race, class, and gender. Doing this work up close and at the point of practice, working to revise a sentence or a phrase, working on how one reads a line, thinking about the consequences of phrasing it this way or that, and doing this work with students, produces gains that are small and local—and, to the profession, largely invisible. This, to me, is why the meeting of composition and cultural studies has been such a great disappointment. The cultural studies course has been quick to teach the critique of commodity capitalism; it has shown almost no interest in teaching students how to work with words (turning them this way and that) as a form of critical practice.

III

The value of Hum 6 is not simply that it seems to authorize or give precedence for the teaching I would like to promote in the Nineties. (Although it does.) The value is not just that Hum 6 connects my graduate training with my present work. (Although it does. And I will confess that it gives me pleasure to see Poirier fondly recalling a freshman course and acknowledging the ways it enabled professionals to think through critical issues.) Hum 6 also functions for me as an important point of reference in the history of composition. Hum 6 is not, of course, a part of our standard accounts of the field and its history. The full argument for its role in composition's history is a complicated one and belongs to a different chapter than this, but let me offer a quick sketch. I want to use Hum 6 (and its relation to the Amherst composition course English 1-2) to think about literature and composition, about competing definitions of "argument," and about the usual sources called on to authorize instruction in logic and argument as part of the English (as opposed to the philosophy) curriculum.

Poirier would have us begin with Emerson to think about linguistic skepticism as part of American thought. I want to make mine a genealogy of instructional practice and so I will begin with Richards and Leavis, the British sources of the New Criticism, who in the Twenties and Thirties radically redefined what it meant to *do* English in school. Our present moment is still driven by the desires and anxieties set into play by their work. Eagleton, in "The Rise of English," phrases it this way:

> No subsequent movement within English studies has come near to recapturing the courage and radicalism of their stand. In the early 1920s it was desperately unclear why English was worth studying at all; by the early 1930s it had become a question of why it was worth wasting your time on anything else. English was not only a subject worth studying, but *the* supremely civilizing pursuit, the spiritual essence of the social formation. Far from constituting some amateur or impressionistic enterprise, English was an arena in which the most fundamental questions of human existence—what it meant to be a person, to engage in significant relations

with others, to live from the vital centre of the most essential values—were thrown
into vivid relief and made the object of the most intensive scrutiny. (31)

This is a dauntingly seductive project, beginning with the belief that
education, education in the use of language, could make people better—better
able to live and better able to live together. Eagleton, finally, has not much
sympathy for the project (which becomes for him associated with Leavis and
the group he gathered at the journal, *Scrutiny*):

> The whole *Scrutiny* project was at once hair-raisingly radical and really rather
> absurd. As one commentator has shrewdly put it, the Decline of the West was felt
> to be avertible by close reading. Was it really true that *literature* could roll back
> the deadening effects of industrial labour and the philistinism of the media? (34)

As the argument went, it was not literature itself that would stem the tide; it
was what one could learn, through proper instruction, by reading literary texts.
And, the fear of mass media was not simply an expression of snobbery or
class-consciousness. For a generation that had learned through World War I
and during the period between the two world wars to understand propaganda
and the effects of control through mass media, there was much at stake in
teaching students to understand from the inside how language worked and to
discriminate between "good" uses of language and "bad." Close reading
became a means of investigation, a way to exercise discrimination in the face
of commercial, political and cultural interests with a previously unheard-of
power to penetrate daily life and produce the "common" sense of the citizenry.

Close reading was a method designed to examine how a text "worked" and
to measure its goals or implications, its version of what it means to be present
in the world, against an idea of the Good. This "good," as with any version of
the good, was contingent and only partially examined. For Leavis it was
represented by a "great tradition" of the English novel and an idealized version
of Renaissance England. For the American New Critics, the Agrarians, the
appropriate texts were modern, ironic and unsentimental; the place was a
conservative, idealized rural South. I am not arguing for the Great Tradition
or the works collected in *Understanding Fiction* or *Understanding Poetry*. As
a seemingly necessary step in the argument, Leavis, among others, grounded
his critical practice in a set of (what were taken as obviously or unquestion-
ably) great examples—as in *The Great Tradition*. And it is for his examples
that Leavis has become an object of criticism. William Cain, for example, says
that Leavis

is a powerful and admirable figure, but I hope I have made clear that his work is too flawed and over-bearing to serve as a model for critical and pedagogical performance. His emphasis on criticism and judgment (as opposed to mere "elucidation") and his concern for general "critical consciousness" (as opposed to academic specialization and disciplinary enclosure) are inspiring and important. But in other respects—his very narrow canon, over-valuation of Lawrence, dismissal of dissent—Leavis is too rigid and dogmatic to stand as the exemplary figure for English studies. (161)

As I say, I am not particularly interested in defending or critiquing Leavis's version of the canon. The examples I am seeking for English studies are not to be found in the library. And so the Leavis-figure important to Cain is less important to me. (Although I will add that words like *overbearing, rigid,* and *dogmatic* do not necessarily carry a negative valence when I cast characters for the scene of instruction. The notion that a dogmatic teacher/ critic only be slavishly followed assumes a student/reader more passive and one-dimensional than I find convincing.) I am not interested in using critics for my examples but classes, assignments, textbooks and methods. Again—I am not trying to recover Leavis, but close reading, for English studies. (A more extended and perhaps less enthusiastic account of Leavis's methods would begin with textbooks like Denys Thompson's *Reading and Discrimination* or E. G. Biaggini's *The Reading and Writing of English.*)

The point I would make is that in the opening moments and at their best, the new critics were polemicists and their interest in the classroom and its methods was political. That is to say, the point of close reading was to enable students to argue with the very forms of understanding produced by the texts they were reading (or writing), to enable them to argue with the forms of understanding they were meant to take for granted, that were meant to be beyond question, outside the interests of the reader or the writer or the classroom. The pedagogy was designed to make visible those productions of selfhood and society, those forms of reading, writing, and imagining produced by contemporary mass culture through literature, radio, film, and advertising. Students, by reading, engaged in an argument with interests and points of view and habits and seductions latent in the words on the page and the "forms, large and small, that reading and writing often fall into." These last words are, again, Poirier's (176). They allow me to highlight the degree to which close reading, or at least one classroom use of close reading, is an exercise in argumentation. One learns to define oneself, at the immediate point of contact, with the arguments built into (hidden in) the "common sense" of the mass culture.

This tradition of argumentation has been the hallmark of a certain kind of "literary education." The tradition is not, however, the same thing as the study of literature—it belongs to particular programs or classrooms, particular ways of doing English. You can trace it through the development of British and American culture studies (both as a critical practice and as a classroom practice, although not necessarily in either—for a discussion of the pedagogy of British Cultural Studies, see Richard Miller).

As I have tried to indicate through my essay, this tradition of argumentation has touched on the history of composition in the United States, particularly through the work of those who taught at Amherst: Bill Coles, Roger Sales, Walker Gibson, and others, including, I think, some of their students and colleagues. The hallmark of this teaching is its method. Student essays are reproduced. They become *the* text or one of the primary texts of the course. Students learn to read their writing closely not to make corrections but to ask how the language works or doesn't work. Revision is a key in these classrooms because writers are always working against the forces evident in their text. And, of course, the work is read against some version of the "good," often defined in terms of what it means to be a person, to engage in significant relationship with others, or to live from the vital center of essential values. By teaching reading, the writing course, as I am imagining it, can teach students to engage in a complex, revisionary argument with the culture as it is present in their own sentences and paragraphs, in their shape and sound, in what they do, and in who or what they point to in allusion. This kind of attention to text and context has been preserved in certain forms of literary education.

This kind of attention is not, however, in the mainstream of composition instruction. Composition has been dominated by a different pedagogical tradition, one that puts almost no premium on close reading, where the student essay, the "product," is an irrelevant or sometimes embarrassing byproduct of the real work of the course, where student writing is read, if it is read at all, primarily for grading or correction or, and this is important, where it is read by the student and the teacher to prepare for the kind of revision that is *not* an argument with the text (and the forces latent in its language) but is rather an acceptance of those forces, a submission. That is to say, in most cases the goal of revision is to perfect or complete or shore up the essay that has begun to complete the work of the culture as it has been brought into play by individual students in a writing class. A reader reads not antagonistically, but to see the patterns that need to be filled or completed.

What happened to close reading in the composition course? Why is it missing? The reasons, of course, are overdetermined; the answers complicated. To mass produce copies of student papers is expensive and awkward. To read closely and carefully demands time and attention from the faculty; this labor is unprecedented and seldom rewarded. To devote class time to "inferior" prose seems wasteful. Within a certain structure of values, English is a system designed to *preserve* the distinction between "great" writing, which deserves close reading, and student writing, which does not.

Another way to think about this is to think about the position of criticism at a key moment in the construction of composition as a professional field. You can, for example, look at the reception of Brooks and Warren's rhetoric (or of Kenneth Burke) to see the ways the profession was trying to stake its claim over and against what was loosely called "literature." The Conference on College Composition and Communication, its journals, and its key figures were eager to cast their lot with linguistics (the science of language) and rhetoric (the reading and elaboration of standard texts). In the reception of *Modern Rhetoric,* which was poorly read and poorly reviewed, one can see the shifts of attention and influence that produced (say) James Kinneavy and Edward P. J. Corbett, even Wayne Booth, as key figures in the recent history of composition, that made it inevitable that composition should turn to philosophy and rhetoric for its models of argumentation, and that made Amherst (or Bill Coles or Roger Sales) almost invisible, or visible only as strange and cranky outsiders. (Look, for example, in the index of Stephen North's *The Making of Knowledge in Composition.*)

Criticism and close reading, including the close reading of student "exercises," Emerson and Frost, Poirier and Brower, Amherst and Harvard—I like to imagine a moment when these could have been important points of reference in the development of composition. Let me be clear, I am not trying to argue against the ways argument is currently figured in the undergraduate curriculum. I think John Gage's work and the curriculum at the University of Oregon make a powerful case for how the introductory composition course can provide intellectual training in argumentation and can be a serious part of the undergraduate curriculum. Nor am I trying to imagine a lost Eden; I am aware of all the limits and difficulties of the kind of course I am associating with Harvard and Amherst. Teaching students to feel the negative pressure of "their own language," to argue with those versions of themselves that come most easily, happily, and naturally through the language and habits of contemporary culture and American schooling, is risky and difficult teaching; its moments of achievement are not nearly so evident as those available in other kinds of writing classes; its problems are often more so. I do, however, want to suggest that there are ways of teaching the introductory course that participate in a tradition of practice where literature and composition, reading and writing, do not necessarily function as opposing terms.

Works Cited

Bartholomae, David, and Anthony R. Petrosky. *Facts, Artifacts and Counterfacts: Reading and Writing in Theory and Practice*. Portsmouth, NH: Boynton, 1986.

————. *Ways of Reading*. Boston: Bedford Books, 1993.

Biaggini, E. G. *The Reading and Writing of English*. New York: Harcourt, Brace and Company, 1936.

Brooks, Cleanth, and Robert Penn Warren. *Understanding Poetry*. New York: Harcourt, Brace and Company, 1938.

————. *Understanding Fiction*. New York: Harcourt, Brace and Company, 1943.

————. *Modern Rhetoric*. New York: Harcourt, Brace and Company, 1949.

Cain, William E. *The Crisis in Criticism: Theory, Literature, and Reform in English Studies*. Baltimore, MD: Johns Hopkins University Press, 1984.

Coles, William E., Jr. *The Plural I—and After*. Portsmouth, NH: Boynton, 1988.

Eagleton, Terry. *Literary Theory: An Introduction*. Minneapolis: University of Minnesota Press, 1983.

Gibson, Walker. "Theodore Baird." *Traditions of Inquiry*. Ed. John Brereton. New York: Oxford University Press, 1985.

Leavis, F. R. *The Great Tradition*. New York: New York University Press, 1960.

Lentricchia, Frank. "In Place of An Afterword—Someone Reading." *Critical Terms for Literary Study*. Ed. Frank Lentricchia and Thomas McLaughlin. Chicago: University of Chicago Press, 1990. 321-39.

Miller, Richard. *Representing the People: Theoretical and Pedagogical Disjunction in the Academy*. Diss. University of Pittsburgh, 1993. AAC9317985.

Miller, Susan. *Textual Carnivals: The Politics of Composition*. Carbondale: Southern Illinois University Press, 1991.

North, Stephen. *The Making of Knowledge in Composition*. Portsmouth, NH: Boynton, 1987.

Poirier, Richard. *The Performing Self: Compositions and Decompositions in the Languages of Contemporary Life*. New Brunswick, NJ: Rutgers University Press, 1992.

————. *Poetry and Pragmatism*. Cambridge, MA: Harvard University Press, 1992.

Thompson, Denys. *Reading and Discrimination*. London: Chatto, 1934.

Varnum, Robin. *Fencing with Words: A History of Writing Instruction at Amherst College During the Era of Theodore Baird, 1938-66*. Urbana, IL: NCTE, 1996.

Index

symmetrical rhetoric and, 6
uncertainty about, 136
Benjamin, Walter, 165, 174-75
Berger, John, 29-30
Berthoff, Ann, 20
Bettelheim, Bruno, 89
Biaggini, E. G., 208
Bitzer, Lloyd, 101-02
Body language, 120
Bolker, Joan, 132, 144
Booth, Wayne, 83, 89, 185, 210
Brady, Judy, 148
Brannon, Lil, 134
Brent, Doug, 73-93, 107, 130
British culture studies, 209
    See also: Culture
Brockriede, Wayne, 46
Brooks, Cleanth, 203, 204, 205, 210
Brooks, Peter, 204
Brower, Reuben, 203, 204, 210
Bruner, Jerome, 159
Bullock, Chris, 130
Burke, Kenneth, 13, 147, 210
Butler, Charles, 4

Cain, William, 207-08
Calvino, Italo, 161, 173
Campbell, George, 13
Carter, Kathryn, 85
Case:
    conceptualizing, 15
    general, 113-14
    judging, 77
    particular, 113-14
    reasonable, 11
Cayton, Mary Kupiec, 144
Change:
    agents of, 101
    Rogerian therapy and, 74-76
Cicero, 103, 105, 107, 111, 113, 116, 118
Cisneros, Sandra, 137
Claim(s):
    assumption of connecting data to, 49
    conflicting, 105-06
    contingent arguments and, 52, 53, 55
    contradictory, 104-06
    evidence for, 19
    generalizations, 37
    incompatible, 111
    qualifier to, 50

Toulmin model and, 57, 58-63, 67
Clarity, reasoned thesis and, 11
Clarkson, Gregory, 139-40
Classes, see Composition classes
Classical Greece, theories of rhetoric in, 6-7
Classical rhetoric, 6-7, 97-122
    combative versus cooperative, 77
    premise of, 100-01
Classism, 139
Classroom communities, 139-43
Clifford, James, 163
Clifford, John, 184-85
Clinchy, Blythe McVicker, 86, 134
Close reading, 201-10
Coe, Richard M., 15, 74, 77, 84, 88
Cognitive conflict, 134
Cognitive growth, 89
Cognitive processes, working class women
    and, 132
Coles, William E., 183-84, 187, 194, 201,
    202, 203, 209, 210
Collaborative inquiry, 134, 142
Colomb, Greg, 102
Color, feminists of, 132
Combative argumentation, 77, 106, 129-30,
    133, 134
Combative metaphors, 51-56, 73
Comley, Nancy, 185
Commentaries, narrator's, 157
Commonplaces, 113-14
Common sense, working class women and, 132
Communication, 119
    asymmetrical, unilateral, 6
    female rhetoric, 127-51
    goal of, 89
    Rogerian therapy and, 75
    social and political nature of, 138
Community:
    argumentation based in, 131
    feminist approaches to argument and,
        139-43
    forming, 103
    of writers, 150-51
Composition:
    classical rhetoric and, 97-22
    cultural studies and, 206
    feminists and, 128-29
    Toulmin model of argument and, 45-70
Composition classes:
    feminist, 127-30, 133-51
    freshman, 98-101

About the Authors

Pamela J. Annas is Associate Professor of English at the University of Massachusetts/Boston. Her publications include articles on pedagogy, *Literature and Society* (Prentice Hall), coedited with Robert Rosen, and *A Disturbance in Mirrors: The Poetry of Sylvia Plath* (Greenwood Press). She is a member of the editorial collective of *The Radical Teacher*.

David Bartholomae (PhD Rutgers, 1975) is Professor of English and Chair of the Department of English at the University of Pittsburgh. He is past Chair of CCCC (Conference on College Composition and Communication) and coeditor of the Pittsburgh Series in Composition, Literacy and Culture. He chaired the second MLA Literacy conference. He has taught twice (once as a Fulbright Lecturer) at the University of Deusto in Bilbao, Spain. He has written widely on composition theory and composition instruction. With Anthony Petrosky, he is coauthor/editor of *The Teaching of Writing* (University of Chicago Press), *Facts, Artifacts, and Counterfacts* (Heinemann), and *Ways of Reading* (Bedford Books).

Doug Brent received his doctorate in Rhetoric and Composition from the University of British Columbia. He is an Associate Professor in the Faculty of General Studies at the University of Calgary, where he teaches courses in rhetoric and composition studies and information technology. He is Director of the Undergraduate Program in Communications Studies and of the Effective Writing Program. He has published articles in journals such as *College English, Textual Studies in Canada,* and *Ejournal* and has published a monograph titled *Reading as Rhetorical Invention: Knowledge, Persuasion and the Teaching of Research Based Writing* (National Council of Teachers of English).

Barbara Emmel is an Assistant Professor and Director of Composition at University of Wisconsin-Eau Claire and an Associate Fellow at Yale University. The focus of her work is on connections between the pedagogy of teaching argumentative writing and the structure of rhetorical and argumentative inquiry. She has published and spoken on the problems of teaching argument and has published articles on the problems of enacting parental leave policies on the level of state and national government. She also publishes poetry and nonfiction.

Jeanne Fahnestock is an Associate Professor in the Department of English Language and Literature at the University of Maryland in College Park, where she has served as Director of Freshman and Professional Writing and of the writing programs overall. She recently instituted a first-year writing curriculum based on classical rhetoric. Her current project concerns figures of argument in the rhetoric of science.

Richard Fulkerson is Coordinator of Composition and Director of English Graduate Studies at East Texas State University, where he teaches courses in prelaw writing, advanced composition, theory and practice of teaching argument, and introduction to logic, among others. He has published and spoken extensively in the field of composition and on connections between argument and composition. His most recent work is a monograph titled *Teaching the Argument in Writing* (NCTE).

John T. Gage is Professor of English at the University of Oregon. He has published and spoken widely on composition, the history of rhetoric, and argumentation.

Paula Resch is a Lecturer in the Department of English at Yale University and Tutor-in-Writing at the Bass Writing Program at Yale. She has written on the ethics of persuasion, historic preservation, and music education, and has led workshops in writing and argument for college writing instructors, business leaders, and graduate students.

Mariolina Salvatori is an Associate Professor of English at the University of Pittsburgh, where she teaches undergraduate and graduate courses in the composition program and in the literature program. She holds a degree in the languages, literatures, and institutions of Western Europe (English, German, Spanish) from the Orientale University in Naples, Italy, and a PhD in nineteenth- and twentieth-century literature from the University of Pittsburgh. She has written on twentieth-century Italian literature, literary perceptions of aging, and the immigrants' experience. Her most recent work concentrates on the interconnections of reading and writing, theory and practice, literature and composition, and on the history of pedagogy. She is the author of *Pedagogy: Disturbing History* (forthcoming, 1996, University of Pittsburgh Press).

Marie Secor is an Associate Professor of English at Pennsylvania State University, where she teaches both graduate and undergraduate courses in rhetoric and composition. She is coauthor (with Jeanne Fahnestock) of *A Rhetoric of Argument and Reading in Argument* (McGraw-Hill) and a number of articles on rhetorical theory and analysis, and is coeditor of the volume *Constructing Rhetorical Education* (Southern Illinois University Press). She is an editor of the journal *Philosophy and Rhetoric* and is currently working on a project linking nineteenth-century logical and rhetorical theory.

Judith Summerfield is a Professor of English at Queens College, The City University of New York, where she also directs The Freshman Year Initiative (FYI), an interdisciplinary center for reform, research, and teaching in the first year. The project has been supported by The Fund for the Improvement of Postsecondary Education, FIPSE. She has published a number of textbooks, including *Frames of Mind* (Random House) and *Negotiations* (McGraw-Hill); and with her late husband, Geoffrey Summerfield, *Texts and Contexts: A Contribution to the Theory and Practice of Teaching Composition* (Random House), which won the MLA Shaughnessy Award. She writes and publishes primarily on narrative, on how and why we tell stories, how tales are shaped by context, and how crucial it is in teaching language to reckon with the daily in addition to the literary. "Is There a Life in This Text?" appeared in Clifford and Schilb, *Writing Theory and Literary Theory,* (MLA). She is at work on a book on narrative and a novel on Dorothy Wordsworth. She has spoken recently at the FIPSE Directors Meetings in Washington, D.C. (1994, 1995) and at the National Conference of the American Association for Higher Education (Spring 1995) on bringing freshmen into the academic culture of the university. In 1994 she won the Queens College Presidential Award for Excellence in Teaching.

Deborah Tenney is a Lecturer in English at Yale University and Tutor-in-Writing at the Yale School of Management. A member of a professional choir in New Haven, Schola Cantorum, which has issued several critically acclaimed recordings, she has published articles on music and the arts.